Jung and Educational Theory

Educational Philosophy and Theory Special Issue Book Series

Series Editor: Michael A. Peters

The *Educational Philosophy and Theory* journal publishes articles concerned with all aspects of educational philosophy. Their themed special issues are also available to buy in book format and cover subjects ranging from curriculum theory, educational administration, the politics of education, educational history, educational policy and higher education.

Titles in the series include:

Jung and Educational Theory
Edited by Inna Semetsky

Researching Education through Actor-Network Theory
Edited by Tara Fenwick and Richard Edwards

The Power in/of Language
Edited by David R. Cole and Linda J. Graham

Educational Neuroscience: Initiatives and Emerging Issues
Edited by Kathryn E. Patten and Stephen R. Campbell

Rancière, Public Education and the Taming of Democracy
Edited by Maarten Simons and Jan Masschelein

Thinking Education through Alain Badiou
Edited by Kent den Heyer

Toleration, Respect and Recognition in Education
Edited by Mitja Sardoč

Gramsci and Educational Thought
Edited by Peter Mayo

Patriotism and Citizenship Education
Edited by Bruce Haynes

Exploring Education through Phenomenology: Diverse Approaches
Edited by Gloria Dall'Alba

Academic Writing, Philosophy and Genre
Edited by Michael A. Peters

Complexity Theory and the Philosophy of Education
Edited by Mark Mason

Critical Thinking and Learning
Edited by Mark Mason

Philosophy of Early Childhood Education: Transforming Narratives
Edited by Sandy Farquhar and Peter Fitzsimons

The Learning Society from the Perspective of Governmentality
Edited by Jan Masschelein, Maarten Simons, Ulrich Bröckling and Ludwig Pongratz

Citizenship, Inclusion and Democracy: A Symposium on Iris Marion Young
Edited by Mitja Sardoč

Postfoundationalist Themes in the Philosophy of Education: Festschrift for James D. Marshall
Edited by Paul Smeyers and Michael A. Peters

Music Education for the New Millennium: Theory and Practice Futures for Music Teaching and Learning
Edited by David Lines

Critical Pedagogy and Race
Edited by Zeus Leonardo

Derrida, Deconstruction and Education: Ethics of Pedagogy and Research
Edited by Peter Pericles Trifonas and Michael A. Peters

Jung and Educational Theory

Edited by
Inna Semetsky

⊛WILEY-BLACKWELL

A John Wiley & Sons, Ltd., Publication

Blackwell Publishing was acquired by John Wiley & Sons in February 2007. Blackwell's publishing program has been merged with Wiley's global Scientific, Technical, and Medical business to form Wiley-Blackwell.

Registered Office
John Wiley & Sons Ltd, The Atrium, Southern Gate, Chichester, West Sussex, PO19 8SQ, United Kingdom

Editorial Offices
350 Main Street, Malden, MA 02148-5020, USA
9600 Garsington Road, Oxford, OX4 2DQ, UK
The Atrium, Southern Gate, Chichester, West Sussex, PO19 8SQ, UK

For details of our global editorial offices, for customer services, and for information about how to apply for permission to reuse the copyright material in this book please see our website at www.wiley.com/wiley-blackwell.

Library of Congress Cataloging-in-Publication Data

Jung and educational theory / Edited by Inna Semetsky.
    p. ; cm
   Includes bibliographical references and index.
   ISBN 978-1-118-29734-6 (pbk.)
   1. Jung, C. G. (Carl Gustav), 1875-1961–Influence.   2. Education–Philosophy.
3. Educational psychology.   4. Psychoanalysis and education.   I. Semetsky, Inna, 1948–
   LB14.7.J855 2012
   370.1–dc23

                   2012002032

A catalogue record for this book is available from the British Library.

The cover design incorporates "Butterfly" © Michail Grobman. Work on Paper, 1965, 29 × 20.

Cover design by Cyan Design.

Set in 10 on 13pt Plantin by Toppan Best-set Premedia Limited

Printed in Malaysia by Ho Printing (M) Sdn Bhd

1   2013

Contents

Notes on Contributors   vi

Introduction: Jung and *Holistic* Education
INNA SEMETSKY   viii

1   **Jung and the Soul of Education (at the 'Crunch')**
SUSAN ROWLAND   1

2   **On the 'Art and Science' of Personal Transformation: Some critical reflections**
RAYA A. JONES   12

3   **The Polytheistic Classroom**
BERNIE NEVILLE   21

4   **Itinerary of the *Knower*: Mapping the ways of *gnosis*, *Sophia*, and imaginative education**
ANTONINA LUKENCHUK   35

5   **The Unifying Function of Affect: Founding a theory of psychocultural development in the epistemology of John Dewey and Carl Jung**
PETER T. DUNLAP   47

6   **Deleuze's Philosophy and Jung's Psychology: Learning and the Unconscious**
INNA SEMETSKY & JOSHUA RAMEY   63

7   **'The Other Half' of Education: Unconscious education of children**
SHIHO MAIN   76

8   **Complex Education: Depth psychology as a mode of ethical pedagogy**
ROBERT ROMANYSHYN   90

9   **Jung and Tarot: A theory-practice nexus in education and counselling**
INNA SEMETSKY   111

Index   120

Notes on Contributors

Peter T. Dunlap is a founder of the *Center for Political Development* located in Petaluma, CA, USA, devoted to helping progressive leaders, their organizations and community groups to attend to the subtle prejudices that restrict the emergent leadership capacities needed at this time in our history. His research focuses on an exploration of the transformative experience toward becoming progressive political leaders. He recently published *Awakening Our Faith in the Future: The advent of psychological liberalism* (Routledge, 2008). Email: centerpd@gmail.com.

Raya A. Jones, PhD, is a senior lecturer in the School of Social Sciences, Cardiff University, UK. Academic specializations include narrative and Jungian approaches to the self, and developmental psychopathology. She served on the executive committee of the International Association for Jungian Studies. Authored and edited books include *Jung, Psychology, Postmodernity* (Routledge, 2007), *Education and Imagination* (Routledge, 2008), and *Body, Mind, and Healing after Jung* (Routledge, 2010). Email: jonesra9@Cardiff.ac.uk.

Antonina Lukenchuk is an associate professor of Educational Foundations and Inquiry at National-Louis University, Chicago, IL. She has a PhD in Linguistics, EdD in Adult Education and MEd in Educational Foundations. Her research focuses on paradigms of research, phenomenology, hermeneutics, critical discourse analysis, cross-cultural studies, transpersonal psychology and service-learning. Among her recent publications is *Living the Ethics of Responsibility through University Service and Service-learning: Phronesis and praxis reconsidered* (2009). She is a *kajukenbo* martial artist and a volunteer in community organizations. Email: Antonina.Lukenchuk@nl.edu.

Dr Shiho Main is a fellow at the Centre for Psychoanalytic Studies, University of Essex, UK, and an associate lecturer in Childhood with the Open University, UK. Her research interests include Jung's views on education and psychological development; history of childhood; and psychological issues concerning children's rights. Among her recent publications is *Childhood Re-imagined: Images and narratives of development in analytical psychology* (Routledge, 2008). Email: smiyag@essex.ac.uk.

Bernie Neville is adjunct professor of Education at Latrobe University, Melbourne, Australia, with a long career as a researcher and teacher educator. His research has focused on the impact of teacher–student relationships on student learning and well-being. His book *Educating Psyche: Imagination, emotion, and the unconscious in learning* examined education through the lens of archetypal psychology. In his recent book, *Olympus Inc.: Intervening for cultural change in organizations*, he applies the archetypal framework to organizational change. Email: b.neville@latrobe.edu.au.

Joshua Ramey (previously known as Joshua A. Delpech-Ramey) is a visiting assistant professor at Haverford College. He is the author of *The Hermetic Deleuze: Philosophy and spiritual ordeal* (Duke University Press, 2012). Ramey is also the editor of 'Spiritual Politics After Deleuze', a special issue of *SubStance* (39.1), and the author of numerous articles on contemporary philosophy, aesthetics and cultural theory. His essays have appeared in *Angelaki*, *Political Theology*, *Discourse* and the *Journal for Cultural and Religious Theory*. Email: jramey@haverford.edu.

Dr **Robert Romanyshyn** is a teacher, writer and psychotherapist trained in phenomenology and Jungian psychology. An affiliate member of the Inter-Regional Society of Jungian Analysts, he is a senior core faculty member of the Clinical Psychology program at Pacifica Graduate Institute, USA. He has published six books, including *The Wounded Researcher* (2007), over 40 book chapters, and edited special journal issues. He has given lectures and workshops at universities and professional societies around the globe. A DVD, *Antarctica: Inner journeys in the Outer World*, is available online at www.jungplatform.com. Website: RobertRomanyshyn.com. Email: RRomanyshyn@pacifica.edu.

Susan Rowland, PhD, is now core faculty at Pacifica Graduate Institute and formerly professor of English and Jungian Studies at Greenwich University, UK. She is the author of books on Jung, gender and literary theory including *Jung: A Feminist Revision* (2002), *Jung as a Writer* (2005) and *C. G. Jung and the Humanities* (2010). Her new book, *The Ecocritical Psyche: Literature, complexity evolution and Jung* is published in 2012. From 2003 to 2006, she was founding chair of the International Association for Jungian Studies. Email: SRowland@pacifica.edu.

Inna Semetsky is adjunct professor at the University of Waikato, New Zealand. She has a PhD in philosophy of education (Columbia University, USA), MA in Family and Child Counseling, and Grad.Dip.Ed in math/science education. She has five entries in the *Encyclopedia of Religious and Spiritual Development* (2006) and has published four books including *Deleuze, Education and Becoming* (2006) and *Re-Symbolization of the Self: Human Development and Tarot Hermeneutic* (2011), as well as numerous articles and chapters, including in International Handbooks. She serves on the board of four academic journals. Among her forthcoming books is *The Edusemiotics of Images: Essays on the Art~Science of Tarot* (Sense Publishers). Email: irs5@columbia.edu.

Introduction: Jung and *Holistic* Education

INNA SEMETSKY

This book assembles nine chapters written by contributors from Australia, USA and the UK who have brought the rich legacy of Carl Jung's analytical psychology to the attention of the international community of educational philosophers and theorists.

In the remarkable book *Awakening the Inner Eye: Intuition in education*, Noddings and Shore (1984) remark on Jung's intuitive function that guides our perceptions and judgments in addition to merely rational thinking. The chapters in this book are written by academics and practitioners that remarkably combine all four of the Jungian functions, including the intuitive, in their approach to research. This uncompromising, holistic and non-reductive, inclusive attitude has allowed the authors to discover a largely untapped area, the dimension of *education* spread through Jung's vast body of works, despite two apparent obstacles to their research. Not only has Jung's analytical or depth psychology as the analysis of the unconscious always existed just on the margins of mainstream theoretical orientations in clinical or counselling practice, but also Jung's legacy still remains largely outside the disciplinary fields in Academia altogether.

This book thus fulfils two novel objectives. First, it brings Jung's corpus into academic discourse in the area of philosophy of education and educational theory. Second, it contributes to articulating the *educational* value of Jung's psychology as a powerful complement to its *therapeutic* value, well known to those Jungians and post-Jungians who work in clinical practice. In fact—as will be seen in the majority of the chapters in this book—the absolute line of division between educational and clinical aspects with regard to Jung's conceptualisations is no longer feasible. Jung's great achievement was his anti-dualistic and unifying approach to what we today call human sciences. Jung's psychology and his emphasis on the learning, individuating, process grounded in human experience strongly parallels John Dewey's educational philosophy, in the framework of which *all* education is always already *moral* education devoted to human *growth*.

Before I present a synopsis of the book's contents, I would like to express my gratitude to many independent reviewers including Maryann Barone-Chapman, Tina Besley, Bill Doll, Peter Fitzsimons, Peta Heywood, Clifford Mayes, and several others who provided their much appreciated professional advice that enabled the selection of essays for publication in this book. Thanks are also due to Susanne Brighouse for her expert technical assistance with the editorial process.

The book begins with Susan Rowland's chapter entitled 'Jung and the Soul of Education (at the "Crunch")'. Challenging the utilitarianism of modernity, Rowland locates education in relation to nature, both human and non-human. She addresses the diminished role of the humanities in education and presents an extensive review of Jungian techniques in the teaching of English as a second language and in Business Studies in universities, as well as in the context of holistic transformative education in

Jung and Educational Theory, First Edition. Edited by Inna Semetsky.
Chapters © 2013 The Authors. Book compilation © 2013 Philosophy of Education Society of Australasia.
Published 2013 by Blackwell Publishing Ltd.

schools. She argues that Jung focused on the problem of being educated as a social being inspired by the creative and artistic potential of the unconscious.

For Rowland, the Jungian approaches to education represent the critique of fragmentation achieved by a 'healing fiction' embedded in a story. She concludes her chapter by presenting the 'visionary' and 'psychological' readings of Jane Austen's Mansfield Park in a university course on literary theory. Rowland's argument is that the Jungian contributions to education are dedicated to aiding psychic wholeness. She discusses 'the educated soul', drawing from the works of two contemporary post-Jungians, Robert Romanyshyn (whose chapter, in one creative stroke, completes this book) and Jerome Bernstein, in the context of the evolution of Western consciousness, alchemy and indigenous (Navajo) culture.

The very concept of Jungian 'soul-speak' in education becomes problematical for Raya Jones in her chapter 'On the "Art and Science" of Personal Transformation: Some critical reflections'. Focusing on the works of several influential post-Jungians, Jones interrogates the concept of transformative learning and addresses the recent call to 'excite children's imagination' in the area of primary education in the UK, as per the Cambridge Primary Review. Taking a critical approach from within a social sciences research perspective, Jones argues that there remains a dissonance between educational goals and those of Jung's therapeutic methods. Jones positions Jung's goal of individuation as becoming a whole person against the background of educational policy in the UK in the tradition of liberal education, and builds up an argument against directly transmitting Jung's methods into pedagogical *praxis* with children.

Acknowledging Jung's science versus art dilemma with regard to modern psychology, Jones emphasises the differences between the reality of the educational settings and that of the therapy room and the difficulty involved in teachers' self-education as a form of Jungian therapy. Jones notes that the discourse on soul psychology in education may impose a subtle coercion, its shadow, given that transformative education generally is understood as emancipatory, and problematises the value-neutrality of the tendency towards taking 'Jung' out of psychotherapeutic settings and into the classroom.

Yet, Bernie Neville's chapter 'The Polytheistic Classroom' does bring Jung into an 'archetypal' classroom populated by the gods of the Greek Pantheon as personifications of the different Jungian archetypes. Neville asserts that the Greek pantheon can provide educators with a pluralist language for talking about a wide range of distinct philosophies, value systems, energies, feeling states, habits of behavior and teaching styles observed in the classroom. For example, the archetypal pattern personified in Zeus is the pattern of power that wants to maintain itself either brutally or benevolently and can both protect and punish; the archetype of Demeter suggests a 'mothering' aspect to a teacher profession; Hermes tends to subvert the conventionally accepted order of things, to disrupt our certainties, and to make changes possible.

Neville notices that each of the Greek gods gives us a different meaning for our being, a different truth, which must be held in balance. Each of the gods represents a different notion of the aims of education or a different perspective on curriculum and, as reflected in current debates on the aims of education, these immortal gods still demonstrate their eternal arguments. Commenting on the phenomenon of ego-inflation as especially important for Jung, Neville remarks that we may find inflations of all kinds in educational systems, in classrooms, and in teachers' personalities. The gods (or archetypes) are many; for Neville, if we follow the advice of the ancient Greeks we will be careful not to neglect any of them as well as not get carried away in worshipping any single one of them.

Antonina Lukenchuk's essay 'Itinerary of the *Knower*: Mapping the ways of *gnosis*, *Sophia*, and imaginative education' connects Jung's theory with several discourses in educational theory on the role of imagination as articulated, for example, by Maxine Greene and Kieran Egan. Lukenchuk finds the close affinity of Jung's claim that reason alone would not suffice with Greene's argument for imagination and arts education and cites Dewey and other philosophers on the role of the arts in developing various faculties of children.

Lukenchuk argues for an integrated educational theory that would also incorporate Gnostic philosophy. She notices the role of the archetypal feminine exemplified in the Gnostic image of Sophia whose 'presence' can be traced through Diotima in Plato's *Symposium*, to Julia Kristeva's works, to Ukrainian lore. Affirming the Gnostic Jung as offering us the knowledge of the heart, she argues that multiple and cross-cultural Jungian discourses should become part of mainstream education, thereby revitalising its philosophical foundations and suggesting new ways of perceiving, knowing, teaching and learning.

While Dewey's educational philosophy is noted in passing alongside Jung in Lukenchuk's essay, Peter Dunlap's essay 'The Unifying Function of Affect: Founding a theory of psychocultural development in the epistemology of John Dewey and Carl Jung' makes Dewey's 'postulate of continuity' central to understanding Jung's developmental theory of knowledge. Dunlap argues that Dewey's and Jung's thoughts converge on the resolution of the subject-object dichotomy prevalent in the positivist paradigm of modernity and moves into a political sphere addressing the potential for more humane social institutions. He demonstrates that Dewey's political philosophy has a psychological wing while Jung's psychology has a political wing, and offers a critique of the cultural identity of political citizenship versus individualism. He identifies 'affect science' as the path to 'affect freedom' that employs the biological, psychocultural, and political functions of our emotions and lists several examples of contemporary cultural leadership and post-Jungian 'political therapy'.

For Dunlap, individual 'political psychologists' need the guidance of a strong institutional form—in terms of educational philosophy, professional ethics, and best practices—in order to establish a range of new professions within community organizations to enable transformative action as an embodied solution to the crises of our time. He concludes the essay by suggesting a type of a social scientist involved in psychoeducational community practice as a potential agent of the transformation of culture.

Inna Semetsky and Joshua Ramey engage the work of Gilles Deleuze as yet another philosophical counterpart to Jung in their chapter 'Deleuze's Philosophy and Jung's Psychology: Learning and the Unconscious'. The value of Deleuze's corpus for educational theory is steadily growing; hence positioning Jung's *psychological* theory against this particular *philosophical* background in education mutually reinforces both novel directions in philosophy of education. Analysing Jung's theory of the archetypes and Deleuze's pedagogy of the concept as two complementary conceptual resources, the authors posit Jungian individuation as becoming-other in the process of (adult) self-education as learning from experiences. Addressing the anti-Oedipal nature of the unconscious for both Jung and Deleuze, the authors emphasise that it is the *collective* unconscious that connects us with the public—social, political, historical, cultural and natural—existence in the world.

The authors' argument is that it is Jung's transcendent function that acts symbolically or *indirectly* (versus immediate representation in consciousness) and, analogously to Deleuze's transversal communication, contributes to creating novel concepts, meanings and values in our practical experience. Addressing what one author (Semetsky, 2010) posits as the *ethics of integration* in education, the authors affirm that the integration of the Shadow is necessary for the educators' *self-education* grounded in Jungian analytical method(s) considered by him to be an eminently educational activity.

Shiho Main in her chapter '"The Other Half" of Education: Unconscious education of children' contrasts the aim of 'the other half' of education, as an indirect unconscious process, with formal curriculum and direct education. She addresses the children's psyche as described by what Jung qualified as *participation mystique*. Arguing that a purely technical education is insufficient, Main nonetheless identifies some problems with Jung's account of the other half' of education.

Main presents Jung's view of children as competent individuals from early on and elucidates a historically controversial hypothesis of ontogeny (the course of individual development) recapitulating phylogeny (human evolution as a species) in the context of Jung's developmental psychology. She bridges the dichotomy between developmental (natural) and symbolic (cultural) aspects in Jung's psychology with regard to the education of children. Asserting that, for Jung, diversity is the expression of universality, she concludes that education in terms of the unconscious process between a student and a teacher does not specify any particular conditions and is therefore inclusive of often marginalised groups regardless of culture, socio-economical background, special needs, etc.; all unified by the purpose of children's well-being.

This essay by Robert Romanyshyn is titled 'Complex Education: Depth psychology as a mode of ethical pedagogy'. While the ethical implications for education, as based on Jung's theory of the unconscious, were also addressed in Semetsky's and Ramey's chapter, it is Romanyshyn who brings the ethical pedagogy to the foreground. Under-cutting the Cartesian dream of reason, Romanyshyn weaves together phenomenology, hermeneutics and Jung's psychology to analyse the unconscious dynamics between a teacher and a student as leading to ethical ways of knowing and being, while remaining careful not to conflate therapy with pedagogy. His central message is that educators have an ethical obligation to take responsibility for their own complex prejudices. Romany-shyn is interested in complex 'characters' implicit in the transference field in a classroom and structures his arguments by reference to his seminal book *The Wounded Researcher* as well as to several earlier practical experiments informed by his formidable Jungian scholarship.

Referring to the *imaginal*, Romanyshyn strengthens the role of this 'third' dimension between the senses and the intellect that enables an embodied way of being in the world within the context of a *complex* mind reaching into nature. His intent is to cultivate a special, even if uncertain, metaphoric sensibility capable of leading one out of linear and literal ways of thinking. Noticing Jung's Gnostic interests, Romanyshyn asserts that a teacher has to be a master of metaphor and argues that ethical education should become a vocation oriented toward the development of individuated human beings who can take up the universal conditions of human existence in a manner that is transformative both of themselves and also of those very existential conditions.

Semetsky's essay on 'Jung and Tarot' presents this ancient cultural practice as an educational and counselling tool that can be used as an aid in the process of Jungian individuation. Her research methodology is a theory-practice nexus that overcomes the Cartesian mind-body dualism. By means of narrating the symbolic meanings of Tarot images we can become aware of the unconscious actions of Jungian archetypes. Thus Tarot hermeneutic functions in the mode of post-formal pedagogy oriented to learning from experiences comprising a 'school of life' filled with meaning.

To conclude, Jung's theory is profoundly postmodern in its denial of the *exclusive* role allotted to the conscious subject. Philosophy of education should take note of the relevance of this idea as well as of Jung's emphasis on self-knowledge and lifelong human development irreducible to perpetual training. Jung was adamant that education should not be confined to schools or stop when a child grows up. In her book *Critical Lessons: What our schools should teach*, Nel Noddings refers to the Socratic 'Know Thyself' principle as the often-disregarded yet necessary goal of education. Noddings emphasises the importance of self-knowledge as the very core of education: 'when we claim to *educate*, we must take Socrates seriously. Unexamined lives may well be valuable and worth living, but an education that does not invite such examination may not be worthy of the label *education*' (Noddings, 2006, p. 10, italics in original). Such *education*, according to Jung, will by necessity bring forth holistic and inclusive pedagogical practice, in which the ethical dimension is embedded and the aim of which highlights bringing up integrated human beings, children and adults alike.

References

Noddings, N. (2006) *Critical Lessons: What our schools should teach* (New York, Cambridge University Press).

Noddings, N., & Shore, P. J. (1984) *Awakening the Inner Eye: Intuition in education* (New York, Teachers College Press, Columbia University).

Semetsky, I. (2010) Towards an Ethics of Integration in Education, in: T. Lovat, R. Toomey & N. Clement (eds), *International Research Handbook on Values Education and Student Wellbeing* (Dordrecht, Springer), pp. 319–336.

1
Jung and the Soul of Education (at the 'Crunch')

SUSAN ROWLAND

> The for-profit university is the logical end of a shift from a model of education centred in an individual professor who delivers insight and inspiration, to a model that begins and ends with the imperative to deliver the information and skills necessary to gain employment. (Stanley Fish, 'The Last Professor'—Stanley Fish Blog—NYTimes.com)

> [T]he actual act of teaching, something I've been doing for more than 50 years now, has not changed at all. In spite of all he new technology the most useful teaching device is still ... a log, with a teacher at one end and a student at the other end. (Tony Steblay in reply to Stanley Fish on the same blog)

> They appear suddenly by the side of the truly modern man as uprooted human beings, bloodsucking ghosts, whose emptiness is taken for the unenviable loneliness of the modern man and casts discredit upon him. (C. G. Jung, *Modern Man in Search of a Soul*, 1933, p. 228.)

Introduction: Education and Controversy

Writing in 2009, at a time of global anxiety and as a university teacher, the world of education appears fraught with universal concerns and to be undergoing its own identity crisis. In the blog quoted above, eminent US English literature professor Stanley Fish associates two major developments in university education. Here the move to a mass model, in which higher education becomes the expectation of more than one third of the population, is inevitably accompanied by the triumph of utilitarianism. Degree education of the masses becomes primarily a means to acquire skills for employment. The corollary at institutional level is that universities are characterized as profit-making institutions. Education is a business. The values of 'useless' study of the humanities are as quickly forgotten as their provision is being eroded.

So the accusation here is of a tragic narrowing of what education means. At the same time, the world faces related crises of climate change and economic meltdown. Indeed, as Robert Romanyshyn pointed out in his many works, we had better pay attention to the coding of our metaphors in which polar ice *melting* suggests more than affinity to capitalist *meltdown*, itself a metaphor often used for nuclear catastrophe. When trying to address the potential catastrophe of nature, routinely there are calls for a revolution in education. By 'education' here, what is referred to is the school system and not the activity in its widest sense.

Jung and Educational Theory, First Edition. Edited by Inna Semetsky.
Chapters © 2013 The Authors. Book compilation © 2013 Philosophy of Education Society of Australasia.
Published 2013 by Blackwell Publishing Ltd.

How can we possibly connect a workplace changing fast via technology and saturated with notions of utility and profit with calls for a new kind of human being? Is education suffering from an overload of social demand and fantasy? From the fantasy that it can save the world while becoming a profitable new industry to replace dying forms of manufacturing? There is a dangerous gulf between 'education' as a locus of fantasies of salvation and what Fish rightly points out is its growing mechanisation and standardisation. Nor is a shift from institutions devoted to learning, to profitable businesses, confined to universities. In Britain in the 1980s, the imposition of a National Curriculum in schools, which significantly homogenised lesson content, was accompanied by the requirement to balance budgets. Schools, for the first time, began to hire managers or accountants.

This article will use the work of C. G. Jung to look at these tensions in education, from the demand that it be part of some kind of social salvation, to the possibilities being explored by Jungians in the classroom today. In particular, the theory and practice of education challenges imagined social boundaries between 'inside' and 'outside' of the institutions and even between inside the self and outside, in cultural creativity. With Jung's help, one might take this sense of provisional or liminal boundaries further and look at education inside the sphere of human existence and also beyond it. Where is education in relation to nature, matter and the non-human?

Jung on Education and Bloodsucking Ghosts

In an article of 1928, 'The Significance of the Unconscious in Individual Education', Jung divides education into three types (Jung, 1954, CW17, p. 149): by example; by norms or rules (collective education); and, significantly, individuation which means coming to terms with one's unconscious. Here Jung is on his core ground. For his ideas are based upon the supreme importance of the unconscious as a source of creativity, and as at least partly, unknowable. All his key notions follow from this initial proposition. Most significantly, this hypothesis of the unconscious renders all other knowledge and argument provisional. To Jung, the assertion of something, anything, as absolute truth is a dangerous fantasy of the ego.

To Jung, subjectivity was a continual process of the ego being challenged, undermined, and remade by the richer creativity of the unconscious. This was 'individuation'. Crucially, he used the metaphor of 'education' as part of a framework of understanding how therapy might aid individuation. While stressing the provisional nature of his findings, and the arbitrary quality of the portrayal of his psychology, he says:

> Be that as it may, I venture to arrange the sum-total of findings under the four heads of confession, explanation, education and transformation. (Jung, 1933, p. 35)

Interestingly, this account of his own methods of psychotherapy deliberately draws upon two social histories, that of religion, specifically confession to a priest, and that of education, presumably of a more individual type. Here, psychotherapy raids collective forms of discourse to set up another collective, the 'rules' of the analytic encounter, in which something very individual is hoped to occur: the individuation of the patient.

Two points could be drawn from this analysis by Jung. One is that 'education' is viewed here as a stage on route toward 'transformation', not as an end in itself. The other point is that, despite Jung's apparent focus upon the individual, collective considerations are innate to his individuation. Of the 'education' stage he says: '[t]he problem which now faces the patient is that of being educated as a social being' (ibid. p.49).

To Jung, the further into the psyche one delves, the more 'collective', and hence 'social', the implications. In suggesting that humans are born with the propensity for certain sorts of images and meanings (archetypes), he theorises a 'collective unconscious'. Cultural life is made up of incarnations of archetypal images. These are energised by the collective inheritance of archetypes, while being coloured by individual and social histories. Jung's psyche is both collective and cultural: it is most profoundly innately creative and partly mysterious. Hence, to him education means coming to terms with one's unconscious in a social context. After all, the unconscious is not only to be found within in dreams. It is also, disconcertingly, to be found projected on to other people, to ideas and ideologies, and social institutions. In fact, the unconscious Other may reach out to us even as the face of nature and the cosmos. In this belief in the projection of a psychic inside to the outside by the independently creative unconscious, Jung appears to have stuck to modernity's paradigm of a division between subject and object, self and world. However, in looking back at the Renaissance discourse of alchemy, and in forming his own ideas about the psyche and material world co-creating meaning (synchronicity), he anticipated new holism. Within holistic educational process, the educator is herself changed.

So who are the bloodsucking ghosts that haunt modernity? They are un-individuated, and therefore, un-educated people. Their un-self-conscious modern existence does not permit them to be remade by the unconscious, and thus they become cut off from it. The more one is cut off from the unconscious, the more one fears it. The greater the fear, the blacker and more powerful the unconscious becomes. Because Jung thinks collectively as well as personally, what is on the individual level someone who has no life of their own, who merely leeches off others, e.g. a bloodsucking ghost, is on a societal level the creator of a terrifyingly material unconscious other. Jung argued that a society not educated to the nature of the unconscious, one that believes only in the reality of matter, creates its own material 'shadow'. Such a shadow, he believed, had become actual substance in weapons of mass destruction.

> [M]an has never yet been able single-handed to hold his own against the powers of darkness—that is, the unconscious ... The World War was such an irruption ... (Jung, 1933, p. 277)

Hence, in Jung's own cultural institution of Jungian psychoanalysis, and also in his psychology, there is a suggestive fluidity or 'deconstruction' of absolute divisions between 'self' and 'world', 'individual' and 'collective', and even 'education of the soul' and 'education of society'. The education of the soul is inevitably involved with the collective, as unconscious dreams and fantasies direct the analytic work into the patient's humanity in a larger sense. For Jung, individuation is healing because Jung believed the psyche was a self-healing entity in which individuation became a drive to ever-greater psychic wholeness. Indeed, he called this wholeness union with, or intimation of, the self. Here self is not ego with a fantasy of separateness from the world; it is self as ever-deeper connectedness to the collective unconscious and the reality of humanity, society and cosmos. Ultimately, Jung is not facilely abolishing the modern individual. He is rather re-situating the human being as only fully her*self* when acknowledging and articulating deep relations to the unconscious psyche, human culture and nature.

What is necessary is not to smash the ego, for that would destroy consciousness and the result would be psychosis on either a personal or mass level. This is precisely what Jung designed his psychology to avoid. He regarded the disaster of Nazi Germany as the result of too little consciousness in the German collective life. Such dire results were caused by too little individuation on a personal and social level. Individuation produces consciousness. Jung's unconscious is a monster if ignored or ill-treated by repression. It is a nurturing (M)other if individuation proceeds as an education in responding to the psyche's creative potential. The consciousness produced by successful individuation is strong enough to work productively with the unconscious as a junior partner. This conscious ego is able to receive its profound fertility in ways that enhance the individual and her world.

Crucially, Jung saw this potential for education and transformation in the individual as *simultaneously* individual and collective. Societies, like individuals, fail or succeed in individuation. Indeed, Jung's interest in the arts pivots upon his perception that the whole socially-located artistic process is a form of collective individuation. He argued that art could be categorised as either 'psychological' or 'visionary'. Like many of his so-called 'opposites', these terms represent poles of a spectrum rather than discrete types. 'Psychological' stands for art where the artist has consciously worked upon a social problem. Here art is an overt expressive *communication* of aesthetic and cultural values drawn from the collective consciousness, the known social consensus.

By contrast, 'visionary' art is deeply evoked by the collective unconscious. It appears to the initial audience as strange, wonderful, shocking, sublime, daemonic or terrifying. Visionary art is hard to 'read', impossible to comprehend, for it calls to its audience for images, voices, intimations, dreams and nightmares that have been lost, forgotten, suppressed or not yet witnessed. Visionary art may be a prediction of social changes to come, or may excavate ancient forms of humanity. What it definitely brings to its culture is the 'other'. It is a form by which the collective unconscious speaks to human beings as individuals, and also collectively as a society. In effect, visionary art *produces* its audience, and *at the same time* is profoundly individual and deeply connected to the social world. For it releases what is powerfully collective, and causes us to know our individuality as liminal as well as precious.

The Educated Soul and Nature: Robert Romanyshyn and Jerome Bernstein

Jung's vision of the educated soul is not confined to the human world. He was fascinated by the borderlands of the psyche. Two post-Jungian theorists have developed what he left largely implicit in his work. Robert Romanyshyn, in publications stemming from his first book, *Technology as Symptom and Dream* (1989), and Jerome Bernstein, in *Living in the Borderland* (2005), both do vital work by looking at the psyche in nature.

Romanyshyn, in particular, explores alchemy, a historical practice that fascinated Jung. He pushes Jung's alchemical studies further by exploring alchemy in relation to meta-phor. Alchemy is popularly understood as the doomed pursuit of turning lead into gold in the Renaissance. More precisely, alchemy is a holistic vision of an educating and transforming practice. For alchemists believed that the material world was inspirited and inspired. Far from God being separate from matter, 'he' was trapped in matter and needed to be freed by complex processes centring on coagulation and solution, solidifying and dissolving. Yet the repeated *solve et coagula* could not be reduced to a purely material process, because the world is not sundered like this. Rather, the alchemist's own soul was involved through philosophical study and poetic meditation upon symbols. Alchemy also sought to bring together feminine and masculine through a 'chymical wedding' of sun and moon.

What is of contemporary significance in this cultural practice, Romanyshyn argues, is the way alchemists believe in the creative linking of psyche, written text, material substance and nature or cosmos. For alchemists, their worldly practice with flasks and test-tubes, etc. (in which they became the precursors of modern chemistry), was a dynamic part of work with the psyche that was itself a marriage of intellect and love, Logos and Eros. Alchemists united parts of human activity that modernity has since divorced, to form divisions such as artistic creativity and science or mathematics, feeling versus rationality, and mind activity with body activity, and psyche as separate from matter. In so doing, alchemists situated humanity in a cosmic web. They saw their work as connecting the human soul to the nature of plants and animals, and the stars. Drawing astrology and magic into their philosophy, they produced a sort of prototype psychology.

Romanyshyn's work explores the potential of what Jung began to intimate about alchemy as a re-visioning of human beings as embedded in nature, rather than as claiming to be of an order 'above' nature as well as a transcendent God who inaugurated dualism, in creating Nature and Man as separate from his own Being. Dualism inevitably manifests culturally as hierarchy, with the founding Father's masculine superiority separate from the 'other', or feminine. Nature too is cut off from the sacred, dis-animated, feminised, and made 'other' to human culture, and even, at times, so repressed as to be the abode of the Jungian shadow, the harbour of demons.

In this parlous antecedent of our present condition of having exploited nature to our own detriment, alchemy represents the survival of a philosophy even older than monotheism. This is known as 'animism', the idea that nature is full of articulate spirits that in certain circumstances are able to communicate with humans. Characteristic of the pre-Christian Celts in Northern Europe, animistic religions are to be found within cultures that have sophisticated ways of caring for and, in turn, being nurtured by, what Westerners symptomatically call, 'natural resources'.

For those who argue that in order to survive and prevent the worst of global warming, we need to totally re-orient the attitudes of Western people by education, it is this fundamental shift from a monotheistic to animistic approach to nature that they mean. It does not necessarily entail the abolition of the three great monotheisms of Judaism, Islam and Christianity, for all three have currents within them capable of renouncing the unethical exploitation of nature. *Genesis*, with its vision of Paradise as a sacred garden, is open to a reading of human, respectful partnership with nature. Such a reading would be in perfect alignment with Jung's vision of individuation of the self in a creative, respectful relation to nature. Jung believes that a creative, mysterious, in-part unknowable unconscious is our root in nature and the cosmos. To return to the needed revolution in Western attitudes to nature, although the problem is in part religious, the solution need not be.

What is required is a revolution in consciousness that re-aligns the social ego, as well as the individual ego, with nature envisioned as *animated*, as having voices, creativity, autonomy, and ethical claims. To some, this will be a religious vision. Jung himself passionately argued that religion is a discourse of the soul, a major means by which the unconscious calls to us.

Art is another such discourse. What is key here is the revolution in psychic orientation to the other, not the actual language (such as religious symbols, poetry, philosophy, gardening, etc.) in which it is enacted. With regard to the collective unconscious as nature within us, Romanyshyn says evocatively: we all have seas and sunshine, and forests in our soul (Romanyshyn, 2007). He argues that the psychoid unconscious, a term coined by Jung for the point where mind and matter meet, is the consciousness of nature.

Jerome Bernstein's *Living in the Borderland* (2005) is both theoretically daring and offers a resonant case study of individual and collective education. Bernstein situates Jung's far more tentative rooting of the human unconscious in nature, in the context of the history of evolution from Darwin to present scientific developments, such as complexity theory. Bernstein shows how monotheism, through the dominant reading of *Genesis*, has created an over-specialised ego for the human species. Following Darwin's logic, species over-specialisation leads to disaster, for it signifies the lack of ability to adapt to a changing environment. Fortunately, there is hope for humanity in a combination of wisdom gleaned from new evolutionary theories, the Jungian psyche, and the far more ecologically sophisticated culture of the Navajo, with which Bernstein has developed lasting connections. Bernstein speculates that his Borderlanders are forerunners of a new evolution in consciousness who have acquired the necessary *reality* of our embedded being in nature. Yet they have done so often without the individuation necessary to bear it. Here analysis is educational, in learning how to bear a transformation that has already happened.

It is suggestive that *Living in the Borderland* includes chapters on the traditions of the Navajo. Here are a people whose culture organically connects education, religion, art and healing. Their indigenous psyche has always lived in the borderland of mind and matter, human and nature, and has walked with spirits and gods. To the Navajo, sickness results from a tear in the fabric of the cosmos. Healing consists of an embodied education, one that mends the psyche, body, culture and vision of their universe back together. The sick person is re-taught stories and chants that are themselves regarded as binding of matter and spirit, reminiscent of European alchemy. By taking part in sand-painting, dance and chanting, the person is re-integrated into a universe where spirits germinate matter and soul, and visit with animals, plants and mountains.

Here too is a holism, a vision of education not as an end in itself, nor as a stage of acquiring skills for a job, but as one process woven into a culture that goes further than Jung or Romanyshyn or Bernstein can in envisioning a culture that has no sense of humans as individuals, nor of nature, as separate from the community of the whole. To Westerners, this evocation of the Navajo is an important reminder of human possibility, and its inclusion in Bernstein's book is an important attempt to redress the denigration of indigenous knowledge by colonial cultures that has been part of the exploitation of the Other, and has impoverished modernity for so long.

While an important education to the non-Navajo reader, it is highly unlikely that the majority culture can straightforwardly assume Navajo norms. Moreover, such a cultural appropriation would be yet another exploitation of Native Americans. Jung, Romanyshyn and Bernstein all stress that for cultures to safely evolve, rather than violently distort, they must re-examine their own heritage for what has been forgotten, repressed or despised. Hence the importance of alchemy to Jung and Romanyshyn, including tracing its influence in the arts and sciences today; and of evolution and the clinic to Bernstein. So that at some point we should look at re-building education where it is supposedly most ubiquitous: in the classroom.

Post-Jungians in the Classroom

In the growth of Jungian research, we do have some real contributions to the contemporary debates about education in an era of crisis. In fact, I am going to argue that this article so far has re-configured the apparent dichotomy between education for individuals *or* the masses and education for utility *or* to transform consciousness. The traditional argument for the *humanities*, which include history, literature, philosophy, music, painting and dance, has been for a humanised society made up of fulfilled individuals who see themselves as serving humanity. In fact, it is arguable that weakening the case for the humanities by suggesting they are *useless* outside the academic setting, and don't help in gaining employment, is a class and economic point, rather than an educational one. If degrees are hard to fund, for the state as well as the individual, then those that reap an immediate financial return will be preferred. It was only when a very small proportion of eighteen-year-olds went to university that degrees were not hard for the state to fund, nor were they hard to finance by the upper middle class. So the humanities can be afforded and their supposed 'humanising' qualities somewhat subsumed into a quasi-class manifesto about educating 'gentlemen'.

This argument works the other way round. Mass higher education is not necessarily inimical to the humanities, only its financing. On the other hand, Jungian analysts are not in the best position to lecture education institutions, since psychoanalysis, of any kind, is less affordable than taking classes. Yet the point remains that Jung's ideas of the psyche undo the conventional assumption that deep educational fulfilment is an individual structure: it is not. Rather, Jungian Studies shows that managing boundaries between inner and outer, self and social, human and nature, means that people cannot be educated either as single beings nor as 'products' disgorged from a education 'system'. Such attempts to re-think the personal and collective in education are behind innovators such as Darrell Dobson in Canada, Lee Robbins in the US, and Elenice Giosa and Claudio Paixão Anastácio de Paula in Brazil.

Jungian Educational Practice in the University

In papers collected in *Psyche and the Arts* (Rowland, 2008), pioneering use of Jungian techniques are explored in universities in Sao Paulo and New York. Elenice Giosa writes in 'The Poetical Word: Towards an imaginal language', of her rejection of an impoverished language of education that has been stripped of its poetic roots in the creative imagination. Her work with advanced students learning English considers language as a symbolic mediator with the deep potential of the learning psyche. Here language is *treated* as a process, not as a final product of grammatical structures. Giosa shifts second language learning from a rational register of Logos, which Jung called a function of cognition, discrimination and separation in the psyche, to one of Eros, Jung's term for connection, empathy and feeling. She uses Jung's Erotic constructions of gender, anima and animus. These terms refer respectively to the unconscious feminine of a man, and the unconscious masculine of a woman. She educates within 'the animic word', from anima or animus, which is a fruit of the dialogical process through the creativity of the psyche released in the seminar. The aim is an Education of Sensibility, a pedagogical expression that re-unites the person with the nature of his or her surroundings. Education in this university classroom becomes part of individuation in which collective change cannot be separated from individual learning.

Also in Brazil, Jungian therapist Claudio Paixão Anastácio de Paula uses Jung to attempt to deepen that most utilitarian of degree subjects, Business Studies. In 'The Serenity of the Senex: Using Brazilian folk tales as an alternative approach to "entrepreneurship" in university education', he describes bringing traditional Brazilian folktales to a class on developing business practices. He uses methods of getting the students to work imaginatively with the stories. Specifically, the lesson is not just an exercise in expanding the learning of the students beyond their business discipline. Rather, Paixão shows that approaching what makes a successful entrepreneur through imaginative, archetypal literature, enhances their capacities to manage the struggles of the commercial world. Lee Robbins in the United States contributes a more explicitly therapeutic orientation to education, still based in the university setting. She works with the Jungian notion of alchemy as a symbolic system uniting psyche and world. Her methods are essentially artistic as well as intellectual, alchemically uniting cerebral and creative modes of learning in a course, which is thereby alchemical in its design. This course alchemically promotes individuation as education and transformation. 'Healing with the Alchemical Imagination in the Undergraduate Classroom' shows the realisation, the making real, of Jung's vision of the alchemical imagination as a third space born between what is perceived as inner and outer reality. This place of alchemical transformation and healing comes to life for a team of students enrolled in a course called 'Alchemy and the Transformation of Self'. Here formal study (Logos) was combined with work with the empathetic imagination (Eros) in subjects ranging from alchemy, to object relations, quantum physics, Buddhist thought and poetics.

These case studies above are evidence of the potential for Jungian ideas to enrich the education of adults. The challenge of working with children, in particular in the school system, has been taken up elsewhere by educationalists such as Austin Clarkson and Darrell Dobson in Canada.

Jungian Education in Schools

Darrell Dobson's sustained study, *Transformative Teaching* (2008), explores an invaluable concept for teachers, the archetype of the teacher-learner, discussed in his book by Austin Clarkson (2002), and taken from Guggenbuhl-Craig's (1971). Ultimately, the idea that the teacher must also be a learner is rooted in Jung's structuring of the therapist as a wounded healer, one who heals himself by the tending to the painful psyches of his or her patients. Dobson's book is about school teachers and about how gaining access to transformative learning methods, through adapting Jung's principles, enables personal growth and self-development, and vice versa.

Transformative Teaching focuses on four truly innovative educators, one of which (engaged in self-reflection) is Dobson himself. One of the enriching aspects of this book is the complex emergence of what might be called the 'wounded teacher'. Dobson portrays a troubled childhood in a difficult family followed by the impulse to rebel negatively as many teenagers do. Some of these teenagers meet wise teachers who know how to structure a creative outlet for what appears to be a suffocating shadow. Fortunate to experience such a high school teacher who could foster his fragile maturity, Dobson shows in this candid account how he has striven to offer a similar transforming capacity to his students through arts practice in the high school classroom. By 'amplifying' (Jung's term) his own professional story through the three others, Dobson provides persuasive qualitative evidence for the value of teaching through appealing to the nascent self of the students, that part of themselves in touch with their potential wholeness. *Transformative Teaching* explores the dialogical perspective, inherent in Jung, that fostering the student means strengthening the psyche of the teacher. The book tells us that exposing talents of the class means psychic engagement.

What is common to all the Jungian approaches to education considered so far is the critique of fragmentation in modern life. Jungian theory and practice tried to overcome this splitting of parts of the self. It does so by a faith in the intrinsically healing creative qualities of the whole psyche. Jung denies that the individual can be *treated* in all senses, including the educational, as apart from the world. Indeed, to treat the individual is to treat the world, in education as well as therapy. I want to end this article by looking at the role of Jung's concept of a 'healing fiction' and how it might work not just in the partnership of therapy, but also in the collective setting of the classroom. Here adapting a Jungian idea about therapy can change the study of literature into an education in psychic transformation.

Healing Fiction as Classroom Practice: Visionary and Psychological Reading of *Mansfield Park* by Jane Austen

Just as the Jungian educators described above use narratives drawn from poetry, stories and myth to structure creative work in the classroom, so did Jung acknowledge that his therapy needed to offer *a story* to the suffering soul. Moreover, the healing soul-story is a fiction. It has to be, if it is to encompass more than the mundane aspects of the person. We need a healing fiction to work as a narrative structure to bring those denied aspects of our psyche to life again.

> Whether the fiction arises in me spontaneously, or reaches me from without by way of human speech, it can make me ill or cure me ... [The doctor] is now confronted with the necessity of conveying to his patient the healing fiction, the meaning that quickens—for it is this that the patient longs for, over and above all that reason and science can give him. (Jung, 1933, pp. 259–60)

The healing fiction, the story with psychic resonance that can unite a fractured psyche, cannot simply be dictated to a class of recalcitrant children but has to be *made* collectively, dialogically, either in the classroom, or with a therapist and/or with a dialogue with the collective archetypes inhabiting the individual. Jung's idea is a contribution to literary theory, as 'healing fiction' goes some way to diagnose the satisfactions of narrative literature down the centuries. It even suggests what its collective cultural function may be. In looking at a pre-Jungian novel, might there be a way of considering its healing fiction for readers *now* as well as for society *then*? Jane Austen's *Mansfield Park* (1814) was written for a very different world of reading and education than that of the 21st century. Can it be used in the classroom today as the basis for creating with students a healing fiction?

My argument is that by re-visioning Jung's categories of literature into forms of reading, there is potential for most literary narrative to be understood as a stimulus to a healing fiction. My suggestion is that instead of worrying about where a literary text fits on the spectrum between conscious engagement with social concerns (psychological) and unconscious articulation of what is forgotten or not yet known (visionary), we try to read literature for both kinds of understanding. In a psychological reading of *Mansfield Park*, we find a novel about women's education. At the time that the novel was written the education of privileged young women was causing concern for its tendency to concentrate upon superficial qualities. A Jungian psychological reading might note that the story considers all three of *his* types of education. The education by rules of daughters of the house, Maria and Julia Bertram, fails to individuate them. They are unable to resist becoming victim to their own illicit desires. On the other hand, despised poor relation, Fanny Price, responds gratefully to education by example and in person by her kindly cousin Edmund.

The education debate remains tantalising entangled by the romance plot. In falling in love with her educator, Fanny has committed the classic 'fortunate' error of the patient in analysis. Yet Fanny does not use this 'mistake' for psychic growth and learn to detach herself from her erotic educator/therapist. She herself takes on more of the educator/therapist role towards Edmund. The novel finally blesses this structuring of sexuality by endorsing the marriage of the two cousins. The transition from education plot to marriage plot could be challenged as failing to respect necessary ethical boundaries. Or, it could be applauded for the way it integrates a powerfully erotic (in all senses) educational process into a final vision of psychic wholeness.

Looking at the novel as a visionary reader is to consider a story of buried trauma, and an even more obscured healing fiction. Edward Said (1993) may have been the first visionary reader of *Mansfield Park* when he pointed to the significant *absence* in the novel of discussion of Sir Thomas Bertram's sources of wealth. Since it is integral to the plot that Sir Thomas leaves his household to visit his estates in Antigua, the absence of any awareness that the entire household lives on the produce of slaves, is morally and politically glaring. Written at a time of political agitation and when the slave trade itself was being abolished, the novel is pregnant with silence on the subject of slavery, Said's criticism is a visionary reading because it makes substantial the way the silences in the novel operate within contemporary politics to generate meanings that cannot be fixed.

Neither psychological nor visionary readings need to be inhibited by questions of authorial intention. In the classroom, one of the ways of liberating the imagination of students is to focus upon the reader as the location where meaning is debated, constructed and imagined. However, Said's visionary excavation of the trauma of slavery may not be the only hope for healing fiction. What Said posits in the novel is the collective shadow of Imperial Britain. Yet the novel offers some hope in the final destination of the individual characters when it sets up the household of Mansfield at the end of the novel as a plausible 'home' for heroine, Fanny Price. To consider a 'shadow' narrative as a healing fiction means that a lot of work is cast onto the reader to imagine some movement towards redemption. The romantic closure (marriage) is explicitly presented as a moral achievement that will nurture the inner psyche as well as the outer worlds of society and nature.

Austen, indeed, is far from 'solving' slavery. Yes, such healing fiction does attempt a *solve et coagula*, a dissolving of slavery (in the story of Fanny) and a solidifying of its horrifying existence, in the silence that may be understood as referring to the suffering in Antigua's sugar plantations. This revised Jungian method of reading can be used in the classroom to invoke a way of encouraging, by education of the psyche, a strengthening transformation. Jung offers ways to combat the modern tendency to de-humanise, even in education, by narrowing what is defined as desirable outcomes. Jungian contributions to education are dedicated to aiding psychic wholeness, which to Jung meant mental health. Since the psyche cannot be excluded from the classroom, Jung's teaching can help us avoid an education in which a portion of the psyche is enslaved.

References

Austen, J. (1814/1998) *Mansfield Park* (New York, Norton).

Bernstein, J. (2005) *Living in the Borderland: The evolution of consciousness and the challenge of healing trauma* (London and New York, Routledge).

Clarkson, A. (2002) A Curriculum for the Creative Imagination, in: T. Sullivan & L. Willingham (eds), *Creativity and Music Education* (Edmonton, Canadian Music Educator's Association).

Dobson, D. (2008) *Transformative Teaching: Promoting transformation through literature, the arts and Jungian psychology* (Rotterdam, Sense Publishers).

Fish, S. (2009) Stanley Fish, 'The Last Professor'—Stanley Fish Blog—NYTimes.com. Available at: http://fish.blogs.nytimes.com/2009/01/18/the-last-professor/

Guggenbuhl-Craig, A. (1971) *Power in the Helping Professions* (Dallas, TX, Spring Publications).

Jung, C. G. (1933) *Modern Man in Search of a Soul* (London and New York, Routledge).

Jung, C. G. (1954) *Collected Works Volume 17: The development of personality*, H. Read, M. Fordham & G. Adler, eds; R.F.C. Hull, trans. (Princeton, NJ, Princeton University Press).

Romanyshyn, R. (1989) *Technology as Symptom and Dream* (London and New York, Routledge).

Romanyshyn, R. (2007) *The Wounded Researcher* (New Orleans, LA, Spring Publications).

Rowland, S. (ed.) (2008) *Psyche and the Arts: Jungian approaches to music, architecture, literature, painting and film* (London and New York, Routledge).

Said, E. (1993) *Culture and Imperialism* (New York, Alfred A. Knopf).

Steblay, T. (2009) Blog Comment 24 on 'The Last Professor'—Stanley Fish Blog—NYTimes.com. Available at: http://fish.blogs.nytimes.com/2009/01/18/the-last-professor/

2

On the 'Art and Science' of Personal Transformation: Some critical reflections

Raya A. Jones

Introduction

On 20 February, 2009, a headline in *The Times* read: 'Schools "failing to fire the imagination" '. Several media sources that day reported on conclusions from the Cambridge Primary Review (CPR), a major inquiry into primary education in England. Interestingly, the condemnation that has fired journalists' imagination is almost inconspicuous in the documents disseminated by the CPR. In their eleventh of twelve recommendations, they urge,

> To excite children's imagination in order that they can advance beyond present understanding, extend the boundaries of their lives, contemplate worlds possible as well as actual, understand cause and consequence, develop the capacity for empathy, and reflect on and regulate their behaviour; to explore and test language, ideas and arguments in every activity and form of thought. In these severely utilitarian and philistine times it has become necessary to argue the case for creativity and the imagination on the grounds of their contribution to the economy alone. ... At the same time, we assert the need to emphasise the *intrinsic* value of exciting children's imagination. To experience the delights— and pains—of imagining, and of entering into the imaginative worlds of others, is to become a more rounded person. (Alexander, 2009, p. 32; italics in the original)

Their contention could be read as an invitation for a Jungian perspective (cf. Jones, Clarkson, Congram & Stratton, 2008). Yet, if Jung excites our own imagination, the excitement might blind us to a dissonance between analytical psychology and education.

This essay considers some aspects of the shadow (in the Jungian sense of the term) of the post-Jungian discourse within transformative learning. In classical Jungian theory, the *personal shadow* is 'the repository of all the aspects of a person that are unacceptable or distasteful to them', though it is not always negative qualities (Casement, 2006, p. 94). Applying the idea to a discourse—i.e. to a system-of-statements that emerges as a collective enterprise by virtue of its texts—the aim of exposing its shadow may be understood as a positive step towards moving that discourse forward.

Jung and Educational Theory, First Edition. Edited by Inna Semetsky.
Chapters © 2013 The Authors. Book compilation © 2013 Philosophy of Education Society of Australasia.
Published 2013 by Blackwell Publishing Ltd.

Jung and Education

Jung's position on individuation and imagination does not necessarily contradict pedagogic goals, but does not directly correspond with them. For instance, does Jung's view of the imagination really accord with what the CPR writers have in mind? When he says that the 'goal of the individuation process is the synthesis of the self' (1940, par. 278), the ideal of a *whole* person—or a person-made-whole—is not the same as the 'rounded' person implied by the CPR writers, which evokes the ideal of liberal education. From the standpoint of education, activating students' imagination would serve the child's mastery of transferable skills, such as communication, problem-solving, expression, and more— and, by implication, the activity's immediate product, such as the picture a child draws, is almost incidental. Jung's technique of *active imagination* is likewise instrumental; but it is a means for confronting one's unconscious. In this context, 'exciting' the imagination would be pointless unless the actual product, such as an image giving form by painting other media, is reflexively engaged with.

It is important to note that Jung built both the praxis and theory of his analytical psychology with a focus on personal growth in adulthood. Telling teachers about his methods, he repeatedly cautioned: 'I must warn you again most emphatically that it would be very unsound to apply these methods directly to children' (Jung, 1928a, par. 111). Although active imagination techniques can be beneficially applied with children (see Clarkson, 2008), Jung assumed a sophistication of self-reflection that is developmentally unlikely in childhood. It involves not only the capacity to reflect on one's feelings, anxieties, or motives (which school-aged children can do), but also one's realization and desire for personal growth, as well as an intellectual grasp of analytical-psychological principles of individuation. Furthermore, according to Jung, the 'individuation process with its problem of opposites' requires a one-to-one relationship, whereby the other person becomes a mirror making possible the confrontation of aspects of one's self that lie outside ego-consciousness:

> This level of insight cannot be reached without the dialectical discussion between two individuals. Here the phenomenon of transference forcibly brings about a dialogue that can only be continued if both patient and analyst acknowledge themselves as partners in a common process of approximation and differentiation. (Jung, 1957, par. 1172)

Such a relationship is fundamentally different not only from that of a teacher and a child, but also from the relationship between two adults where one is positioned as teacher and the other as student, because a different set of rights and duties is reciprocally assigned when people acknowledge themselves as partners in an educational process as opposed to therapy. Other important distinctions include the fact that, notwithstanding private tuition, teachers' interactions with students always place the student within a classroom group (even when advising the student individually); and the student's progress is evaluated, often quite publicly, against formal benchmarks. The 'lived' reality of the educational setting is unlike that of the therapy room.

Addressing the International Congress of Education in 1923 and 1924, Jung did not impart a psychologist's advice about teaching or learning. In the epilogue appended to the last of those lectures two decades after delivering it, he admits: 'About education in general and school education in particular the doctor has little to say from the standpoint of his science, as that is hardly his business' (1946, par. 228). This hardly means that he had nothing to say—but he spoke as a clinician. One of the 1924 lectures concerns the aetiology of psychopathology in children. The lecture makes some important points, but today it offers little that hasn't been developed more extensively in non-Jungian frameworks. His most direct consideration of pedagogy is found in the 1923 lecture; but his advice boils down to telling teachers to work on improving their own character, for children learn from adults by example—and, having established that, he urges educators (like any adult) to self-educate in the basics of analytical psychology as a step towards their own personal growth. Jung is at his best, most original and still fresh, when speaking about individuation in adulthood.

In effect, following his advice would take the teacher outside the classroom and into the therapist's room. A post-Jungian strand within transformative learning, in the context of adult education, presents an interesting case of a reverse movement: taking 'Jung' out of psychotherapy and into the classroom. For brevity's sake, I shall focus only on some writings by John Dirkx, who has done the most to develop an approach inspired by James Hillman's post-Jungian psychology. This approach fosters awareness of the role of emotions in learning, and specifically the power of emotionally loaded images (e.g. Dirkx, 2001a, 2001b). It is precisely this awareness which ought to alert us to the play of images in our own campaigns, if we are campaigning for 'Jung' in education.

The Power of Images

Dirkx (1998) identifies four strands of the conceptual framework associated with labels such as transformative or transformational learning or education, strands which overlap and cross-influenced each other: (1) transformation as consciousness-raising (associated with the work of Freire), (b) transformation as critical reflection (associated with Mezirow), (c) transformation as development (associated with Daloz), and (d) transformation as individuation, attributed in the first instance to Boyd (e.g. 1991). As Dirkx put it,

> [Boyd's] concern is primarily with the expressive or emotional-spiritual dimensions of learning and integrating these dimensions more holistically and consciously within our daily experience of life. According to Boyd, adult learners do this by making the unconscious conscious, becoming aware of aspects of themselves of which they are not conscious. (Dirkx, 1998, p. 3)

Dirkx and a few others extended Boyd's approach to 'a frankly more spiritual perspective' (ibid., p. 4). In his own work, Dirkx has sought to understand better 'the role that fantasy and imagination play in transformative learning and how these processes guide learners to deeper understandings of themselves in relation to the subject matter or texts they are studying and to their world' (ibid., p. 4).

To make an obvious point, images enter pedagogy in two functionally different ways, objective and subjective. For example, Plato-as-Socrates provides several analogies to communicate his ideas about the nature of the soul or mind (depending on how the word *psyche* is translated). Suffice it to cite *Theaetetus*, where he elaborates two in quick succession: the soul is first described as containing a block of wax upon which sense-impressions are made; second, it is likened to an aviary where all sorts of birds represent 'pieces of knowledge' flying in every direction, 'some in flocks apart from the rest, some in small groups, and some solitary' (Plato, 1992, §197e). Those are objective (or inter-subjective) images insofar as anyone familiar with wax or birds would understand what Socrates is trying to say in a similar way. Neither analogy is asserted by Plato as the 'correct' model of the mind. And both are the wrong tools if we want our students to get a picture of the variety of conceptual models in modern psychology. Towards this goal we may note that some psychologists liken the mind to a computer, some liken the person-ality to an organism, or liken the self to a narrative or a text, and so forth; and also note that heated debates ensued from disagreements about the 'correct' image. However, the Socratic analogies (and likewise modern metaphors) also have a subjective effect. To me, the aviary has poetic potency that the block of wax doesn't. I could intellectualize about it—e.g. quoting Jung ('Birds are soul-images': 1952, par. 315) and amplifying it with mythological and other examples—or simply be content with liking to hold this image in my mind. It has the homely feel of watching birds flocking down to the bird-table in my garden. It also 'rings true' experientially: working on a paper, it sometimes feels like birds flocking about in my head, and I'm trying to get them into some linear flight pattern. So the aviary makes me smile. My point: it has an *aesthetic*, a 'feeling' effect, which may reveal something about me; but this effect has little if anything to do with its utility (or not) for me as a teacher or student of psychology.

I've drawn out that distinction as a prelude to emphasizing again the dissonance between educational and 'Jungian' goals. Arguably, Dirkx's most important message is to point out the subjective function of images—including images (or imagos) that have no manifest 'pictorial' content, but make their presence in emotional reactions to some classroom situation. In terms of pedagogy (or andragogy), it is not clear what teachers can do about it. Should I make my students (who major in social-sciences disciplines) read certain novels, listen to great pieces of classical music, and so on, hoping that they'll find these as inspiring as I do? What would be the pedagogic purpose, given that I want them to get to know (in a short time) the works of Jung, Freud, Piaget, and more? I agree with Dirkx (1998) that reading novels, listening to music, etc., may 'open up a realm of being that is barely visible to our waking ego consciousness' and that it is 'this realm of being that is expressed in learning through soul' (p. 82). But to take upon oneself, as a teacher, the role of someone who opens doors to such mysteries is a fantasy of power (cf. Guggenbühl-Craig, 1971)—a self-delusion that could turn dangerous, for confronting the unconscious can be highly disturbing.

Secondly, 'learning through soul' reiterates the truism that we learn better when we find the content highly engaging—and why something is highly engaging is not always consciously known—but by overstating the subjective function of images, the pragmatic and ego-conscious purpose of learning something is dismissed as if it were irrelevant. *Self-directed learning* has been generally identified as a main feature differentiating adult education from the education of children. The factor of *choice* should also be taken into account. Not all my students could be described as 'self-directed' learners, but all of them enter post-compulsory education out of choice, investing money and time, and typically with a career in mind. Commenting on the commodification of adult education, Lauzon (1998) has suggested that 'education for the marketplace' is based on 'a psychology of the *empty-self*, a self that only finds fulfillment through consumption' (p. 318; italics in the original). He makes a passionate case for a psychology of the soul, which is 'about healing and becoming whole again … a way of knowing … of understanding and constructing meaning in the world … of acting in the world' (ibid., p. 319). This repositions the adult learner as someone in need of healing—irrespective of whether this adult knows it—and positions the teacher as morally bound to guide students' journey of individuation, irrespective of what those adults expect out of education. The discourse of soul psychology in education thus imposes a subtle coercion—its shadow, given that transformative education generally is understood as emancipatory.

A Short Detour to the Pragmatics of Science

A practitioner's review of the transformation-as-individuation framework would consider the pragmatic utility of what its proponents are saying. The cogency of the argument made by exponents of transformation-as-individuation, and whether the premises upon which it rests have what could be called scientific validity, may be critiqued independently of any practical utility. One of its truth-claims is that 'Self-knowledge, or knowledge of ourselves and the world, is mediated largely through symbols rather than directly through language' (Dirkx, 1998, p. 3). This statement has the structural trappings of a testable hypothesis; that is, generating predictions that could be confirmed or refuted in experimental or quasi-experimental procedures if only scientists could figure out how to gauge the relative effects of words versus images vis-à-vis self-knowledge. The 'frankly more spiritual' approach is suspicious of the scientific method. In contrast, Boyd (1991) used the traditional scientific method to investigate transformation in small groups, finding a pattern that could be described as an orderly succession of archetypes. If the pattern is shown to recur with regularity greater than chance in many groups, such knowledge may help teachers to anticipate the dynamics of classroom groups. It is rigorous research pertaining to the *art* (or craft) of a profession in which psychology is applied.

There is a crucial difference between seeking to establish what 'works' best in practice (including the utility of abstract principles and models such as identified by Boyd) and seeking to understand why or how something works. The latter constitutes the *science* of psychology. Different criteria apply when judging the value of Jungian ideas for the art of transformative education than when judging their viability vis-à-vis a scientific explanation. Although Jung referred to analytical psychology as a science, he placed it firmly within the domain of art (as defined above) when introducing it to teachers:

> Analytical psychology is eminently practical. It does not investigate for the sake of investigation, but for the very immediate purpose of giving help … . We could as well say that abstract science is its by-product, not its main aim, which is … a great difference from what one understands by an academic science. (Jung, 1928b, p. 348–9)

The 'abstract science' of analytical psychology consists of concepts which are imported 'back' into the praxis of classical Jungian analysis as if these were a scientific explanation, but which have not been subjected to the scientific method. This fact does not render them meaningless; but Jung's abstract science 'might be correct in the way that a literary novel, poem, musical piece or abstract painting is correct. That is, as a whole coherent unto itself, all its elements in perfect relation to each other' (Jones, 2007, p. 14).

Jung indeed recognized the problems inherent in applying the natural-scientific paradigm to the study of the psyche, problems which he regarded as the dilemma of modern psychology. Noting that an 'unbreakable' rule in scientific research is to accept something as known only insofar the scientist can make 'valid statements about it'—where valid 'simply means what can be verified by facts'—Jung contended that psychology 'does not exclude the existence of faith, conviction, and experienced certainties of whatever description, nor does it contest their possible validity ... [but] completely lacks the means to prove their validity in the scientific sense' (1948, par. 384). Given that dilemma of psychology, the belief that self-knowledge is 'mediated largely through symbols rather than directly through language' remains a belief: a matter of faith, conviction, and an experienced certainty for some—and disputed by others.

Many social scientists would beg to differ with statements such as Dirkx's. An extreme opposite truth-claim is staked by discursive psychologists, who equate the self with the first-person singular pronoun. As commented upon in Jones (2007, p. 65), 'The idea of the self as a grammatical operator is incommensurable with Jung's view of the self as arising from the natural psyche and encompassing "both the experienceable and the inexperienceable" '. Less extreme, but highly influential in the social sciences, has been George Herbert Mead's view of the self as a product directly and solely of language-mediated social interactions (see Jones, 2007, for Mead's view in relation to Jung's).

Soul-speak as Ideology

We are entered into soul-speak immediately when encountering the title of Dirkx's (1997) paper: 'Nurturing Soul in Adult Learning'. What exactly is 'nurturing the soul'? It is explained at the end of the introduction:

> It is a view of learning through soul, an idea centuries old reemerging in this age of information, giving voice in a deep and powerful way to imaginative and poetic expressions of self and the world. But the soul dimensions of transformation have received little attention in our study of adult learning. Our journey of self-knowledge also requires that we care for and nurture the presence of the soul dimension in teaching and learning. In this chapter, I develop a view of what it means to attend to, understand, and facilitate learning through soul, of nurturing and caring for soul. (ibid., p. 80)

While the word *soul* is mentioned five times in the above four sentences, we don't find out what Dirkx means by it till later (quoted below). In the meantime, the word has already auto-defined itself for us in accordance with its personal associations. It has acted upon us like a poetic image which, as Bachelard (1994 [1958]) put it, 'sets in motion the entire linguistic mechanism. ... After the original reverberation, we are able to experience resonances, sentimental repercussions, reminders of our past. But the image has touched the depths before it stirs the surface' (p. xxiii). Dirkx may call that rhetorical effect an experience of soul. He explains the term:

> It is easier to see what is meant by *soul* through examples of common experiences than through a specific definition. Being awestruck by a brilliant sunset, captured by the majestic beauty of a rising full moon, or gripped by the immense pain and helplessness we feel for a child trapped deep inside an abandoned well are experiences of soul. (1997, p. 81)

This pertains to what William James (1884) spoke of as 'the *aesthetic* sphere of the mind, its longings, its pleasures and pains, and its emotions' (p. 188, italics in the original). However, to supplant James's 'aesthetic sphere' with 'experiences of soul' is to do more than merely use a different label. *Soul* is not a neutral term. It is a most powerful emotionally loaded image.

As I read him, Dirkx is not suggesting that educators should abandon the 'traditional, technical-rational perspective' with its focus on manifest content (1997, p. 81). He seeks to redress the balance, hence avers that personal transformation should be 'informed by a sense of mythos, as well as logos' (ibid., p. 87). He encourages learning experiences 'through the lens of mythos rather than logos' (ibid., p. 81). And he speaks evocatively—with subtle connotations of Eastern mysticism—of 'the *way* of mythos' (ibid., p. 80; my italics). But here the shadow makes its ironic play. While emphasizing wholeness, seeking to redress the one-sidedness of education, soul-speak is entrenched in the myth of a mythos-versus-logos dichotomy, having us believing that true meaning can be achieved only through one or the other. To speak of soul is to take a high moral ground (who can argue against nurturing the soul?). Soul-speak evokes a narrative, a storyline, of deep dark mysteries which open up to followers of the Way of Mythos; and to those enticed by the evocation, soul-speak shines a light which casts Logos in the deep shade of a bleak, frigid, soul-less intellectual realm.

The way-of-mythos narrative could be viewed as a myth in Barthes's (1993 [1957]) sense of the term. To Barthes, the 'very principle of myth' is that 'it transforms history into nature' in the eye of the myth-consumer; 'what causes mythical speech to be uttered is perfectly explicit, but it is immediately frozen into something natural; it is not read as a motive, but as a reason' (ibid., p. 129). In other words, myth is a form of speech that hides nothing but distorts. In soul-speak, the ideal of personal transformation is frozen into a notion of a psychological process in touch with innermost human nature, our very soul. Such mythical speech converts into 'nature' the historicity of human lives and personalities, as well as denying its own historicity as a discourse peculiar to late-modern Western (middle-class and mostly white) society.

It is a quirk of history that certain individuals found Jung or (more directly) Hillman inspiring, and have been in a position to import depth-psychological insights into education. What I have called soul-speak is separate from the art and science of personal transformation. Arguably, work such Dirkx's would not lose its poignant contribution to educational practice if it were stripped of soul-speak, though it might lose its rhetorical power. Yet, by focusing on soul—with connotations of Nature, the pan-cultural and a-historical—this discourse makes its own historicity almost untellable. As Christopher and Hickinbottom (2008) say in their critique of positive psychology, 'There is, quite simply, no such thing as a value-neutral, culture-free psychology' (p. 565).

A Closing Reflection

Jung may have the 'final' word here. He attributed to Heraclitus the discovery of the 'most marvellous of all psychological laws: the regulative function of opposites ... sooner or later everything runs into its opposite' (1943, par. 111). Heraclitus's wisdom—and Jung's—was to point to necessary dualities, like day and night, dark and light. The mythos-versus-logos dichotomy, in which the transformation-as-individuation approach is entrenched, could be transcended when the two 'ways' are recognized as a necessary duality within the history of ideas in modern society.

References

Alexander, R. J. (2009) *Towards a New Primary Curriculum: A report from the Cambridge Primary Review. Part 2: The Future* (Cambridge, University of Cambridge Faculty of Education).

Bachelard, G. (1994) *The Poetics of Space* (Boston, MA, Beacon Press) (Original work published 1958.)

Barthes, R. (1993) *Mythologies* (London, Vintage). (Original work published in 1957.)

Boyd, R. D. (1991). *Personal Transformation in Small Groups: A Jungian perspective* (London, Routledge).

Casement, A. (2006) The Shadow, in: R. K. Papadopoulos (ed.), *The Handbook of Jungian Psychology* (London, Routledge).

Christopher, J. C. & Hickinbottom S. (2008) Positive Psychology, Ethnocentrism, and the Disguised Ideology of Individualism. *Theory & Psychology*, 18, pp. 563–589.

Clarkson, A. (2008) The Dialectical Mind: On educating the creative imagination in elementary school, in: Jones R. A., Clarkson A., Congram S. & Stratton N. (eds), *Education and Imagination* (London, Routledge).

Dirkx, J. M. (1997) Nurturing Soul in Adult Learning, *New Directions for Adult and Continuing Education*, 74, pp. 79–88.

Dirkx, J. M. (1998) Transformative Learning Theory in the Practice of Adult Education: An overview, *PAACE Journal of Lifelong Learning*, 17, pp. 1–7.

Dirkx, J. M. (2001a) The Power of Feelings: Emotion, imagination, and the construction of meaning in adult learning, *New Directions for Adult and Continuing Education*, 89, pp. 63–72.

Dirkx, J. M. (2001b) Images, Transformative Learning and the Work of Soul, *Adult Learning*, 12, pp. 15–16.

Guggenbühl-Craig, A. (1971) *Power in the Helping Professions* (Dallas, TX, Spring).

James, W. (1884) What is an Emotion?, *Mind*, 9, pp. 188–205.

Jones, R. A. (2007) *Jung, Psychology, Postmodernity* (London, Routledge).

Jones, R. A., Clarkson A., Congram S. & Stratton N. (eds) (2008) *Education and Imagination* (London, Routledge).

Jung, C. G. (1928a) Child Development and Education, *The Collected Works of C. G. Jung* (Vol. 17) (London, Routledge & Kegan Paul).

Jung, C. G. (1928b) Analytical Psychology and Education, in: H. G. Baynes & C. F. Baynes (eds), *Contributions to Analytical Psychology* (London, Kegan Paul).

Jung, C. G. (1940) The Psychology of the Child Archetype, *The Collected Works of C. G. Jung* (Vol. 9i) (London, Routledge & Kegan Paul).

Jung, C. G. (1943) On the Psychology of the Unconscious, *The Collected Works of C. G. Jung* (Vol. 7) (London, Routledge & Kegan Paul).

Jung, C. G. (1946) Analytical Psychology and Education, *The Collected Works of C. G. Jung* (Vol. 17) (London, Routledge & Kegan Paul).

Jung, C. G. (1948) The Phenomenology of the Spirit in Fairytales, *The Collected Works of C. G. Jung* (Vol. 9i) (London, Routledge & Kegan Paul).

Jung, C. G. (1952) Symbols of Transformation, *The Collected Works of C. G. Jung* (Vol. 5) (London, Routledge & Kegan Paul).

Jung, C. G. (1957) Forward to Michael Fordham: New Developments in Analytical Psychology, *The Collected Works of C. G. Jung* (Vol. 18) (London, Routledge & Kegan Paul).

Lauzon, A. (1998) In Search of a Future: Adult education and the psychology of the soul, *International Journal of Lifelong Education*, 17, pp. 318–327

Plato (1992) *Theaetetus* (Indianapolis, IN, Hackett).

3
The Polytheistic Classroom

BERNIE NEVILLE

Archetype

The concept of archetype is central to Jung's understanding of the universe and the place of human beings in it. It is one of the most important ideas to have emerged in the 20th century, an idea with enormous implications for the way we think about ourselves.

In his writing, Jung swings through a number of variations on the notion of archetype. At times he was careful to point out the distinction between the archetypes as such and the archetypal images through which we become aware of them. At times he seemed most interested in their physical manifestation, in instinct or pathology. At times he described them as our archaic heritage—a 'living system of reactions and aptitudes that determine the individual's life in invisible ways' (Jung, *Collected Works*, 8, para. 339). He argued that 'they can only be explained by assuming them to be deposits of the constantly repeated experiences of humanity' (Jung, *CW*, 7, para. 109). At other times he emphasized that they were not inherited habits, or even inherited ideas, but inherited *possibilities* of ideas and behaviour. All of our ways of perceiving, thinking, feeling, valuing and behaving are shaped by particular possibilities.

More recently archetypal psychologists like Michael Conforti have argued that it makes most sense to think of archetypes as fields which predate the existence of matter, and out of which matter and form emerge. Others, like Anthony Stevens, argue that the archetypal patterns in human behaviour are the result of evolutionary adaptation. If we see these two ideas as contradictory it may say less about the nature of archetype than it does about the nature of our thinking. What is important here is the notion that the universe we live in is patterned in specific ways, and that these patterns can be detected even in apparently trivial aspects of human experience.

We experience these patterns in our instincts, our habits and our emotions. For Jung, their most obvious cultural manifestation is in images to which we collectively attribute power and meaning. Our ancestors personified them as gods. James Hillman suggests that if we want to understand ourselves we should see through our behaviour all the way to the god image and the god-story in which it is embedded. And we need to experience these god-stories the way our ancestors did, not just as interesting stories which we hear and remember and tell to our children, but as grand narratives within which we live our lives.

Before his break with Freud, Jung had developed the notion of the complex, a group of interconnected ideas and feelings which exert a dynamic effect on behaviour. While complexes could be pathological, they could also be healthy, normal components of the personal psyche. As Anthony Stevens puts it, Jung saw them as 'the functional units of which the ontogenetic psyche was composed' (Stevens, 1982, p. 65). James Hillman

Jung and Educational Theory, First Edition. Edited by Inna Semetsky.

argues that Jung's key contribution to psychology was not his discovery of the complex but 'his radical, personified formulation of them' (Hillman, 1977, p. 20). Referring to his labelling of complexes with names like 'Wise Old Man','Great Mother', 'Child' and 'Anima', Jung explains that:

> ... the fact that the unconscious spontaneously personifies ... is the reason why I have taken over these personifications in my terminology and formulated them as names. (Jung, *Collected Works*, 9,1, para. 514)

It was only later, when he became convinced of the importance of collective unconscious processes and developed his theory of archetypes, that he came to see complexes as 'personations' of archetypes. Their autonomy, feelings, intentions and patterns of behaviour seemed to be grounded in archetypal 'persons'.

> We are obliged to reverse our rationalistic causal sequence, and instead of deriving these figures from our psychic conditions, must derive our psychic conditions from these figures ... . It is not we who personify them; they have a personal nature from the very beginning. (in Hillman, 1977, p. 22)

It has become fairly conventional in Jungian and post-Jungian writing, especially since the publication of Hillman's *Re-visioning Psychology* (1977), to use the gods of the Greek pantheon as a language for talking about complexes and archetypes.

For Jung the gods are indispensable to the life of the psyche.

> All ages before us have believed in gods of some form or other. Only an unparalleled impoverishment of symbolism could enable us to rediscover gods as psychic factors, that is, as archetypes of the unconscious. (Jung, *Collected Works*, 9, 1, para. 50)

But, as Hillman points out, today that is precisely where we do discover the gods—in the unconscious psyche—and because of this unconsciousness we are 'unable to distinguish gods from archetypes. Therefore, a description of the archetypes and the classical descriptions of the gods ... have to be analogous' (Hillman, 1977, p. 36).

Associated with the complex in Jung's thinking was the phenomenon of inflation: 'the state of egocentric exhilaration which can follow the eruption into consciousness of highly charged unconscious (particularly archetypal) components' (Stevens, 1982, p. 298). We can likewise talk of inflation when a nation or culture is taken over by a particular archetypal energy. We may find inflations of all kinds in educational systems, in classrooms, in teachers' personalities. When we look at teachers and the classrooms in which they work we may find both the wisdom that comes with embracing the perspective of a particular god, and the pathology which comes with excessive worship, where the teacher is inflated by the energy of one god at the expense of all the others.

The Greek pantheon can provide us with a language for talking about a wide range of distinct philosophies, value systems, energies, feeling states, habits of behaviour and teaching styles as they can be observed in the classroom. It is a language which is not dominated by a single educational philosophy or theory but welcomes contradictory perspectives. The gods are many, and if we follow the advice of the ancient Greeks we will be careful not to neglect any of them—and not to get too carried away in worshipping any single one of them.

Great Zeus

The archetypal pattern personified in Zeus is the pattern of power, the power which brings order to chaos, maintains itself brutally or benevolently, can both protect and punish and provides security as well as fear. Autocratic administrators or teachers may embody the positive qualities of Zeus, in providing staff or students with the security of clear expectations and unambiguous rules, or they may embody his negative qualities in their suppression of dissent. The Zeus-dominated curriculum ensures that what is taught is what is already known and judged to be important. The Zeus-dominated bureaucracy protects teachers and students from chaos. Human beings generally prefer order, even autocratic order, to chaos. The Zeus-inflated teacher or principal believes that he (usually he) does not have to answer to anyone. He makes all the decisions. He punishes those who offend him and rewards with those who please him.

William Glasser (1990) describes the 'quality school' as one where children's basic needs for power, belonging, freedom and fun are satisfied. Children and adolescents no longer simply need power; they are aware when they haven't got enough, and inclined to demand it. If the teacher does not offer them any power, they manufacture it through defiance, resistance or apathy. In the quality classroom, where Zeus' children Athene and Dionysos have a place, students are involved in decision-making, take leadership roles, initiate action and experience responsibility. They don't need to satisfy their need for power in ways that damage themselves and others.

The teacher's Zeus energy keeps the teacher in charge, even when she conducts her classes in a radically democratic fashion. There are times when we need Zeus' authority to deal with crisis, or to keep the classroom safe. However, to keep ourselves nice we need something from the other gods as well.

Glorious Hera

Hera, for the classical Greeks, was the Queen who shared in the power of King Zeus, the Wife who remained loyally in the background while the divine Husband attended to the affairs of the universe. 'Lady' is a fitting title for her. It denotes her dignity and the honour due to her as queen of the gods. In the Greek imagination, she represents social stability. Homer and the other poets depict her as the god of marriage and the family, the god of all those familial and social bonds and shared expectations which keep a society from exploding into fragments. To use the language of the *quality school*, Hera puts a high value on *belonging* and *power*, but has no interest in *freedom* or *fun*.

We find her in the notion that the task of teachers is to educate their students in the appropriate ways of behaving in our society. She abhors change. She attaches no value to creativity or personal growth. Her priorities are responsibility, loyalty, respect, commitment, honour, stability, dignity. For the teacher who worships her, the school and profession command complete loyalty. There is no place in Hera's world for individuals who give priority to their own satisfaction and personal fulfilment. Every member of the school family must put commitment and loyalty to the school ahead of personal whims and satisfactions. Hera loves pointing this out to people.

The child who knows how to 'fit in' may flourish in the Hera style of classroom, because 'fitting in' is what it is about. The teacher who knows how to 'fit in' will flourish in the school where Hera is worshipped. She will treat senior members of the 'family' with respect. She will not criticize the school to outsiders. She will appreciate that there is a 'proper' way of doing things. If she has any ideas that challenge the established way of doing things she will be wise to keep quiet about it.

Mother Demeter

Jung found that the image of *mother as container* is universal in human experience. When he looked to mythology and religious belief he could find stories of the Mother Goddess which matched the observations that he and Freud had made about our infantile attachment to mother and our conflicting needs to escape from mother's embrace and remain in it.

There is clearly a pattern in human affairs which we call mothering, and Demeter personifies it. She gives birth, she suckles, she provides, she is anxious for her child, she grieves, she gives her child the love and support necessary for growth. This is a psychological pattern as well as a biological one, and men as well as women share in it. Teaching is a profession where mothering skills are often needed. For some children, the school and classroom provide the only container where they feel safe.

Teachers with strong Demeter values take mothering seriously. Central to their image of themselves is their task of providing a safe and supportive environment for their students. They take responsibility for the care of their students, exercising the power of the carer and nourisher. Rather than, 'Do what I say because I say so' which is the message of Father Zeus, Mother Demeter says, 'Trust me. I know what is best for you'. However, when we find schools seriously devoted to mothering their students, protecting and nourishing them in a cycle of mutual affection and dependence, we may be concerned that children will not grow up 'tough' enough for the 'real' world. We can see readily enough the negative aspects of the goddess in Demeter-inflated teachers who cannot bear to let their children grow up. However, awareness of Demeter's pathology leaves some educators unable to acknowledge the positive Demeter aspects— nurturance, protection, sacrifice, love. Demeter's right to be reverenced may be acknowledged in the infant class, where mothering needs little excuse, but it tends to be resisted elsewhere in the schooling system.

The myth of Demeter suggests that if mothering is not honoured, Earth is not honoured, and if Earth is not honoured we all die.

Bright-eyed Athene

Athene is the goddess of balance, of normality, of common sense. Unlike the numerous gods of the bizarre, who manage to make our lives exciting, Athene represents our tendency to avoid extremes. She is a goddess with attributes which we are now inclined to stereotype as masculine. She is, for instance, a god of war. Not vehement, sword-wielding, blood-lusting warfare, waged for the violence and the glory of it (like Ares, the other Olympian war god), but cool, intelligent, calculating, strategic warfare, waged to defend one's city and citizens. She is also a god of peace, and of the civilized living that comes with peace. She teaches us the arts and sciences which form the basis of this civilization. She also teaches us that we must fight to defend them. She is the goddess of the democratic process. She has little interest in relationships, except in so far as they have strategic value.

Athene has many disciples in the education system. They believe in doing things well. They believe in participative decision-making. They use cooperative teaching methods. They see schooling as an apprenticeship in democracy. They are delighted when they find themselves teaching a group of children or adolescents who are really prepared to take responsibility for their behaviour, and are happy to negotiate curriculum and rules of classroom conduct with them. They favour a problem-solving approach to curriculum. In their teaching, they like to use a lot of group work, not because relationships are important, but because group work is a very efficient method of teaching.

As administrators they have a great deal of faith in consensus. Their preferred way of developing strategies or dealing with problems is a collaborative approach that recognizes and utilizes people's different kinds of expertise. Too much emotionality is frowned on. Principals who are committed to the values of Athene put great store by the professional expertise of their staff.

The pathology of Athene can be found where students have learned Athene's lesson of non-engagement but not the point of that non-engagement, which is to enable a clear-sighted and focused attack on a critical problem. It is apparent also in schools where democratic processes are so central that no decision can ever be made until everyone's opinion has been taken into account—with the result that often decisions are not made at all, or Zeus decides to ignore every one's opinion and just do it his way.

Shining Apollo

Apollo is the eldest son of Zeus, the symbol of what it meant to be Greek and civilized: art, music, poetry, science, respect for law, athletic prowess, a sense of moderation. He is, besides, the god of prophecy and healing. However, the myth of Apollo shows him to be very inept when it comes to relationships.

If we look at the basic assumptions behind traditional notions of education, we will find Apollo, the god of clarity, understanding, enlightenment and order claiming our attention and demanding our worship. However, Apollo's claim to this domain has been under challenge for some time. It used to be assumed without question that, while there were certain skills which everyone ought to learn, and certain habits that everyone ought to acquire, the real purpose of education was knowledge, understanding, even wisdom. This fantasy is hanging on grimly nowadays, in the face of a challenge from other more fashionable gods.

In the classroom Apollo establishes order and the rule of law. Not autocratic do-it-because-I-say-so law (which is the law of Zeus), but rational law, based on a reasoned estimation of what constitutes good and bad behaviour. He is the god who gives children and adults the capacity to think clearly, to understand how the world works, to find meaning, to organize their lives in an ordered way. He demands that we seek moderation in all things and look at the world in a detached and reasonable way.

Teachers or principals who are sensitive to Apollo values will place a high value on a rational approach to their work. Individual whims and impulsive decision-making are strongly discouraged and emotional outbursts are looked on with distaste. It is assumed that all problems can be solved and all crises dealt with through the application of cool intelligence. The pathology of Apollo emerges in a tendency to dogmatism and rigidity. Once the Apollo-inflated principal or teacher sees the way things are, he or she has little tolerance for those who cannot. He (usually he) wants things to be obvious, and has little patience with ambiguity and illusion. He is inclined to insist that people accept his assessment of a situation, because its reasonableness is perfectly clear to him and those who can't see this must be stupid or bloody-minded. Apollo's pathology also emerges in his hostility to women, whom he marginalizes as trivial, intuitive, emotional, sensual and irrational. In mythology, Apollo appears to be unable to have any sort of satisfactory relationship with a female—goddess, nymph or mortal—except with his mother and sister. Apollo's is not the only truth. Each of the gods gives us a different meaning for our being, a different truth, and all these meanings and truths must be held in balance.

Artemis the Huntress

Artemis, or Diana as the Romans called her, is the goddess of sisterhood. She is the virgin goddess of the woods and mountains, the goddess of the moon, a goddess who is both a hunter and a protector of animals. She has neither the need nor the desire to make herself pleasing to men or to give them power. As goddess of wild animals she shares their natural grace, their ability to live in harmony with nature and their fierceness. As goddess of childbirth she has a special role in the protection of children. As a nature-goddess she is clearly distinguished from Demeter, as the virgin forest is distinguished from the nurturing earth.

An Artemis education is based on an ideal of companionship rather than hierarchy, natural rhythms rather than abstract order. It values its difference, sees itself not only as special, but also as constantly under threat from an outside world which would destroy it. The bonds between people are based as much on the sharing of an ideology as on intimacy. Teachers in such an environment are expected to be passionate about their mission, and they want their students to share their passion. They don't have much respect for formal management structures, and value intuition more than logic.

The values of Artemis, the heroic feminine (she is associated with the Amazons), provide an essential counterbalance to the images of the masculine hero which have played a dominant part in Western culture. Artemis brings us a very different vision of educational priorities: to develop in children sense of community, a love of wilderness, ecological sensitivity and a respect for non-human creatures.

Both girls and boys, both women and men, have suffered from the devaluation of the qualities peculiar to Artemis: the ability to live within the rhythms of nature, to move lightly over the earth, to deal with crises precisely and gracefully, to build community, to be self-contained, to protect the weak. The truth of Artemis, that we must live in harmony with nature, not in opposition to it, is one which must be fought for, ruthlessly if need be.

Artemis exercises her influence over her disciples through personal power. She is not dependent on roles and structures, but on a sort of animal bonding which is sometimes called charisma. Teachers who have this power, should recognize it as a gift, but a dangerous one. It can help them immeasurably in the work, if they can acknowledge it without embarrassment. It can also enable them to do great harm, if they refuse to acknowledge it or if they identify with it too completely. Artemis must be worshipped, but so must her brother, Apollo.

Golden-haired Aphrodite

Aphrodite is the goddess of beauty and sensuality. She is overtly and unselfconsciously sexual. She believes in fun, in immediate gratification, in the ultimate power of beauty. She has none of Hera's concern for respectability and social obligations. She is irresponsible and self-indulgent, careless of the consequences of her actions. She gets plenty of attention in popular culture, but she does not get much acknowledgment in an education system dominated by other gods.

Unfortunately, there are not many classrooms where educational activity is driven by the pursuit of beauty, where poems are read, stories are told, photographs are looked at, mathematical formulations are admired, scientific experiments are performed, systems of government are examined, objects are crafted, languages are practised, simply because they are beautiful. Many schools force the worship of Aphrodite to be carried on in secret, if at all. Furthermore, many of us, teachers and students, are starved of beauty in the places where we work.

Teachers who are under the influence of Aphrodite will not stay in the profession unless they can find beauty and pleasure in their work. They want teaching to be fun for them and fun for their students. Yet, as Glasser argues, the world which children and adolescents take seriously is the world in which they can have fun. If they find all their fun outside the classroom, they'll do their learning outside the classroom.

One way in which Aphrodite makes herself present in the classroom is through seduction. Good teachers are all involved in seduction. They want to seduce their students into learning. They present their subject as attractively as possible so their students will share their own love for it. They are also involved, consciously or unconsciously, in presenting their own personalities attractively, for it important to them to be liked by their students. It requires no great effort to imagine the ways this can tip over into to the negative. Exploitative sexual seduction in 'helping' professions such as teaching, counselling, medicine and the ministry is too common to be ignored.

We need to recognize that Beauty is a powerful and demanding goddess in her own right. It may not be conventional any more to think of beauty as a goddess, or even as an instinct or drive or need, but she/it has had a powerful part in shaping our culture and our sensibility. The Greek myths warn that she ruthlessly punishes those who ignore her. She certainly has her pathology—sexual seduction, bitchiness, vindictiveness, superficiality, self-obsession and self-indulgence, inability to tolerate the grittiness of reality—and her influence must be balanced by the presence of other, more responsible gods. Nevertheless, without her education has no charm and provides no delight.

Winged Eros

The power of Eros is felt by humans and gods alike, in their propensity to fall obsessively in love. It is felt in both the delight and the anguish of intimacy. Eros is singularly the god of the drive to union, of relationship, and of the creativity which is generated by relationship. The Greeks of classical times imagined Eros as an adolescent boy, for their experience of love included more than the simple drive to union. Eros was unpredictable and irresponsible and destructive as well as delightful and creative. We find Eros in the classroom where the teacher is convinced of the critical importance of relationships. We find him in the teacher who is able to say that she loves mathematics, loves Shakespeare, loves teaching, loves her pupils. Eros is easily recognized in the work of the teacher who goes to great pains to establish a climate of non-dependent trust in his classes, who genuinely loves his students and has their good always in mind.

In the classroom dominated by Eros, the highest value is intimacy. The ideal emotional climate is positive, supportive, free of risk. Notions of hierarchy have no place in Eros' value system. What makes the classroom a great place to grow and learn is the relationship between teacher and students. Content and process are secondary to the satisfactions of relationship, the satisfaction of belonging. It is love which makes teaching creative and productive.

Eros pathology readily appears when Eros is the only god being honoured. If intimacy and openness are good, we might suppose that more intimacy and openness are better, and that still more openness and intimacy are better still. However, experience of closeness is not always as unambiguously positive as this. Sometimes, relationship maintains its intensity while reversing its meaning. Teachers and students can get so caught up in with relating to each other that they forget that their purpose in being together is to learn something. Unless Eros is accompanied by more responsible gods like Hera and Apollo, he may become destructive.

Ares the Warrior

Ares wasn't a particularly popular god among the Greeks. As a war-god, Ares represents battle-fury, blood-lust, the exhilaration of conflict and conquest. Most Greeks preferred to give their devotion to Athene, who personified intelligent, strategic warfare.

Ares is recognized easily enough in his negative aspect. The centuries are strewn with the consequences of Ares-pathology, both personal and tribal, and we have good reason to be suspicious of him. However, Ares has a significant place in our classrooms. He is the god of energy, of vehemence, of conflict, of challenge, of action. If as teachers we are devotees of Athene or Eros we are not likely to have much time for Ares. If we are committed to the values of cooperation, relationship and dialogue, we are likely to give conflict and competition no place in our classrooms.

It is certainly not a good idea to hand over the classroom entirely to Ares; he is emotionally immature and not very smart. Classrooms where children and adolescents are taught that life is all about competition are destructive both for those who always win and those who always lose. Nevertheless, the classroom where Ares is properly worshipped is full of challenge and excitement; conflict is not avoided but welcomed and enjoyed; the satisfactions of competition are acknowledged; children are encouraged to be passionate about the things that matter to them; teacher and students revel in each other's energy. Intellectual subtleties may be neglected, but there is real engagement in what is happening.

It is particularly important that Ares be given some attention in the education of girls. When Pandora, the first woman, was crafted by Hephaistos, the gods each gave her a gift. Ares' gift was the fire which flickers within her. It is a fire which the patriarchal gods prefer to keep under strict control. Our society generally makes sure that most boys pick up more than enough of Ares values. Girls, on the other hand, are not encouraged to engage in the friendly physical rough and tumble that boys grow up with; they are taught not to assert themselves, or fight for their rights; they do not get a chance to learn the rituals of 'fighting fair'. Yet both men and women are incomplete without Ares, just as both women and men are incomplete without Artemis. To allow Ares to be undeveloped and unacknowledged in us is to risk having him run out of control. To deny him proper worship in the classroom is to invite the emotional and physical violence which characterize his pathology.

Crippled Hephaistos

Hephaistos is the only god who works. He is the divine blacksmith, the god of craftwork. His status as a god rose and fell with political and economic conditions in ancient times, as in our own. He is represented in the Iliad and Odyssey as a crippled and comical god of metal-working. His role as husband to Aphrodite shows how deeply he is obsessed with beauty, and the myths reveal how little reward he gets for his devotion. Hephaistos is the ugly god, who creates beauty through pain and tedium. He is the god who drives the dancer or gymnast or musician or sculptor to craft something beautiful through the aches and pains of practice and performance, and to bear the calluses and other physical deformities that are the price of this obsession.

Hephaistos is honoured in the arts, but gets little worship in the normal classroom. There is too little value put on beauty to expect children or adolescents to endure pain to create it. In a commodity-driven society such as our own there is too little value put on any sort of crafting to give it a respected place in the classroom. Teachers who are committed to teaching the crafts of living and who regard their own profession as a craft are really a bit old-fashioned, like Hephaistos and his mother, Hera.

The Hephaistos stories are told and retold in teachers' staff-rooms. There is the story about teaching being a greatly undervalued profession, whose practitioners slave day and night down at the forge while fancier, more fashionable gods enjoy themselves upstairs in the palace. There is the story about how all problems can be solved by working harder. There are stories about trapping Hera or Ares or Aphrodite in compromising or embarrassing situations and having a good laugh at their expense. Hephaistos complains a lot about the way he is treated but he stays where he is, for he has no doubt that he is superior to those who lord it over him.

Aunty Hestia

Hestia is another fire-god, but the fire which she personifies is the domestic fire. She dwelt in the hearth which was the focus of each home, and in the communal fire which was the focus of each village or city.

Hestia is the centre of things. She is the centre of the individual, the centre of the family, the centre of the city, the centre of the world. She represents the place of stillness from which we come and to which we go, the focus towards which everyone faces, the point around which everything revolves. She does not enter into the squabbles of the gods, but sits quietly and works at her weaving. She is quiet and self-effacing, but demands considerable honour. It was to Hestia that the Greeks said 'grace' before and after their meals.

There are societies whose notions of education give Hestia a central place, where 'just sitting' is regarded as a legitimate activity. Obviously, our mainstream society is not one of them. There is not much value placed on introversion, on stopping to rest in what is essential. Things have been falling apart for so long that there is little sense of a focal point around which everyone is happy to gather from time to time. Yet Hestia, like the other gods, represents both an individual and a collective need. Where she is present in the classroom she gives children the sense of containment they yearn for.

Some people learn to satisfy this need through meditation. Indeed, meditation is gaining more and more legitimacy as the pace of life increases. 'Just sitting' is a permissible activity in the most unlikely places. However, schools generally manage to keep themselves remote from such activities. When teachers want to argue for the value of meditation in the classroom, they are forced to fall back on utilitarian arguments, and provide evidence of the way meditation will increase their students' attention and performance. Yet there is a Hestia perspective on education which does not rely on such arguments. Many teachers are able to manifest the presence of Hestia in the serenity of their classrooms, in their students' balance and focus and in the ease with which they learn.

Where Hestia is worshipped too obsessively we get inertia. Yet, given due honour, Hestia gives us an extraordinary experience of focus. Our students are totally focused on what they are doing. The outside world disappears. Past and future disappear. Time appears to stop. The experience may be rare, but even in its rarity it makes our work deeply rewarding.

Dancing Dionysos

The worship of Dionysos seems to have been imported into Greece from Asia. The authorities found his worship somewhat unsettling and did not at first approve of it. Here was a god to be worshipped through mystical rites, whose followers sought ecstatic communion with him, who ran enthusiastically into the mountains to give themselves over to madness and orgiastic celebrations. Eventually, however, the worship of Dionysos was incorporated into the state cults; the god of license and chaos was worshipped side by side with Apollo, god of order and moderation. In particular, the development of the theatre came under his sponsorship, so that the exploration of the most intense human experience was pursued through a sophisticated and highly structured art form.

The authorities are still suspicious of Dionysos, and acknowledge him very reluctantly. He gets very little honour in schooling, and that only on the fringes of the curriculum. For one thing, Dionysos has no respect for authority and no regard for social expectations, and schools are supposed to turn children into good citizens. He is the god of growth and go-with-the-flow and do-my-own-thing. He brings both joy and grief. He is the god of the adrenaline charge, the god of tragedy, of feeling, of play, of suffering, of exhilaration, of charisma, of performance, of ecstasy, of newness, of freedom. It is hardly necessary to point out that there is not much ecstasy apparent in schools. Dionysos would have our students dance, sing, perform, be creative and spontaneous, experience the animal flow of life, be utterly engaged in what they are learning, experience both fun and freedom—but there is little time for such things in most schools now.

One fruit of this neglect is apathy, the absence of feeling. Another is the uncontrollable explosion of feeling whose expression has been frustrated. If policy makers in education persist in their primitive, narrow, simple-minded worship of the marketplace, and if civilized teachers stop resisting the pressure to join in this worship, we will find that we are performing education not as farce but as tragedy.

We can think of the gods as representing instinctual needs or drives. We may not often think of ecstasy and intoxication in terms of needs or drives, unless we are focusing on addiction. Yet there seems to be plenty of evidence that we have a psychological need for at least an occasional experience of ecstasy or intoxication, a need to escape from the ordinariness of existence. Historically people have sought and found such experience in religious ritual, in sexual orgasm, in the exhilaration of battle or in hallucinogenic drugs. We are familiar enough with the consequences when students seek ecstasy in dangerous ways—through train-surfing, risky sex, alcohol or other drugs—yet we are not generally inclined to see this as a substitute for the ecstatic religious experiences which have ceased to be accessible. Fortunately we can still seek ecstasy and intoxication in lots of less problematic ways as we let ourselves be caught up in the joy of play, or in the tribal enthusiasm of a football match, a concert, a religious celebration or a dance party. Or we can try mountain climbing or jumping out of planes. One of the most useful things a teacher can do for adolescents is to teach them ways to have fun without getting drunk or stoned.

Prometheus the Saviour

The image of Prometheus the Titan has been enormously significant in European consciousness. He is the creative mind. He is the god who created man (not woman), who took humanity's side against the will and wrath of Zeus. He is the hero who defied the patriarchy in the name of individual freedom, who brought light into our darkness. He is the saviour who sacrificed himself for the sake of mankind, the benefactor who brought the gift of technology down from heaven, the teacher who showed us how to use our intelligence to take control of the world. He is the individual who proclaims his and our right to be an individual.

In the 19th century, the capitalist version of the Promethean myth expressed the fantasy of achieving freedom from poverty through the development and management of technology. This has proved remarkably resilient, in spite of the fact that any one who wants to look can see how our obsession with technology has brought us to a point where we may have damaged the planet irreversibly and put the future of the species at risk. Any one who wants to look can see that technology has proved at least as effective an instrument of enslavement as it has been an instrument of emancipation. It has become increasingly clear that belief in the inevitability of progress has little evidence to support it. Yet the fantasy survives. The primary purpose of education, we are told, is the skilling of our society.

When the Promethean fantasy takes over education we hear a great deal of talk about technology, as we might expect. We also hear talk about education as an instrument of social change, of emancipation. But most of all we find ourselves immersed in a rhetoric of skilling and training. The Prometheus' view of education is a very simple one: skilling brings empowerment for the individual and productivity for the society, and the simplest and most efficient and most technically sound way of teaching skills is through training. It is also the way most congenial for those who perceive human beings as machines.

Training as a mode of education can be satisfying and useful. Or it can be boring and irrelevant. There is a dimension to our humanity which is machine-like, which responds to having our buttons pushed, learns through repetition and rehearsal and exalts in the power that we find in new skills. Yet there is more to education than teaching skills. Those who are stuck in Prometheus myth think that we can solve the social and ecological problems of the planet by being clever and developing our skills, and they fail to see that in a world of accelerating change the skills we teach our students today may prove inadequate or irrelevant by tomorrow.

Hermes the Salesman

If there was any god more popular in classical times than Aphrodite, it was Hermes, the god of travellers, shepherds, thieves, merchants and scholars. He is a very slippery character, an opportunist without any respect for conventional morality, a trickster, a liar and a thief. He is elusive, unpredictable and mischievous. He is also very charming. The Greeks believed him to be friendly to mortals, but they were careful not to trust him too much.

In recent years Prometheus' myth of progress has been replaced by Hermes' myth of the marketplace, and Hermes, god of the marketplace, has taken a strong hold on our consciousness. This is manifested in the way we now look at education. The marketplace is becoming the dominant metaphor. Teachers in times past have been seen as custodians of the culture (Zeus), developers of social responsibility (Hera), givers of parental care (Demeter), providers of understanding (Apollo), protectors of the fragile and vulnerable (Artemis), guides to the appreciation of beauty (Aphrodite), defenders of civilization (Athene) or facilitators of personal growth (Dionysos); now they are asked to be retailers of marketable skills. Many educational institutions are now happy to take their offerings into the market and to hawk them to whoever will buy. They happily base curriculum decisions not on what best serves the culture, or what most intelligently examines it, but on what sells best.

In the Hermes-driven classroom, there is plenty of interest in communication, but not so much concern about what is worth communicating. There is plenty of interest in the process of learning, but not so much concern about what is worth teaching. In such a classroom the learning of dry facts is not regarded very highly. Students don't have to accumulate knowledge. What matters is being able to access the information you need and getting it to serve you. Teachers and students get their buzz out of being clever rather than being learned, finding ways to 'beat the boredom', constantly moving on, being entrepreneurs rather than workers or artists. Hard work and critical thinking have no place in the classroom.

Hermes subverts the conventionally accepted order of things, disrupts all our certainties, unties all our knots, and makes change possible. Schools, and education systems generally, get stuck in repeating themselves, doing things the way they have always done them simply because this is the way they have always done them. We need Hermes' gifts of flexibility, adaptability and imagination, his readiness to let go of what has been taken for granted, even his opportunism and persuasiveness, to initiate change. In a world where we are told 'change is the only constant' a Hermes consciousness is essential. But in education as in business, it must be balanced by the other gods or it will quickly bankrupt us.

Hermes does not hold to values of his own. Zeus tells us to respect rightful authority; Apollo tells us to act rationally; Hera tells us to fulfil our social obligations; Aphrodite tell us to pursue beauty; Artemis demands that we live in harmony with Nature; Hephaistos tells us that work is honourable; Eros insists that we love one another; Dionysos challenges us to become fully ourselves; Athene tells us to keep things in balance; Prometheus requires us to use our intelligence to make a better world; Ares wants us approach our tasks with passion; Hestia gently suggests that we stay centred, not get fussed, and focus on what is essential.

Hermes insists that we worship all the gods.

Conclusion

Zeus and his family, who dwelled on Mount Olympus, were not the only gods demanding worship. Pan and Persephone, Hekate and Herakles, the Graces, the Muses, the Fates and the Furies, were all alive in the Greek imagination, and they are still competing for our attention when we turn our minds to wondering about the point of education.

Each of the gods has his or her special gifts to give. Each represents a different notion of the aims of education, a different perspective on curriculum. Each appears differently in the personalities of teachers and in their ways of teaching and learning. Each is present in her or his distinctive form in the truths we adhere to, in the instincts which drive us and the visions which draw us, in teaching as in the rest of our lives. In our current arguments about the purposes of education and the best ways of providing it, the ancient and immortal gods are still involved in their old arguments.

While we must honour them all, we are unlikely to honour them all equally. We each have particular gods which shape our personality, our values and our perceptions. And while there is no single god who can claim the classroom as his or her personal sphere of influence, some of them may have a greater claim on it than others. However, we run an awful risk if we give all our devotion to our favourite god and neglect the others. We may like to see the eternally squabbling gods simply as colourful images, and their worship simply a useful metaphor to help us explore a multi-dimensional approach to education. On the other hand we may wish to take them more seriously, to acknowledge that the Greeks, like other polytheistic cultures, knew something about cosmology and psychology which we have forgotten. However we may think about them, we neglect them at our peril.

References

Glasser, W. (1990) *The Quality School* (New York, Harper Collins).
Jung, C.G. (1973) *Collected Works* (Princeton, NJ, Princeton University Press).
Hillman, J. (1977) *Re-visioning Psychology* (New York, Harper Colphon).
Stevens, A. (1982) *Archetype: A Natural History of the Self* (London, Routledge).

4
Itinerary of the *Knower*: Mapping the ways of *gnosis*, *Sophia*, and imaginative education

ANTONINA LUKENCHUK

> One more thing we must know, because we had forgotten to discuss it: teach us concerning man! (Jung, *The Seven Sermons to the Dead*, cited in Hoeller, 2006)

'The Breath of Possibility': Imaginative Education and Jungian Motifs

Growing up, I remember myself as a highly imaginative and impressionable child. The modest circumstances of my life forced me to look for wonders in books, music, theatre, movies, or nature. I turned to introspection at the time when most children were interested in exploring their bodies. My biggest fear is to lose the sense of wonder that has been nourishing my mind and soul for as long as I can recall. It seems like yesterday that I stood on the staircase leading toward the grand university entrance holding my breath and hardly believing that I was *really* accepted to the place that I could only dream about. Although initial moments of excitement quickly turned into the more prosaic things of the university life with its requirements and routines, I managed to sustain my natural curiosity and find ways to release my imaginative powers.

By fate or perhaps due to a series of incidents, I have become involved in the field of education, in various capacities, for over two decades. Although for the most part educational 'gains' seem to outweigh the 'losses', I share my concerns for today's education with Maxine Greene (2000, 2001) and her followers who insist that we have to break with the 'technical, the measurable, with the fearful ideas of effectiveness and efficiency', and instead, make 'discovery possible again' (Greene, 2001, p. 63). Education should be indeed 'the breath of possibility', as Greene would have it; and children must 'make their own use of what has been taught; children must go beyond what has been learned—to do what might be called untaught things' (Greene, 2001, p. 137). Greene urges us to release our imagination in order to renew educational purposes and our common world: 'Imagination may be a new way of decentering ourselves, of breaking out of the confinements of privatism and self-regard into a space where we can come face to face with others and call out, "Here we are"' (Greene, 2000, p. 31).

Kieran Egan (1988, 1997, 2005, 2006) expresses similar concerns about the state of contemporary education in Western societies. The failure of today's schools to provide the most rudimentary education to many students signifies the crisis of public education. To

Jung and Educational Theory, First Edition. Edited by Inna Semetsky.
Chapters © 2013 The Authors. Book compilation © 2013 Philosophy of Education Society of Australasia.
Published 2013 by Blackwell Publishing Ltd.

Egan (1997), current educational problems are due to the absence of a coherent philosophy of education, a philosophy that embraces different kinds of understanding: somatic, mythic, romantic, philosophic, and ironic. Education can 'best be conceived as the process of developing each of these kinds of understanding as fully as possible' (Egan, 1997, p. 6). Egan proposes a radical change in educational curricula that should not be seen strictly as a 'body of knowledge' (knowledge about science, history, mathematics, geography, etc.), but instead, teaching young children to employ 'mythic understanding' in getting an 'initial grasp on the world and on experience', and recognizing school teachers and themselves as the 'storytellers of [...] culture' (Egan, 1997, p. 64). Our dependence on reason alone certainly does not suffice. When we teach children, we 'should bear in mind their potentially rich imagistic and emotional mental activity, and we should design programs that will support and develop those capacities' (Egan, 1997, p. 62).

Remarkably, contemporary educators such as Greene and Egan reiterate Jungian ideas on the nature of being and the multiple ways of knowing, seeing, and feeling. More than half a century ago, Jung claimed that being in the world means to be conscious of one's being. Without consciousness there would be no world; 'consciousness is a precondition of being' (Jung, 2006, p. 48). Jungian discourses on the imaginary overlap with Greene's conception of imagination and arts education as providing 'opportunities for perceiving alternative ways of transcending and of being in the world' (Greene, 2000, p. 142). Much like Jung who believed that 'reason alone does not suffice' (2006, p. 98) in dealing with our personal or societal problems, Greene claims that we ought to consider 'multiple conceptions of what it is to be human and alive' (2000, p. 43).

Jungian motifs and their educational iterations can be found in the works of French philosopher, poet, and educator Gaston Bachelard (2005) who once said that when imagination works, everything works! Bachelard believed that imagination is primal and fundamental, and that we perceive the world first and foremost through our imagination's spectacles. Imagination is an active, dynamic, and unifying force in the human soul. Like Jung, Bachelard associated life with archetypes and interpreted them as symbols of reality. He appealed to the archetypal elements of earth, fire, air, and water to create breathtaking poetic images that convey unlimited potential of imaginative language: 'Imagined images are sublimated archetypes rather than reproductions of reality. The human psyche forms itself first and foremost in images' (Bachelard, 2005, p. 3).

Collingwood (2005) echoes Bachelard's conception of imaginative education by advocating for arts education: 'Art is the kingdom of the child: and anyone who wants to enter that kingdom must enter it as a child. Hence we can say that not only is every child an artist, but every artist is a child' (p. 75). Art is the teacher of humanity: 'It is only in a society whose artistic life is healthy and vigorous that a healthy and vigorous scientific life can emerge' (Collingwood, 2005, p. 78). Collingwood thinks of the problem of suppressing our creative and emotional powers as the problem of education:

> The general aim is that the child should become able to speak his mind, to utter itself clearly and accurately in every medium that it handles. A child so trained will need no dope, for it will be able to do something better with its emotions than to stimulate them artificially. It will be able to express them, and so to understand the expressions of other people. Children so trained may or

may not turn out great artists; they may or may not turn out learned scholars; but they will begin life sane. (2005, p. 304)

Dewey's classical work *Art as Experience* (1934/2005) reaffirms the value and power of arts and imaginative education as a 'full and intense experience' (p. 138), the only 'gateway through which meanings can find their ways into a present interaction', and the 'conscious adjustment of the new and the old' (p. 283). The leitmotif of the imaginary as the conscious *and* embodied experience that brings unity and fullness to our lives as individuals and communal beings seems to permeate and connect the works of Jung with those of Dewey and other educators who seek to transform schools into more hospitable and exciting places that are full of possibilities 'embodied in works of art that are not elsewhere actualized' (Dewey, 2005, p. 279).

Jung's idea of the collective unconscious finds affinity with Dewey's conception of the works of art as 'signs of unified collective life', and a 'remaking of the experience of the community in the direction of greater order and unity' (Dewey, 2005, p. 84). Art is the 'extension of the power of rites and ceremonies to unite men, through a shared celebration, to all incidents and scenes of life;' art 'renders men aware of their union with one another in origin and destiny' (Dewey, 2005, p. 282).

The relevance of Jungian thought to contemporary education is precisely in what Greene calls a 'breath of possibility'—the possibility of embracing life in its fullness and totality of human experience, which means tapping into the realms of conscious *and* unconscious, actual *and* transcendental, physical *and* metaphysical. To conceive of a truly inclusive philosophy of education and inclusive curricula means to conceive of possibilities for integrating the language of different kinds of understanding of our cultures, histories, identities, and states of mind. I concur with Egan who advocates for an integrated conception of education which, in my view, presupposes the term *holistic* that alludes to esoteric vocabulary. Jung's esoteric leanings are widely known and explored, and it is specifically Gnostic Jung that interests me most in the context of this paper.

Gnostic Jung and Esoteric Iterations

Esoteric philosophy represents an unbroken tradition from the Egyptians, Hebrews, and Greeks, through the Christian West, and continuing to the present. Central to esoteric world traditions is the system of 'the One' that cannot be properly expressed in words and that has different interpretations specific to different cultures. The One is the supreme God that emanates in the form of the Intellect or Nous which further emanates in the Soul. It exemplifies the union of human beings with the Infinite, the unity of human consciousness with infinite reality, '*unio mystica*, spiritual nuptials, *copula spiritualis*, in which man tries to lose his identity in an immensely greater life than his own—the life of God, an all-embracing life' (Baumgardt, 1961, p. 5).

Although Jung's work still remains a subject of conjecture, many conceive of him as an esoteric writer. During his lifetime, Jung 'shrouded the origins of his discoveries in a mantle of caution that often bordered on Hermetic concealment' (Hoeller, 2006, p. 3). Jung is said to have gone through a series of intense mystical experiences between 1912 and 1917. Reportedly, even his handwriting changed drastically during that time. Jung's experiences of the time resulted in his two explicitly esoteric works—*Aion* and *The Seven Sermons to the Dead*.

In *Aion* (1950/1978), Jung presents a history of the Western imagination in such manifestations as Gnosticism, alchemy, astrological symbolism, and Christianity mapping the psyche's dimensions of space-time (*upwards* and *outwards*). *Aion* is the name of Mithraism's god who rules over time and the astrological calendar. The title suggests a factor that transcends the time/space continuum that governs ego-consciousness. In *Aion*, Jung endorses the coming of a new age, an 'Aion of Aquarius' that signifies a unity of space and time, and 'syzygy' of anima and animus—the 'two halves of the totality formed by opposites from which divine child is born as the symbol of unity' (Jung, 1978, p. 31). *Aion* abounds with comparative analyses of different symbols (fish, water, serpent, etc.) relevant to Jung's conception of psyche's unity. His appeal to Gnosticism is especially pronounced. In Gnosticism, fish, for instance, represent the driving force of the coming world of consciousness (Aquarius) symbolic of the time/ space continuum. 'By far the most fruitful attempts to find suitable symbolic expressions for the self were made by the Gnostics' (Jung, 1950/1978, p. 269). Gnosticism is the teaching of Gnostics (Gr. *gnostikoi*) denoting those who have *Gnosis*, or inner knowledge: Gnosis is known as the knowledge of the heart.

Jung's exploration of Gnosticism continues in *The Seven Sermons to the Dead* first published in 1917. Jung attributed the authorship of *Sermons* to Gnostic sage Basilides who taught in Alexandria in Hellenistic Egypt around CE 125–140. Opinions about *Sermons* differ. When Jung was questioned about it later in his life, he called the work his 'youthful indiscretion' (Hoeller, 2006, p. 8). The *Sermons* are small in size and written in an exceptionally coded symbolic language. Perhaps the most enigmatic notion of S*ermons* is *Pleroma* which signifies the ultimate fullness of Being. In *Sermons*, Jung proposes a model that goes beyond the binary division of anima-animus, and Eros-Logos. He develops an elaborate analysis of the transformation of human spirituality and sexuality: 'Spirituality receives and comprehends. It is feminine and therefore we call it MATER COELESTIS, the heavenly mother. Sexuality generates and creates. It is masculine and therefore we call it PHALLOS, the heavenly father' (*The Fifth Sermon*, in Hoeller, 2006, p. 55). The woman, therefore, is not totally ruled by Eros: the principle of Logos is quite powerful in her and makes her more insightful and intuitive.

The essential love-object of Jung's *Sermons* is the secret, Gnostic self-knowledge, and the ultimate stage of the development of human sexuality is the mystical marriage. Gnostic Jung, perhaps despite himself, urges us to bring forth our own *Aion* that encompasses all levels of human experience and embraces both the masculine and feminine modes of human expression. True to his time, Jung realized that the world still marginalized the feminine on different levels, yet he was never afraid to assert the spiritual and psychic importance of the Goddess within. Jung's insights into the Divine Feminine provided a 'springboard for many seekers of Sophia to find effective approach to the Goddess' (Matthews, 2001, p. 329). Understood primarily as the archetypal image, *Sophia* (literally 'wisdom' in Greek) does not have to be identified exclusively with the transcendental. In fact, contemporary poststructuralist and post-Jungian thinkers (e.g. Butler, 2004; Rowland, 2002) draw from (and revise) Jung to expand on their feminist theories and specifically on the construction of the female subject/identity.

Julia Kristeva, a Bulgarian-French poststructuralist, psychoanalyst and writer, has created perhaps some of the most original renditions of the feminine (e.g. Kristeva, 1980, 1986, 1987) that are not entirely incompatible with Jungian archetypes. Although a comparative analysis of feminist theories is beyond the scope of this paper, some tentative arguments on the female subject and identity formation will be further explored in the discourses on the archetypal feminine as the power of *both* transcendental and embodied wisdom.

In Search of *Sophia*: The Way of the Lost Goddess

Sophia has been revealing herself to different people with different traditions and religions throughout the history of humankind. She is:

> ... the great lost Goddess who is veiled, blackened, denigrated, and ignored most of the time, or else exalted, hymned, and pedestalled as an allegorical abstraction of female deity. She is allowed to be a messenger, a mediator, a helper, a handmaid; she is rarely allowed to be seen in charge, fully self-possessed and creatively operative. (Matthews, 2001, p. xxv)

The Wisdom Books of the Old Testament relate to the theme of Wisdom (Hebrew: *Chokmah*; Greek: *Sophia*), which is personified as a female figure. Gnostic Philo of Alexandria (13 BC–43 CE) repeatedly used the concept of *Sophia* (on a par with *Logos*, *Nous*) drawing from the Old Testament. He claimed that God created Sophia at the beginning of creation and then together with Her created the entire universe. For Jung, Sophia is 'the *Sapientia Dei* [...], feminine nature that existed before the creation' (Jung, 1952/1973, p. 24). She is 'the Johannine Logos', the 'feminine human of the metropolis par excellence', a 'reflection of Ishtar', the 'vine, the grape, the vine flower', the 'Beloved' (Jung, 1952/1973, p. 26). Sophia is personified as the Holy Ghost or the Grail Goddess.

Greek philosophers wrestled with the questions of the origins of the world, the role of the divine wisdom/Sophia in the eschatological schemata, and the relationship between Sophia and Logos. Pythagoras, who is traditionally considered to be the first self-proclaimed 'lover of wisdom', is instrumental in the Western Sophia tradition. In Plato's *Symposium*, we encounter Diotima, the 'great priestess of Mantineia, the wise stranger whose sacrifices had saved Athens from the plague, who dictates to Plato the ideal, idealized, and in that sense "Platonic" concept of love' (Kristeva, 1987, p. 71).

Kristeva's (1987) rendition of Diotima represents, in my view, a compelling argument from both psychoanalytic and poststructuralist critical feminist perspectives in support of the power of Sophia incarnate—the power that has become overshadowed and most often overtaken by the masculine Logos in the West for centuries. In contrast to the male-dominated structure of the possession-love, Diotima epitomizes 'uniting-love' principle. Diotima's love is a 'daemon', a 'unifying go-between, an agent of synthesis' (Kristeva, 1987, p. 72). Still, Diotima embodies the power of Phallus and 'hands it over to the philosopher whose task it is to possess it, to conquer it, and to use it to enslave or educate' (Kristeva, 1987, p. 74). Assuming that Sophia is power/wisdom in her own rite, she *is* indeed it, yet without having to assert herself among 'philosopher kings'.

In Christianity, an identification of *Sophia* and *Logos* was concealed for centuries due to the so-called 'Arian controversy'. Arius was the Bishop of Alexandria who regarded Logos and Sophia as equal generative principles of creation. Eventually, the Church fathers condemned the ideas of Arius, and Sophia's image almost lost its initial significance. Schipflinger (1998), one of the most recognized authorities in Sophiology (the study of Sophia in different religions, cultures, and philosophies), argues that the exclusion of Sophiology from official theology 'left a vacuum within theology which heretical movements consistently tried to fill' (p. 65). Ironically, however, Sophia has never, in fact, been 'lost': she is fully embodied in the word 'philosophy' (*philosophia*), the word that in some languages (e.g. Slavic) carries an explicit connotation of a female gender.

In Ukrainian (one of the Slavic languages), for instance, both *phileo* ('love') and *Sophia* are of a female gender, as well as many other words symbolizing female empowerment. *Sophia* is revered in Eastern Orthodoxy as *Hagia Sophia*, the 'Holy Wisdom', and it represents an exceptionally powerful female archetype of the Jung's collective unconscious in Ukrainian culture. She is a 'God-bearer', but more importantly, she legitimizes woman's power and her proper (and often dominant) place in society. My identity has been partially shaped by the Ukrainian cultural context until the 1990s, which certainly accounts for my personal understanding and internalization of the feminine. However, an impressive and well-acclaimed scholarship on Slavic Sophiology (e.g. Bulgakov, 1993) supports the arguments for a unique position of the feminine and woman's empowerment in ancient Slavic cultural traditions that still remain relevant to the formation of personal and cultural female identities in today's Ukraine. More importantly, with regard to the context of this paper, the Slavic conception of Sophia bears striking resemblance to the Jungian archetypal feminine.

Most Jungian works refer to the four interrelated aspects of the Divine Feminine: Hawwah/ Eve (biological woman), Helen of Troy (erotic woman), Mary (spiritual woman, virgin mother), and Sophia (the wise woman, the world soul) who embodies all of these roles. Eve corresponds to 'the woman and her seed'; Mary, the virgin, 'is chosen as a pure vessel for the coming birth of God' (Jung, 1952/1973, p. 36). There are thirty-two symbolic attributes of the Virgin identified in the Litany of Loreto (e.g. Lovable Mother, Seat of Wisdom, Mystical rose, Morning star). These attributes 'show how the soul-image (anima) affects the conscious attitude. She appears as a vessel of devotion, a source of wisdom and renewal' (Jung, 1982, p. 7). Jung claims that the Church Fathers were greatly influenced by Gnostic ideas:

> The worship of Mary was a vestige of paganism which secured for the Christian Church the heritage of the Magna Mater, Isis, and other mother goddesses. The image of the *vas Spientiae*, vessel of wisdom, likewise recalls its Gnostic prototype, Sophia. (Jung, 1982, p. 19)

According to Jung, every man carries within him the eternal image of woman, just as every woman has her inborn image of man. However, the Western mind 'has never yet devised a concept [...] for the *union of opposites through the middle path*, [...] that most fundamental item of inward experience' (Jung, 1982, p. 94). Jung's search for anima/ animus syzygy in the Western tradition reflects intense dynamics:

> The recognition of the anima gives rise, in a man, to a triad, one third of which is transcendent: the masculine subject, the opposing feminine subject, and the transcendent anima. With a woman, the situation is reversed. The missing fourth element that would make the triad a quaternity is, in a man, the archetype of the Wise Old Man, and in a woman, the Chthonic Mother. These four constitute a half immanent and half transcendent quarternity, an archetype which I have called the *marriage quaternio*. The self, on the other hand, is a God-image. (Jung, 1982, p. 166)

Jung's archetype of the Self embodies 'supraordinate personality' that represents a distinction between 'the ego, which extends only so far as the conscious mind, and the *whole* of the personality, which includes the unconscious as well as conscious components' (Jung, 1982, p. 148). Sophia, in Jungian terms, thus incarnates *imago Dei*, the female archetypal Self, and a supraordinate personality.

Jung's most elaborate analysis is that of the Mother archetype. Like any other archetype, the mother archetype 'appears under an almost infinite variety of aspects' (Jung, 1982, p. 109). Jung develops his ideas of the mother archetype around the Greek myth of Demeter-Persephone and her three-fold nature: maiden (Kore), mother (Demeter), and a wise woman (Hecate). Demeter represents Primordial and Earth Mother, fertile, and full of potential. Kore is:

> ... a woman that is generally a double one, i.e. a mother and a maiden, which is to say that she appears now as the one, now as the other. Kore often appears in woman as an *unknown young girl* [...], the *dancer*, in which case the 'maiden' appears as the *corybant, maenad*, or *nymph*. (Jung, 1982, p. 145)

Hecate represents a 'daemonic' supraordinate female personality, the queen of the underworld, the shadow. Demeter and Kore, mother and daughter, share the most intimate connection. They extend the feminine consciousness both upwards and downwards. Their ties produce the feeling that life continues through generations—the feeling of *immortality*. The individual's life is 'elevated into a type, indeed it becomes the archetype of woman's fate in general. The individual is rescued from her isolation and restored to wholeness' (Jung, 1982, p. 149).

The unique triadic nature of the feminine described by Jung through the Demeter-Persephone myth finds its affinity in Kristeva's semiotic and psychoanalytic formation of the female subject. Demeter-Persephone appears to be a 'unifying go-between' goddess; she is Kristeva's 'subject-in-process', never fixed in time, moving inwards and outwards, descending to the Underworld and being resurrected again to her maidenhood. The imagery of Demeter-Persephone metamorphoses is reminiscent of Kristeva's *chora*—an explicitly feminine (often referred to as a womb), rhythmic and amorphous space that symbolizes the cycle of deaths and rebirths. Kristeva borrows the concept of *chora* from Plato and renders it as a 'non-expressive totality formed by the [body] drives and their states in a motility that is as full of movement as it is regulated' (Kristeva, 1986, p. 93). *Chora* is neither signifying nor signified. *Chora* is the "place where the subject is both generated and negated" (Kristeva, 1986, p. 95).

In asserting the primacy of the ethical dimension in psychoanalysis, Kristeva appeals to motherhood that represents, simultaneously, an unconditional (transference) love and a separation of the two subjects in their amorphous relationship. The Demeter-Persephone myth portrays a perpetual cycle of deaths and rebirths, whereas the female subjectivity is being formed, deconstructed, and reconstructed all over again: as Hecate becomes violently separated from her mother Demeter, she acquires hew own, 'dae-monic', self ('supraordinate' personality), which requires further (second order of) reconstruction into maiden Kore, the subjectivity sustained and produced by love. The goddess thus becomes restored to wholeness.

As noted above, Sophia reveals itself in powerful ways in Slavic cultures. Sophia is both an incarnation of Slavic pagan goddess and *imago Dei* in Orthodox Christianity. The history of Slavic people shows that Slavs have accommodated their Christian traditions with a variety of pagan beliefs throughout the centuries. Throughout modern history, Ukrainian folklore has played a vital role of informal education in the formation of Ukrainian culture and national identity. Ancient and modern Ukrainian cultural tradi-tions, beliefs, and customs continue to spark creativity in contemporary writers, com-posers, and thinkers. To this day, one of the most popular Ukrainian female archetypal images is that of *Berehynya*, a pagan goddess-protectress of the hearth and home, who shares many features with the Greek goddess Demeter. The image of *Berehynya* is deeply ingrained in the Ukrainian collective unconscious.

According to Jung, archetypes are related to myths, fairytales, and esoteric teachings. Myths and fairytales 'give expression to unconscious processes, and their retelling causes these processes to come alive again and be recollected, thereby re-establishing the connection between conscious and unconscious' (Jung, 1950/1978, p. 180). Like the Jungian Mother archetype, *Berehynya* is a multi-faceted goddess. At times, she acquires the form of a wood-nymph, mermaid, or nixie, each an 'instinctive version of a magical feminine being, the *anima*' (Jung, 1969, p. 25). The Ukrainian version of a maiden goddess Kore is *Mavka*, the main character of a famous drama *Forest Song (Lisova Pisnia)* (1911/1985) written by Lesia Ukrainka, a pen name of Larysa Kosach-Kvitka (1871–1913). Interestingly, Mavka is an embodiment of a specifically Ukrainian mytho-logical image and, at the same time, a universal archetype of the *maiden*. Ukrainka's knowledge of world mythological traditions could have contributed to the creation of the character of Mavka that exceeds its native origins. Because of her fluency in German, Ukrainka might have been well familiar with Jung's writings. Whether this remains true or not, Mavka, in my view, personifies Kore, a 'vulnerable goddess', a woman 'in-between' (Jung), and a 'subject-in-process' (Kristeva). The *maiden* is 'often described as not altogether human in the usual sense; she is either of unknown or peculiar origin, or she looks strange or undergoes strange experiences, from which she is forced to infer the maiden's extraordinary, myth-like nature' (Jung, 1982, p. 147).

Mavka's harmonious existence with this exuberant universe goes undisturbed until the moment when she meets the peasant youth Lukash who gets lost in the woods. Hiding among the trees, Mavka watches Lukash struggling to find his way out. Lukash pauses for a moment and begins to play his flute. Enchanted by the music, Mavka decides to disclose herself and help Lukash find his way home. They enter into a playful dialogue and soon discover mutual attraction. Pierced by Cupid's arrows, Mavka acquires a human soul. Because of her deep love for Lukash, she decides to leave the forest and make her way in the world of people. In this world, Mavka finds nothing but disillusionment. The *real* world of people is filled with pragmatism, scheming, and cheap and narrow morals. Her pure love for Lukash is insulted and profaned. His calculating mother brings the cheap and gaudy Kalyna, whom she prefers as her daughter-in-law, into her home. Lukash cannot stand up for himself and surrenders to his mother's will. He soon loses his gift for music. Without Mavka, Lukash becomes a rough and dull fellow. Mavka's sorrow becomes unbearable. She runs to the forest that once was the equilibrium of her life, disturbed, full of fear and pain, almost unrecognizable:

> (*Wood Goblin*)
>   Daughter, daughter,
>   how hard the punishment for your betrayal ... !
> (*Mavka, raising her head*)
>   But whom have I betrayed?
> (*Wood Goblin*)
>   Your very self.
>   You left the crowning heights of forest-land,
>   descended to the petty lowly pathways.
>   And what do you now look like? Like a servant,
>   a hired hand who, through her bitter toil,
>   wishes but to earn a piece of happiness,
>   and failed. And only utter shame
>   prevented you from living like a beggar.
>   Remember how you looked that special night
>   when your great love was born and came to flower?
>   Oh, then you truly seemed Queen of the Forest,
>   with crown of stars that gleamed in your dark
>   hair–
>   Good Fortune then reached out her eager arms
>   and brought you many a gift that magic night! (Ukrainka, 1985, p. 155)

Mavka's fate explicates the myth of Persephone and her three-fold aspect as maiden, mother, and Hecate. The story is told that Demeter's daughter Kore (or Persephone) was once abducted by Hades who dragged her down to his underworld kingdom. The heartbroken Demeter ventured to search for her daughter and, because of that, the usual growing seasons were disrupted. Zeus was called upon and eventually intervened. He arranged with Hades for Kore to be returned to her mother. Upon her return home, Kore confessed that while in the underworld she ate a pomegranate, the food of the dead and a symbol of the marriage union between a man and a woman. Demeter got furious and vowed that no crops should ever again grow on the earth. Zeus eventually arranged an agreement between both parties where Kore would spend three months with Hades, as Queen of the Underworld (Hecate), and the remaining nine months on earth with her mother. She spent the winter months in Tartarus and returned to the earth at the beginning of Spring.

Like Persephone, Mavka is positioned 'in-between' the two worlds and is forced to reclaim her identity through trials and loses. Her demise reveals the dark side of Hecate's nature. She is doomed to spend her time in the 'underworld' for as long as she betrayed her true nature as Kore, the maiden and the queen of the forest, the subjectivity sustained and produced by pure and unconditional love. In essence, the finale of *Forest Song* is tragic: wise Uncle Leo dies, Lukash's house burns down, and he seems to have lost his mind and is marked for death. Mavka dies, but her farewell soliloquy is permeated with the hope that the human soul is indestructible. Life is eternal as is nature itself; for after autumn and winter, spring comes again and the end becomes a new beginning. Mavka's return is inevitable; everything passes by, but love and beauty abide ...

Conclusions

Jungian thought can hardly be restricted to the field of his practice alone; it certainly has far more reaching implications: cultural, philosophical, spiritual, and educational. Jungian depth psychology:

> ... is more than a therapeutic discipline, just as Gnosticism is more than an ancient religion. Both are the expression at their particular levels of existential reality of a Gnosis, a knowledge of the heart directed toward the inmost core of the human psyche and having as its objective the essential transformation of the psyche. (Hoeller, 2006, p. 33)

Shortly before his death, Jung had a dream in which he saw a boulder on a high place lit up by the sun. Carved into a stone, were the words: "'Take this as a sign of the wholeness you have achieved and singleness you have become." Perhaps the archetypal gods thus presented the aged Gnostic with a final token of their regard and affection' (Hoeller, 2006, p. 217).

An integration of Jungian discourses into mainstream education can revitalize its philosophical premises and the ways of knowing/seeing, teaching, learning, and co-inhabiting the magical world that we call school. If our classrooms are to be 'nurturing and thoughtful', as Greene would have it, we must 'want our students to achieve friendship as each one stirs to wide-awakeness, to imaginative action, and to renewed consciousness of possibility' (Greene, 2000, p. 43). It is Jungian thought that can bring a 'breath of possibility' to education and heighten its consciousness. Jung's theory of the collective unconscious corresponds and undoubtedly contributes to what Dewey believed in and desired for a 'unified collective life' and a 'shared celebration' of diverse individuals, their rites and traditions. Jung Gnostic offers us the 'knowledge of the heart'—so necessary and so lacking in what we teach and learn in today's schools. Finally, *Sophia* reminds us of the missing feminine link in 'the fullness of being'.

An exploration of female aspects of Jungian archetypes in different cultural traditions such as Ukrainian, for instance, can enrich feminist and gender studies by introducing the female images that can empower women cross-culturally. Sophia, with its many facets, is a potent force that brings equilibrium to the lives of all seekers and lovers of wisdom:

> Reclaimed by feminists, political activists, spiritual pioneers and women in need of nourishment, the names of the Goddess are sounded again. However, the realm of the Goddess does not belong to women alone but to all. In the initial stages of reclaiming the Goddess as an image of empowerment, role

model, archetypal pattern, blueprint for wholeness, image of womanhood and symbol of liberation, women have chosen to reclaim and honor this home-coming alone. Women's Mysteries belong to women, Men's Mysteries belong to men, but Transcendental Mysteries belong to humanity. (Ozaniec, 2003, p. 354)

On a final note, the transcendental messages of Jung expressed in his *Seventh Sermon* can (and perhaps should) be translated into a more gender inclusive language:

At night the dead came back again and amidst complaining said: 'One more thing we must know, because we had forgotten to discuss it: teach us concerning [wo]man!'

—[Wo]man is a portal through which one enters from the outer world of the gods, demons and souls, into the inner world, from the greater world into the smaller world. Small and insignificant is [wo]man; one leaves her/him soon behind, and thus one enters once more into infinite space, into the microcosm, into the inner eternity. (cited in Hoeller, 2006, p. 58)

References

Bachelard, G. (2005) *On Poetic Imagination and Reverie*, C. Gaudin, trans. (Putnam, CT, Spring Publications Inc.).

Baumgardt, D. (1961) *Great Western Mystics: Their lasting significance* (New York, Columbia University Press).

Bulgakov, S. (1993) *Sophia: The wisdom of God. An outline of sophiology* (New York, Lindisfarne Press).

Butler, J. (2004) *The Judith Butler Reader* (Malden, MA, Wiley-Blackwell).

Collingwood, R. G. (2005) *The Philosophy of Enchantment: Studies in folklore, cultural criticism, and anthropology* (Oxford, Oxford University Press).

Dewey, J. (1934/2005) *Art as Experience* (New York, Perigee Books).

Egan, K. (1988) *Imagination and Education* (Maidenhead, Open University Press).

Egan, K. (1997) *The Educated Mind: How cognitive tools shape our understanding* (Chicago, IL, University of Chicago Press).

Egan, K. (2005) *An Imaginative Approach to Teaching* (San Francisco, CA, Jossey-Bass).

Egan, K. (2006) *Teaching Literacy: Engaging the imagination of new readers and writers* (Thousand Oaks, CA, Corwin Press).

Greene, M. (2000) *Releasing the Imagination: Essays on education, the arts, and social change* (San Francisco, CA, Jossey Bass).

Greene, M. (2001) *Variations on a Blue Guitar: The Lincoln Center Institute lectures on aesthetic education* (New York, Teachers College Press).

Hoeller, S. A. (2006) *The Gnostic Jung and the Seven Sermons to the Dead* (Wheaton, IL, Quest Books).

Jung, C. G. (1950/1978) *Aion Researches into the Phenomenology of the Self*, 2nd edn., R. F. C. Hull, trans. (Princeton, NJ, Princeton University Press).

Jung, C. G. (1952/1973) *Answer to Job*, R. F. C. Hull, trans. (Princeton, NJ, Princeton University Press).

Jung, C. G. (1969) *The Archetypes and the Collective Unconscious*, 2nd edn. *The Collected Works*. Vol. 9, part I, R. F. C. Hull, trans. H. Read, M. Fordham & G. Adler, eds (Princeton, NJ, Princeton University Press).

Jung, C. G. (1982) *Aspects of the Feminine*, R. F. C. Hull, trans. (Princeton, NJ, Princeton University Press).

Jung, C. G. (2006) *The Undiscovered Self*, R. F. C. Hull, trans. (New York, A Signet Book).

Kristeva, J. (1980) *Desire in Language: A semiotic approach to literature and art*, T. Gora, A. Jardine & L. S. Roudiez, trans. (New York, Columbia University Press).

Kristeva, J. (1986) *The Kristeva Reader* (New York, Columbia University Press).

Kristeva, J. (1987) *Tales of Love*, L. S. Roudiez, trans. (New York, Columbia University Press).

Matthews, C. (2001) *Sophia: Goddess of wisdom, bride of God* (Wheaton, IL, Quest Books).

Ozaniec, N. (2003) *The Kabbalah Experience: A practical guide to kabbalistic wisdom* (London, Watkins Publishing).

Rowland, S. (2002) *Jung: A feminist revision* (Cambridge, Polity).

Schipflinger, T. (1998) *Sophia-Maria: A holistic vision of creation*, J. Morgante, trans. (York Beach, ME, Samuel Weiser, Inc.).

Ukrainka, L. (1985) *Forest Song* (Kyiv, Ukraine, Dnipro Publishers).

5

The Unifying Function of Affect: Founding a theory of psychocultural development in the epistemology of John Dewey and Carl Jung

Peter T. Dunlap

Introduction

At the beginning of the 20th century much consideration was given to the possibility that evolutionary theory could be applied to human culture. Psychology was one of the sciences taking up this exciting possibility. In Europe, psychology emerged from the experimental work of Wilhelm Wundt and others as well as from the later development of psychoanalysis by Sigmund Freud. While quite interested in the opportunities for research founded in experimental psychology, Wundt turned his attention to the issues of cultural evolution/development from within the frame of his 'Volker psychology' (Buxton, 1985, p. 39).

In America psychology was pioneered by the wide-ranging interests of William James who was influenced by Wundt's experimental psychology as well as his own exploration of the flora and fauna of the natural world, shaped by his studies of natural history with Louis Agassiz (Richardson, 2006, p. 48). James' interest in the idea of 'adaptation' placed the psychology of the individual within an evolutionary frame. James' student John Dewey extended James' interest in individual adaptation by applying it to the development of human culture. Dewey asserted that the relationship between the biological and the psychocultural was developmental and governed by a 'postulate of continuity' (Dewey, 1938, p. 23), which did not allow for any breaks of 'kind' between these phenomena. Joining this pioneering group of psychological thinkers was Carl Jung who also adhered to the concept of developmental continuity between the biological and the psychocultural.

Both Dewey and Jung were more attentive to the developmental connection between biological, psychological, and cultural phenomena. Applying his 'postulate of continuity', Dewey worked out a theory of human development that began in the biological and moved toward the psychocultural through the interaction between an emerging modern individuality and democratic institutions. Working somewhat less overtly with the idea of continuity, Jung asserted that psychological experience is 'analogous' to biological experience (McDaniel, 2009), that both developed through a process of 'differentiation', which takes place psychoculturally as gifted individuals become aware of what the

Jung and Educational Theory, First Edition. Edited by Inna Semetsky.
Chapters © 2013 The Authors. Book compilation © 2013 Philosophy of Education Society of Australasia.
Published 2013 by Blackwell Publishing Ltd.

collective culture represses and these individuals then channel this awareness into much-needed 'communicable ideas' (Jung, 1919, pp. 314–315).

Unfortunately, the effort these thinkers put into working out the developmental relationship between the biological and psychocultural did not draw significant institutional support. Instead, the disparity between individual and cultural experience could not be contained within a single institutional enterprise (Polkinghorne, 1983, pp. 22–24); and, problematically following the natural sciences, psychological and cultural experience were relegated to distinct disciplines. By the second generation interest in this idyllic topic begin to fade in the face of the institutional pressures that required clear vocational forms for the emerging field of psychology (Bellah *et al.*, 1985, p. 299). While second-generation thinkers like Erik Erikson continued to explore the connection between cultural and individual development, such as in his idea of 'psychohistorical' development, there was an overall sense that imagining such a connection was naïve and it was set aside along with the discredited idea that ontogeny recapitulates phylogeny (Erikson, 1968, p. 27).

Fortunately the divergence between the disciplines that study biological, psychological, and cultural experience narrowed over the course of the 20th century with many of the seeming disparities effectively accounted for through research. Prior to turning to this research I will review the common epistemological and theoretical interests of Dewey and Jung.

Dewey and Jung Converge upon the Idea of the *Objective Capacity* of the Subject

Much of modern philosophy, particularly epistemology, addresses the question of how the human *subject* is adequate to its *object*. Simply put, this question is about how we can say we 'know' the world. Building on Kant's epistemological turn and James' naturalism, Dewey resolved this question by defining 'experience' as an intimate relationship between 'knowers' and 'knowns' (Dewey, 1925, p. 8; Dewey & Bentley, 1949). Dewey would say that we know the world through our *experience* of it. Historically this would raise the objection, 'how can you be certain?' In response Dewey wrote a book, *The Quest for Certainty*, in which he critiques this quest, asserting that such a desire is a result of a less advanced stage of human development that struggles with bearing doubt (Dewey, 1929c).

Like Dewey, Jung also recognizes our trouble with doubt, he writes: 'Everything in us that still belongs to nature shrinks away from a problem, for its name is doubt, and wherever doubt holds sway there is uncertainty in the possibility of the divergence of ways' (Jung, 1930, p. 388).

Instead of searching for an ultimate certainty Dewey argues for an acceptance that knowledge is determined by the needs of a people in different circumstances at a given time in history. With this in mind Dewey wrote:

> We recognize that as observers we are human organisms, limited to the positions on the globe from which we would make our observations, and we accept this not as being a hindrance, but instead as a situation from which great gain may be secured. (Dewey & Bentley, 1949, p. 80)

From this position the human subject is not defined based on its limits, rather on its possibilities. After several centuries of focusing on containing or accounting for the limits of individual subjectivity, Dewey's own epistemological turn is a relief. Previously the quality of scientific understanding was thought to be determined in relationship to the extent to which the individual's subjective experience could be excluded leading to 'scientific neutrality' and the 'spectator theory of knowledge', which resulted in the positivist's paradigm of science (McDaniel, 1980–88). Following Dewey, we can say that we've stuck to this paradigm long enough and it is time to reconsider the role of subjectivity in the determination of scientific and other forms of cultural knowledge.

From Dewey's 'pragmatic' epistemological approach, individual subjectivity is the means through which we acquire knowledge, not as certainty but as warranted assertion. Dewey takes this further when he claims that it is due to the development of subjectivity that we have a deepening objective experience of the world.

> Until some acts and their consequences are discriminatingly referred to the human organism and other energies and effects are referred to other bodies, there are is no leverage, no purchase, with which to regulate the course of experience ... in this sense the recognition of 'subjects' as centers of experience together with the development of 'subjectivism' marks a great advance. (Dewey, 1925, p. 13)

This argument extends Dewey's resolution of the modern subject/object dichotomy, as it implies a developmental process through which objectively useful cultural knowledge co-emerges with individual subjectivity. Carl Jung takes a similar stand from a more overtly psychological perspective when he writes:

> The further we go back in history, the more we see personality disappearing beneath the wrappings of collectivity ... the collective attitude hinders the recognition and evaluation of a psychology ... because the mind that is collectively oriented is quite incapable of thinking and feeling in any way other than by projection. What we understand by the concept of 'individual' is a relatively recent acquisition in the history of the human mind and human culture. (Jung, 1921, p. 10)

Jung's desire for an 'objective psychology' is based on the idea that the differentiation of the individual leads to a wider range of objective experiences.

> Nowhere is the basic requirement so indispensable as in psychology that the observer should be adequate to his object, in a sense of being able to see not only subjectively but also objectively ... The recognition and taking the heart of the subjective determination of knowledge ... is fulfilled only when the observer is sufficiently informed about the nature and scope of his own personality. He can, however, be sufficiently informed only when he has in large measure freed himself from the leveling influence of collective opinions and thereby arrived at a clear conception of his own individuality. (Jung, 1921, pp. 9–10)

In this statement Jung parallels Dewey epistemologically in his recognition of the value of subjectivity in determining objective, trustworthy experience. Also, like Dewey, Jung's statement implies a developmental process that he is more explicit about as he describes the means by which the individual becomes a source of objective experience, that is, through self-awareness, thus pulling itself out of an undifferentiated, collective state of consciousness.

The Developmental Continuity between the Biological and the Psychocultural

For both Dewey and Jung the development of subjectivity is a source of an expanding objectivity. Both thinkers assert that this process is developmentally continuous, having its roots in biological experience and extending into psychocultural experience. Jung expresses this continuity through his assertion that the psychological sciences are grounded in biology, 'The separation of psychology from the basic assumptions of biology is purely artificial, because the human psyche lives in indissoluble union with the body ...' (Jung, 1936, p. 114).

Dewey does the same more overtly by asserting a 'postulate of continuity:'

> The idea of continuity is not self-explanatory. But its meaning excludes complete rupture on one side and mere repetition of identities on the other; it precludes reduction of the 'higher' to the 'lower' just as it excludes complete breaks and gaps. The growth and development of any living organism from seed to maturity illustrates the meaning of continuity ... The application of the postulate of continuity ... means that a reasonable account shall be given of the way in which it is possible for the traits that differentiate deliberate inquiry to develop out of biological activities not marked by those traits. (Dewey, 1938, pp. 23–24)

For Dewey the assertion of continuity between the biological and psychocultural has the purpose of drawing attention to the active, adaptive, and developmental nature of mental phenomena—both individually and culturally with science representing the conscious use of intelligence to solve human problems. For both Dewey and Jung, it is not just the human subject that develops, but it is actually the ecosystem in which the individual is found that develops as well. This is a direct challenge to the positivist paradigm that had asserted that we discern truth through a passive perception of a pre-existing world, which Dewey challenges,

> The function of intelligence is therefore not that of copying objects in the environment, but rather of taking account of the way in which more effective and more profitable relations with these objects may be established in the future. (Dewey, 1931, p. 30)

Dewey says that what begins as an adaptive biological activity, in human beings, becomes 'teleological'.

> The adaptations made by inferior organisms, for example the effective and coordinated response to stimuli, become teleological in man and therefore give occasion to thought. Reflection is an indirect response to the environment, and the element of indirection can itself become very great and very complicated.

But it has its origin in biological adaptive behavior and the ultimate function
of its cognitive aspect is a prospective control of the conditions of the environment. (Dewey, 1931, p. 30)

Jung also attached to human behavior a purposive nature. Using the terminology of
clinical psychology Jung speaks of the 'unconscious' as having both a historical and
prospective function. He writes, 'The unconscious has a Janus-face: on one side its
contents point back to a pre-conscious, prehistoric world of instinct, while the other side
it potentially anticipates the future' (Jung, 1939, p. 279).

Both theorists also address the question of how the individual develops by means of a
process of internalization during which group activities get brought into the awareness of
individuals such that they are then able to repeat these actions on their own, thus forming
more complex identities analogous to that first experienced by the group as a whole.
Dewey writes, 'No process is more recurrent in history than the transfer of operations
carried on between different persons into the arena of an individual's own consciousness'
(Ratner, 1939, p. 842).

For Jung the process of internalization is significantly more complex than implied by
Dewey. Following his studies of native peoples, Jung describes the way in which ritual
activities harness affective and imaginal experience to channel instinctive energy toward
the cultivation of the will to 'work', which is essentially developmental and leads to the
formation of individual identities (Jung, 1928/1960, pp. 41–5).

From More Complex Individual Identities to More Humane
Social Institutions

Both Dewey and Jung credit the differentiation of individual identity with the potential
for the growth of more humane social institutions. For Dewey this process is governed by
increasingly complex uses of science as the 'naturalization in use' of our intelligence to
support educational programs that activate more self-aware individual and institutional
identities (Dewey, 1929a, p. 30). For Jung, science opens the possibility of an 'objective
psychology'; however, Jung does not emphasize education, he is more interested in the
change that can come about in the individual through psychotherapy (Jung, 1921, p. 8).
While Dewey recognized the difficulty of forming humane institutions and championed
the liberalization of social and political forms, Jung attempted to find a different path to
freedom: psychological freedom. While seemingly disparate, I have come to think of both
of these as distinct responses to the fragmenting experience in Western societies between
our 'public' and 'private' lives (de Tocqueville, 1945; Bellah *et al.*, 1985; Samuels, 1993;
Burack, 1994; Dunlap, 2008). In this respect the difference between Dewey and Jung is
representative of two larger currents in the political development of Western culture that
responds to this public/private split. Each stands near the apex of unique institutional
forms addressing this split and helping to differentiate *the languages of liberalism* that
would shape the 20th century.

In my research I associate Dewey with the language of 'political liberalism' and his
identity with that of the 'political individual' who pursues religious, political, and economic freedom through political, educational, scientific languages that articulate egali-
tarian values as the basis of our personal and institutional actions (Dunlap, 2008, p. 165).

This is in contrast with Jung's language of what I call 'psychological liberalism' spoken by a 'private-psychological person' that pursues psychological freedom through scientific research and psychotherapy and a general retreat from the public sphere (Dunlap, 2008, p. 22). And, at the meeting point between these two distinct languages of liberalism lies a possible integration of the two.

Dewey's insight into the developmental nature of knowing, that is, the role that the modern individual is capable of playing in the creation of cultural knowledge, is focused, for one, on the development of a publicly-minded, educated citizen. While overtly focused on education and the life of citizenship, Dewey also emphasizes the psychological nature of these enterprises when he writes: 'The problem of constructing a new individuality consonant with the objective conditions under which we live is the deepest problem of our time' (Dewey, 1929a, p. 32). He expresses this psychological dimension even more overtly when he identifies the task to be the formation of 'a new moral and psychological type' (Dewey, 1929a, p. 83). Dewey sought to resolve the political issues of our time through his interest in creating such *psychological citizenship*.

While Dewey's politics has this psychological wing, Jung's psychology has a political wing. Jung pursued an image of an individuating person free of the authoritarian control previously exercised by the collective force of tradition and its troubling internalization. However, despite Dewey's psychological interests and Jung's political interests no Angel materialized between these two wings in the 20th century. Dewey's image of a new 'psychological and moral type' is too abstracted, offering little reason for the 'political individual' of his time to attend to the internal work of forming a new psychological identity. Similarly, Jung's individuating 'psychological person' is too introverted; it's middle-income comforts and determination to be outside of the materialistic mass culture preclude any devoted citizenship. Neither cultural identity differentiated by these social scientists embodied the leadership capacities of psychological and political citizenship needed by their time.

Until there was such an image that could bring together Dewey's sense of political justice and his educational agenda with Jung's insight into the internal turmoil of the modern psyche the public/private divide could not be bridged. In the 21st century the project remains just this and begins with the identity of the social scientist.

The Modern Identity and Its Impact on the Identity of the Social Scientist

Like all men and women of any age, both Dewey and Jung were influenced by current attitudes toward the identity of the social scientist including the contemporary attitude that the scientist needed to minimize the impact of their subjectivity on scientific inquiry. While both thinkers challenged much of the positivist paradigm they could not anticipate the extent to which their cultural milieu crept in by means of their restricted under-standing of the psychocultural function of human emotion. This restriction limited their ability to extend their intuition about the developmental continuity between biological and psychocultural experience.

In his book *Liberalism and Social Action* Dewey describes how Enlightenment sensibility fostered the idea of individual independence. This included thinking of the individual as coming into the world as a 'blank slate', having the 'natural rights' to determine their own political and cultural relations through 'social contracts' (Dewey, 1929b, p. 4). A new 'psychology' collaborated with the rising laissez-faire liberalism by privileging the functions of sensing and thinking to support an emerging scientific and cultural milieu, while deprecating the cultural function of emotion in order to break the authoritarian grip of unjust social roles that had been maintained through emotion-laden interactions. In combination, the new politics and psychology supported political freedom through the differentiation of our thinking and sensing capacities. Through European Rationalism and British Empiricism this 'reasoning' and 'sensory' freedom was institutionalized, which transformed the political landscape of that time (Dunlap, 2008, p. 129). About this political freedom Christian theologian Paul Tillich writes:

> We must understand what this reasoning was. It was not [just] a calculating reason, which decides whether to do this or that, depending on which is more advantageous. Rather, it was a full, passionate, revolutionary emphasis on man's essential goodness in the name of the principle of justice. (in Wilber, 1995, p. 381)

While the emergence of reasoning and sensory freedom liberalized Western culture, the deprecation of emotion has since taken its toll. A rising wave of contempt for emotion as 'sentiment' broke authoritarian social chains but left us prejudiced against emotion and unable to use it effectively to maintain human connections. This troubling but possibly necessary development relegated emotional experience to the 'private-life of children, women, and artists, while reserving reason and sensory experience for the world of men and public discourse' (Dunlap, 2009). This deprecation of emotion is institutionalized in the Utilitarianism of James and John Stuart Mill. J. S. Mill describes his father's suspicion toward emotions, which he asserted perpetuated the authoritarian social order through 'sentimentality' (Mill, 1873/1989, pp. 56, 97).

This dilemma/circumstance in the political development of Western culture has contributed to the rise of a modern individual disconnected from its community. Alexis de Tocqueville identified and chronicled the rise of this individuality, its retreat from the public sphere into a private life, leaving control of the polis to whoever could manipulate it.

> Individualism is a mature and calm feeling, which disposes each member of the community to sever himself from the masses of his fellows and draw part with his family and his friends, so that after he has thus formed a little circle of his own, he willingly leaves society at large to itself. (de Tocqueville, 1945, p. 98)

While the rise of this privacy reflects one trajectory of the positive growth of individualism it also seeds the failures of democracy leading to a 'mass mindedness' (Jung, 1958, p. 379). The instability of the modern identity was also characterized by Dewey:

> The unrest, impatience, irritation and hurried that are so marked in American life are inevitable accompaniments of a situation in which individuals do not find support and contentment in the fact that they are sustaining and sustained

members of a social whole. They are evidence, psychologically, of abnormality ... only an acute maladjustment between individuals and the social conditions under which they live can account for such widespread pathological phenomena. (Dewey, 1929a, p. 56)

For Jung this mass mindedness is made all the worse by the modern imbalance between thinking and emotion. Jung described how repressed emotion within an individual who is rootless gives rise to psychic epidemics such as what brought Germany to its incandescent peak before plunging it into the flames of Allied bombers. What was needed were '... values in the conscious mind of the individual which would have enabled him to understand and integrate the [mass emotional] reaction when it reached consciousness' (Jung, 1946, p. 223).

While the privileging of thinking and sensing supported a blooming Enlightenment, both were reduced to a passive recording of nature. In combination with the disconnect from emotion, passive thinking and sensing functions restrict the identities of citizens and scientists alike. What an intolerable dilemma! Expected to show restraint, without feeling, while passively reporting the inhumanities in the world they love. What soul-price has the social scientist paid for positivism's false objectivity?

What would happen if we learned to work more actively with our subjectivity, with our emotions? Is there a way that this could lead to acts of cultural leadership or to an expanded role for the social scientist as cultural leader? Isn't the impoverished identity of the social scientist part of our frustration, reflecting our inorganic position in culture? Because of the deprecation of emotion as a source of cultural knowledge and the assumption that thinking and sensing could only be passively utilized, no active moral citizenry emerges between Dewey's rational, well-educated 'political individual' and Jung's introspective, private 'psychological person'. Is there a way to imagine emotion playing a nobler role in the identity of the social scientist and in the life of the citizen? To answer that question we need a better understanding of the nature of human emotion.

Affect Science: The Path to 'Affect Freedom'[1]

What is the role of emotion in the life of the human individual and culture? We live at a time when Enlightenment sensibilities are being questioned as we challenge the unreflective view of the supremacy of rationalism. Much developmental theory focuses on the maturation of rational capacities. Yet many, including Jung, Charles Darwin, William James, Sigmund Freud, Melanie Klein and others, draw attention to the functioning of emotions in human development. Freud views these capacities as instinctive, rooting them in our biology. James describes emotions as 'bodily changes' that let us know that we have been affected by something (McCutchan, 2006, p. 48). Klein asserts the importance of both love and hatred in the process of the child's differentiation in relation to a primary caregiver (Burack, 1994, p. 32). Jung asserts a subtle view, attributing emotions with the capacity for making value distinctions; that is, determining what is important and unimportant to us in our environment and in our society or species experience. And finally, cognitive theorists are learning to define emotion as linked to 'self-awareness and cognitive evaluation' and speak about the way the self is constituted by emotions and narratives (Lewis, 2000, p. 623). However, with the development of 'affect science', it is becoming clear that the complexity of our emotional life requires an even more complete understanding of how they function at intrapersonal, interpersonal, sociopolitical, and even evolutionary levels. In the 1950s and 60s, Stanford scientist Sylvan Tomkins identified 'affect' as the biological portion of emotion, which led to the emergence of the field of 'affect science'. Tomkins identifies nine primary affects most having a range of intensity presented in the chart below (Table 1).

These affects are biological responses taking place as fixed patterns, having identical features in the old and young alike, and are common to the species, as well as to other mammals (Scherer, 1994, p. 172; Lazarus, 1994, p. 163). They are rooted in the biological functioning of the limbic system, and are in a functional relationship with many other brain structures and other aspect of physiology (Scherer, 1994, p. 172). The affect system is thought to have an evolutionary significance in how it prepares an organism physiologically to respond to its environment, making it 'adaptive phylogenetically' (Frijda, 1994, p. 116) and a means of 'action readiness' and 'resource mobilization' (Clark & Watson, 1994, p. 136).

Affect also functions socially allowing, 'the organism to communicate signals of evaluative reactions and behavioral intent to others' (Scherer, 1994, pp. 127–130). For example, 'distress cries alert community members to the need for help, whereas shouts of excitement or joy invite others to join in the hunt or feast' (Clark & Watson 1994, p. 132).

From clinical psychology we draw on how psychotherapists have learned to use their emotions to 'assess' the nature of their client's suffering. Simultaneously, recent work in cognitive science and political psychology draws attention to way emotions function 'politically', which is helping open conversation more widely about the positive role of emotions in our communal life (Westen, 2007; Lakoff, 2008). In addition, historian William Reddy focuses on the positive role of emotion in bringing about the advances of democratic culture, which takes place through what he calls the advances of 'emotional liberty' (Reddy, 2001, p. 129).

Positive
interest—excitement
enjoyment—joy
Neutral
surprise—startle
Negative
fear—terror
distress—anguish—grief
anger—rage
embarrassment—shame
disgust
'dissmell' (related to contempt)

Table 1: The nine affects (biological basis of emotion)*

*Adapted from Donald Nathanson's presentation of the work of Sylvan Tomkins (Nathanson, 1992, p. 59).

In my own work as a political psychologist working with the leadership of social change organizations I summarize the understanding of the biological and psychocultural function of emotion as follows: in addition to using emotion to *assess* our circumstance it also functions to *direct attention*, *motivate action*, and to *connect to others* (Dunlap, 2008, p. 15). In this work I have seen first hand the difficulty the progressive leadership of our communities has in using their emotional experience to lead, which is also the social scientist's dilemma. However, based on the sound epistemological and theoretical foundation of Dewey and Jung it is possible to imagine a role for the social scientist as community leader supporting the differentiation of the emerging capacity for 'affect freedom' in order to give birth to Dewey's 'new moral and psychological type' through the formation of a psychological citizenry (Dunlap, 2008, p. 14). Affect freedom is the capacity to draw from and use a full range of the biological, psychocultural, and political functions of our emotions (Dunlap, 2008, p. 15).

Affect Freedom, Cultural Leadership and Psychological Citizenship

Both Dewey and Jung were determined to use the social sciences to activate human development. However, the two personify the cultural divide within the 19th and 20th centuries between two liberalizing cultural influences, which I have referred to as 'political' and 'private-psychological' liberalism. Unfortunately, the life of the 'political individual' is still too controlled by an over-identification with his rational capacity; Lakoff and Westen's research captures how rationalism is the 'bane of liberalism' (Lakoff, public lecture, 25 March 2005). While the 'psychological person' begins to use her emotions for what they are for she does this almost exclusively in her private life, foregoing applying this capacity in her life as a citizen. Fortunately, it is possible to integrate these two within a new individual identity, that of the 'psychological citizen', and within the new institutional form of what I call a 'public-psychological liberalism'. This integration is difficult to focus on, as it requires seeing how emotion has functioned over the course of the last several centuries. However, Dewey and Jung's historical vision successfully identified the traces of this process of psychocultural development. If we think of the differentiation of 'reasoning' and 'sensory' freedom as new sources of culturally valid knowledge that are 'emergent capacities' arising through the psychocultural development of Western culture, then we might think of 'affect freedom' as a more recent emerging capacity also being differentiated as a source of culturally valid knowledge.

As a source of cultural knowledge, affect freedom supports the emergence of individual and organizational identities capable of using emotion to assess both their private and public life circumstances, to direct attention, the motivate action, and to help us come together as a people. In the following chart (Table 2) I present this model of psychocultural development.

Following this rough idea of the trajectory of these psychocultural developments of Western culture we can see the way in which the biological experience of emotion is developmentally continuous with our individual and cultural experience.

> The emergence of the identity of the modern individual is taking place through the functional differentiation of 'reasoning', 'sensory', and now 'affect

Differentiation of Emergent Capacity	*Institutional Support*
↑ **Affect Freedom** emerges early 1800s	**Psychotherapy and Culture** • Sigmund Freud (1930) asserts that humanity's nature is *passionate, irrational* in *Civilization and its Discontents*. • Carl Jung (1928/1960) uses archetype and affect to understanding processes of individual and cultural differentiation. • Andrew Samuels (1993) develops the idea of political emotions. • Diana Fosha (2000) focuses on a therapist active use and display of affect. • William Reddy (2001) offers a historical account of the rise of 'emotional liberty'. • Aftab Omer (2005) asserts that affect is source of emergent capacities. • John Beebe (2008) asserts the importance of affect as 'objective sympathy' **Scientific Study of Emotion** • Charles Darwin (1872) begins the scientific study of the function of emotion. • Sylvan Tomkins (1950s) identifies the biology of emotion in 'affect science'. **Revolution and Reform** • Political use of emotion for moral development of Western culture (emphasis on grief, shame, and guilt): political and social reform movements starting in the late 1700s running through 20th century.
↑ **Sensory Freedom** emerges late 1600s	• **John Locke's** 'empiricism' declares that the individual is self-determining and not obligated to feudal lords. This position is developed through the idea that we are born as a blank slate, sensory experience discovers natural laws, thinking and sensing are trustworthy, emotions are not to be trusted.
↑ **Reasoning Freedom** emerges early 1600s	• **Rene Descartes'** 'rationalism' finds freedom in differentiated thought. While typically characterized by the phrase 'I think therefore I am', a more accurate rendition is offered by Jungian John Beebe: 'I think therefore I'm free' (Dunlap, 2008, p. 168). According to Descartes the individual has an immortal soul and can be a source of original thinking.
↑ **Religious Freedom** emerges to direct instinct and impulsivity	• Knowledge comes through revelation and is expressed in sacred texts, which supports emergence of *mythic order*. The individual is not valued, nor can individual experience lead to valid knowledge. Affect, fear and shame in particular, are used to control individual impulsivity.
↑ **Limbic freedom**	The development of the Mammalian brain expands range of an organism's time and space relations.

Table 2: Emergent capacities and their institutional support [Adapted from Dunlap, 2008]

freedom'. What has made this process so painful and difficult is the extent to which the advance of political development seemingly required the sacrifice of emotion and its capacity for connectivity in order to consolidate the gains of reasoning and sensory freedom ... Affect can be restored as a dimension of trustworthy human experience and it can be extended as the emergent human capacity for affect freedom, which supports our ability to discern and act on cultural knowledge. (Dunlap, 2009)

There are several prominent psychological educators working in this terrain to consolidate an image of 'psychological citizenship' working at the interface between the psychology and politics of emotion. San Francisco Jungian John Beebe goes beyond the traditional psychotherapist's use of emotion for assessment to include the therapist's display of her emotions (Beebe, 2008). Beebe notes that the therapist's display of emotion as 'objective sympathy' provides a patient with a direct encounter of emotion enabling them to learn to use their emotions for what they are for. Beebe also shows how political leaders like Hillary Clinton and Barack Obama are *showing* levels of affect freedom not seen in previous generations of political leadership. Following Beebe we can consider the need to follow these acts of cultural leadership by developing the educational practices that could support a wider and deeper cultural use of this emerging capacity for affect freedom.

Political psychologist and Jungian analyst Andrew Samuels encourages his students and other participants in his 'political clinics' to use their imaginations and emotions to assess and creatively respond to the political and cultural crises of our time. He models for us what it might mean to do 'political therapy' in our communities (Samuels, 2001, p. 159; 1993, p. 55).

Aftab Omer, president of the Meridian University of Psychology and Business, identifies the way in which acts of cultural leadership expose repressed affect in politically oppressive circumstances (Omer, 2005). Omer also identifies the way in which specific practices confront this suffering and transmute affect into a range of human capacities. For example, Omer notes how: a practice of mourning transmutes grief into compassion; encouragement transmutes fear into courage; conflict resolution transmutes anger into loving fierceness; and accountability transmutes shame into having a conscience (Omer, 2002). The following historical events exemplify Omer's insight:

> Martin Luther King exposed himself to physical violence and incarceration in order to draw the attention of the nation and the world to the shame of the American people's treatment of African Americans ... King's acts of cultural leadership transmuted his own and his follower's fear into courage and the American people's shame into a rudimentary conscience, one capable of recognizing the social trauma of prejudice and our own active and passive perpetuation of this horror. (Dunlap, 2009)

Based on the work of these recent theorists it is possible to offer the following understanding of the political development of Western culture, particularly the current day circumstances of our political culture.

The Psychoeducational Practices of a Transformative Political Psychologist

Currently the field of political psychology is a subfield of the discipline of political science. The research completed in this field supports the application of psychological knowledge to the goals of political science. Political psychology has made invaluable contributions to our knowledge of politics including 'the development of political attitudes, the perception of political leaders, the sources of party identification, and attribution of traits to enemies and allies, the relationship between ideology, attitude, and act, social trust, and the attractions of authoritarianism' (Alford, 2002, p. 198). The practitioners in this field embody the best of Dewey's political individual and have built substantial institutions based in the values of political liberalism.

However, the unintended passivity/neutrality of the social scientist enters into the identity of the political psychologist who, according to political psychologist Fred Alford, offers only 'understanding' and 'no solutions' (Alford, 2002, p. 195). This troubled stance carries forward into the recent work of Lakoff (1996; 2004; 2008) and Westen (2007) both of whom have generated new ideas about the political function of emotion but neither of whom use their insights to imagine more developed, advanced 'political identities' for the social scientist or the progressive community and its activists. While helpfully focusing on the public use of emotion, they fail to imagine into the relationship between political identity, emotion, and political development. While their work helps create educational programs that inform existing progressive groups of how to 'frame' their political work, it does not embrace Dewey's vision, however abstract, of forming a new 'psychological and moral type'. While the work of Lakoff, Westen and others is invaluable, the critique offered here goes to the question of the potential role of the social scientist in intervening in political culture. What would happen if the political psychologist imagined into existence the capacity to intervene in political systems, paralleling the role of a psychotherapist in clinical practice (Samuels, 1993, p. 55)?

Currently the field of clinical psychology brings to the table the idea that the social scientist, as psychotherapist, is capable of activating the psychological and moral development of her clients. As expressed in the governing images of Luke's 'physician heal thyself' or of the 'wounded healer', psychotherapists are expected to achieve some modest level of self-reflection and self-development. While circumscribed by the limits of just treating individuals, this image can be pulled forward and combined with the identity of the political psychologist.

From political psychology we can draw forward the need to understand political culture. From clinical psychology we can draw forward the opportunity to intervene in this culture as an agent of transformation. This hybrid image grounds Dewey's idea of the social scientist as a new 'psychological and moral type' combining the interests of understanding and intervention into an image of psychocultural development. Incorporated in this image is a new psychological and moral type of 'practitioner/citizen' who takes responsibility for her own and her community's political development.

These new types of practitioners/citizens could engage their communities in order to help them face the perfect storm of environmental degradation, social injustice, the abuses of power, and economic collapse. These practitioners/citizens can extend the *passive objectivity* derived from 'reasoning' and 'sensory' freedom into an *active objectivity* discerned through the emerging capacity for affect freedom, which activates a public use of emotion.

Through the activation of affect freedom a practitioner/citizen could help bridge the cultural divide between science and governance, which has limited the current psychocultural development of Western culture. This is a task recognized by both Dewey and Jung and, while their shared theory of knowledge did not mature into clear practices, that is changing. Following Samuels, Omer, and others, there are numerous 'educational', 'healing', and 'community engagement' learning practices that are helping people to reconnect to their own political histories, to each other, and to strengthen their political identities (Dunlap, 2008, p. 244). In my own work with progressive organizations and their leadership I've established practices that draw attention to a range of 'subtle prejudices', such as those against authority, religion, and even psychology that are rooted within 'political wounds' suffered by progressive groups over the last few hundred years that continue to haunt their political effectiveness (Dunlap, 2008, p. 267). While this work is new and promising it is also challenging.

The work ahead will be difficult and risky. As the 2009 American healthcare reform debate showed with its emotional reactivity and the ease with which that volatility was manipulated, it is no simple matter to use our emotions in public. Progressives are caught between the reactive emotionality shown by the political Right (their indulgence in anger and contempt and their fear mongering) and their own overly-rationalized identity with its neutered emotionality.

Currently there are numerous individuals who are exploring the opportunity for a professional identity between politics and psychology, one that works to expand the emotional intelligence of the progressive community. Whether as political consultants, cultural coaches, leadership trainers, or what I think of as 'transformative political psychologists' these new practitioners/citizens will need the guidance of a strong institutional form helping to establish an educational philosophy, professional ethics, best practices, and other forms of standardization needed in order to fully establish a range of new professions within our organizations and communities.

In the work ahead there is a role for a transformative political psychologist to engage the citizens in their communities, including other social scientists, educators, and activists in the work of transforming political culture. Whether at academic conferences, in classrooms, city council meetings, or the board rooms of our nonprofits, we have the opportunity to attend to each other, to heal the political wounds that are rooted in each of our personal and political identities, and thus to pursue human freedom through our political development. Such transformational work will activate the affect freedom needed for us to become embodied solutions to the current crises of our time.

Note

1. The concept of 'affect freedom' is derived from my dissertation research, (2003) 'Destiny as Capacity: The transformation of political identity in human development', Meridian University, Petaluma CA.

References

Alford, F. (2002) Group Psychology is the State of Nature, in: K. Monroe (ed.), *Political Psychology* (Mahwah NJ, Lawrence Erlbaum Associates).
Beebe, J. (2008) Objective Sympathy, Keynote address to the International Conference *Beyond Ego Psychology: Journeys of the Heart East and West* (Ryukoku University, Kyoto Japan).

Bellah, R., Madsen, R. Sullivan, W. M., Swidler, A. & Tipton, S. M. (1985) *Habits of the Heart* (Berkeley, CA, University of California Press).

Burack, C. (1994) *The Problem of the Passions: Feminism, psychoanalysis, and social theory* (New York, New York University Press).

Buxton, C. (1985) *Points of View in the Modern History of Psychology* (Orlando, FL, Academic Press).

Clark, L. & Watson, D. (1994) Distinguishing Functional from Dysfunctional Affective Responses, in: P. Ekman & R. Davidson (eds), *The Nature of Emotion* (New York, Oxford University Press).

Darwin, C. (1872) *The Expression of the Emotions in Man and Animals* (Oxford, Oxford University Press).

Dewey, J. (1925) *Experience and Nature* (New York, Dover).

Dewey, J. (1929a) *Individualism Old and New* (New York, Capricorn Books).

Dewey, J. (1929b) *Liberalism and Social Action* (New York, Capricorn Books).

Dewey, J. (1929c) *The Quest for Certainty: A study of the relation of knowledge and action* (New York, Minton, Balach and Co.).

Dewey, J. (1931) *Philosophy and Civilization* (New York, Minton, Balach & Co.).

Dewey, J. (1938) *Logic the Theory of Inquiry* (New York, Holt, Rinehart, and Winston).

Dewey, J. & Bentley, A. (1949) *Knowing and the Known* (Boston, MA, Beacon Press).

Dunlap, P. (2008) *Awakening Our Faith in the Future: The advent of psychological liberalism* (London, Routledge).

Dunlap, P. (2009) An Emerging Cultural Psychology: The psychological scientist as cultural leader, in: *International Journal of Jungian Studies* (London, Routledge publishers) in review.

Erikson, E. (1968) *Identity, Youth and Crisis* (New York, W.W. Norton).

Fosha, D. (2000) *The Transforming Power of Affect* (New York, Basic Books).

Freud, S. (1930) *Civilization and its Discontents*, J. Riviere, trans. London: Hogarth Press and Institute of Psycho-Analysis.

Frijda, N. (1994) Emotions Are Functional, Most of the Time, in: P. Ekman & R. Davidson (eds), *The Nature of Emotion* (New York, Oxford University Press).

Jung, C. (1919/1960) The Psychological Foundation of Beliefs in Spirits, in: *The Structure and Dynamics of the Psyche*, *The Collected Works of C.G. Jung*, vol. 8 (Princeton, NJ, Princeton University Press).

Jung, C. (1921/1971) *Psychological Types*, *The Collected Works of C.G. Jung*, vol. 6 (Princeton, NJ, Princeton University Press).

Jung, C. (1928/1960) On Psychic Energy, in *The Structure and Dynamics of the Psyche*, *The Collected Works of C.G. Jung*, vol. 8 (Princeton, NJ, Princeton University Press).

Jung, C. (1930/1960) The Stage of Life, in *The Structure and Dynamics of the Psyche*, *The Collected Works of C.G. Jung*, vol. 8 (Princeton, NJ, Princeton University Press).

Jung, C. (1936/1960) Psychological Factors Determining Human Behavior, in *The Structure and Dynamics of the Psyche*, *The Collected Works of C.G. Jung*, vol. 8 (Princeton, NJ, Princeton University Press).

Jung, C. (1939/1959) Conscious, Unconscious, and Individuation, in *The Archetypes in the Collective Unconscious, The Collected Works of C.G. Jung*, vol. 9.i (Princeton, NJ, Princeton University Press).

Jung, C. (1946/1964) The Fight with the Shadow, in *Civilization in Transition, The Collected Works of C.G. Jung*, vol. 10 (Princeton, NJ, Princeton University Press).

Jung, C. (1958/1964) Flying Saucers: A modern myth, in *Civilization in Transition, The Collected Works of C.G. Jung*, vol. 10 (Princeton, NJ, Princeton University Press).

Lakoff, G. (1996) *Moral Politics* (Chicago, IL, University of Chicago Press).

Lakoff, G. (2004) *Don't Think of an Elephant* (White River Jct., VT, Chelsea Green Publishing).

Lakoff, G. (2008) *The Political Mind* (New York, Viking).

Lazarus, R. (1994) Universal Antecedents of the Emotions, in: P. Ekman & R. Davidson (eds), *The Nature of Emotion* (New York, Oxford University Press).

Lewis, M. (2000) *The Handbook of Emotions* (New York, Gilford Press).

McCutchan, R. (2006) *Awakening the Spirit of Osiris* (Sarasota, FL, Profits Publishing).

McDaniel, S. (1980–88) *Coursework in the Psychology and Philosophy Departments* (Rohnert Park, CA, Sonoma State University).

McDaniel, S. (2009) *The Transactional Developmental Model*: Part one, section two, Available at: http://www.stanmcdaniel.com/pubs/development/development.html

Mill, J. S. (1873/1989) *Autobiography* (Harmondsworth, Penguin Classics).

Nathanson, D. (1992) *Shame and Pride: Affect, sex, and the birth of the self* (New York, W.W. Norton).

Omer, A. (2002) *Definitions in Imaginal Psychology, Dissertation guide* (Petaluma, CA, Meridian University).

Omer, A. (2005) The Spacious Center: Leadership and the creative transformation of culture, *Shift: At the Frontiers of Consciousness*, 6, pp. 30–33.

Polkinghorne, D. (1983) *Methodology for the Human Sciences* (Albany, NY, State University of New York Press).

Ratner, J. (1939) *Intelligence in the Modern World* (New York, Modern Library).

Reddy, W. (2001) *The Navigation of Feeling* (Cambridge: Cambridge University Press).

Richardson, R. (2006) *William James* (New York, Houghton Mifflin).

Samuels, A. (1993) *The Political Psyche* (London, Routledge).

Samuels, A. (2001) *Politics on the Couch* (London, Profile Books).

Scherer, K. R. (1994) Evidence for Both the Universality and Cultural Specificity of Emotion Elicitation, in: P. Ekman & R. Davidson (eds), *The Nature of Emotion* (New York, Oxford University Press).

de Tocqueville, A. D. (1945) *Democracy in America*, vol. 2 (New York, Alfred Knopf).

Westen, D. (2007) *The Political Brain: The role of emotion in deciding the fate of the nation* (New York, Public Affairs).

Wilber, K. (1995) *Sex Ecology and Spirituality* (Boston, MA, Shambhala).

6

Deleuze's Philosophy and Jung's Psychology: Learning and the Unconscious

Inna Semetsky & Joshua Ramey

Introduction

In his recent book 'Deleuze and The Unconscious', Christian Kerslake (2007) brings to the front the oft-neglected yet powerful presence of Jungian inflections in Gilles Deleuze's philosophy. Considering the place Deleuze's corpus presently occupies in educational theory (e.g. Peters, 2004; Semetsky, 2006; 2008), this paper aims to extend the link between Deleuze and Jung towards discovering an under-explored dimension in Carl Jung's thought as related to philosophy of education and against the background of Deleuze's conceptualizations, especially with regard to the role of the unconscious, or affective, dimension (cf. May & Semetsky, 2008) and experiential learning.

Some conceptual shifts need to be presented at the outset. More often than not education is equated with formal schooling thus *a priori* marginalizing the realm of human development and, specifically, adult development. Adult education, under the slogan of life-long learning, has been transformed into 'frightful continual training ... continual monitoring of worker-schoolkids or bureaucrat-students. They try to present it as a reform of the school system, but it's really its dismantling' (Deleuze, 1995, p. 175). In the same way that corporations have replaced factories, an abstract concept of life-long learning replaces the problematic of human development. By turning exams into continuous assessment, education itself is 'turning ... into a business' (Deleuze, 1995, p. 179). In this manner, new forms of schooling become the means to provide a continuous stream of human capital for the knowledge economy. If and when human capital replaces humans, then, as Deleuze argues, individuals become replaced by 'dividuals', a market statistic, part of a sample, an item in a data bank. Yet, it is *individuation* proper as a process of subject-formation that remains at the core of Deleuze's philosophy and Jung's psychology alike and, we contend, is what human development as a process of learning from experience is all about.

Self-education

Individuation was defined by Jung as a process of *self-education* in which both unconscious and conscious aspects of life-experiences are integrated completely. Jung was explicit that education should not be confined to schools nor education should stop when a child grows up. Presenting his *depth* psychology as a method of/for self-education, Jung (1954) was adamant that self-knowledge remains an indispensable basis of self-education and emphasized an *indirect* method for attaining such inner self-knowledge by means of its symbolic mediation in the analytic process:

> There are ... many extremely psychic processes which are unconscious, or only indirectly conscious ... there is ... something as impersonal as a product of nature that enables us to know the truth about ourselves ... . Of the unconscious we can learn nothing directly, but indirectly we can perceive the effects that come into consciousness. (Jung, 1954, p. 49)

Both Jung and Deleuze were anti-Oedipal—and anti-Freudian—in defying the reduction of the unconscious dimension to a single master-signified represented by the Oedipal complex overlaid exclusively by sexual symbolism. The true means of communication between the conscious mind and the unconscious is by virtue of symbols thereby exceeding a solely linguistic expression grounded in a propositional, conscious, thought: 'symbols act as *transformers*, their function being to convert libido from a "lower" into a "higher" form' (Jung CW 5. 344); a 'lower' meaning its psycho-sexual, Freudian, form and a 'higher'—reaching toward a deeper, spiritual and numinous, dimension. Unconscious contents, for Freud, could always be reduced to sexual origins of familial dramas. There is no deeper inner meaning to dreams, for example, but rather a single content indicating the contours of the inhibited or traumatized personal desire. For Deleuze and Guattari, however, the unconscious is plurality or multiplicity that does not belong to the scope of traditional psychoanalytic thought. It is the unconscious as multiplicity that ultimately connects us not with private but public—social, political, and world-historical—existence. Over and above the personal unconscious, it always deals with some collective frame and is 'a productive machine ... at once social and desiring' (Deleuze, 1995, p. 144).

For Jung too, the unconscious is irreducible to its personal dimension. The *synthetic*—indirect and interpretive—method of Jungian *analytical* psychology (not a contradiction in terms!) is grounded in the *transcendent* function that creates a symbolic bridge between the realm of the unconscious and the phenomenal world of human experiences. Synthetic method reflects the dynamical and evolutionary approach to knowledge oriented to the creation of meanings and, for Jung, a 'psychological fact ... as a living phenomenon ... is always indissolubly bound up with the continuity of the vital process, so that it is not only something evolved but also continually evolving and creative' (Jung CW 6. 717) as a function of our life-long learning from experience *per se*. Even if our existence emerges from and within family dynamics, 'there are non-oedipal, anoedipal currents that begin as early as Oedipus and continue just as long, with another rhythm, in a different mode of operation, in another dimension, with other uses of *syntheses* that feed the autoproduction of the unconscious—unconscious-as-orphan, the playful unconscious, the meditative and social unconscious' (Deleuze & Guattari, 1983, p. 100; italics ours). The unconscious cannot be reduced to psychoanalytic drives or instincts as well as 'playing around all the time with mummy and daddy' (Deleuze, 1995, p. 144). Unconscious formations are to be brought into play because an individual 'family drama depends ... on the unconscious social investments' (Deleuze, 1995, p. 20) in, as Deleuze calls it, *delire* that may manifest in a diverse regime of signs such as dream interpretation in Jungian analysis.

Affects and Experience

The totality of human experiences reflected in worldwide myths and folklore led Jung to postulate the existence of an *objective* psyche shared by humankind (Jung, 1959) and 'populated' by the archetypes implicit in the field of what he called the *collective uncon-scious*. Jung addressed this deepest level as *psychoid* and asserted that it is at this level where, in a holistic manner, body and mind, *physis* and *psyche*, become united as two different aspects of one world, *Unus Mundus*. Jung insisted on a multiplicity of inner, spiritual, meanings for the unconscious that would have exceeded its overt, even if latent, meaning posited by Freud as repressed. These deep evolving meanings express them-selves through the archetypal images that act as *symbolic transformers* capable of making the unconscious contents manifest at the level of conscious awareness. According to Jung's depth psychology, the unconscious 'archetypes [as] ... structural elements of the psyche ... possess a certain autonomy and specific energy which enables them to attract, out of the conscious mind, those contents which are better suited to themselves' (Jung CW 5. 232), thus helping us achieve a much wider scope of awareness than rational thinking alone in terms of reasoning from premise to conclusion is capable of providing. The collective unconscious encompasses future possibilities, and '[a] purposively inter-preted [image such as in dreams], seems like a symbol, seeking to characterize a definite goal with the help of the material at hand, or trace out a line of future psychological development' (Jung CW 6. 720) toward 'the Self' as the archetype of wholeness repre-senting the ultimate purpose of individuation when the unconscious becomes fully integrated into consciousness.

Jung commented that Freud 'was blind toward the paradox and ambiguity of the contents of the unconscious, and did not know that everything which arises out of the unconscious has ... an inside and an outside' (Jung, 1963, p. 153)—quite in accord with the critical thinking of Gilles Deleuze who presented the relationship between con-sciousness and the unconscious as *enfolded*. Deleuze defined the very *outside* of thought as 'a moving matter animated by ... movements, folds and foldings that together make up an inside: they are not something other than the outside but precisely the inside *of* the outside' (Deleuze, 1988a, p. 97): the fold. The process of individuation is artistic and creative and ultimately enables 'the conquest of the unconscious' (Deleuze, 1988b, p. 29) during its own constructive process. The dynamic subject's complex rules of formation are defined by the intensive capacity 'to affect and be affected' (Deleuze & Guattari, 1987, p. xvi). Affects are not simple personal feelings but 'becomings that spill over beyond whoever lives through them (thereby becoming someone else)' (Deleuze, 1995, p. 137): *becoming-other*. It is something enfolded in the singular event of the archetypal nature that 'forces us to think. This something is an object not of recognition but a fundamental "encounter" [that] may be grasped in a range of affective tones: wonder, love, hatred, suffering' (Deleuze, 1994, p. 139) leading to our learning from experience embedded in this particular event when it begins making sense for us. 'Thinking' via affects—as partaking of four Jungian functions that enrich rational thought with sensing, feeling and intuition—enables one to access the very depth of the psyche or '*an unconscious of thought* [which is] just as profound as *the unknown of the body*' (Deleuze, 1988b, p. 19; Deleuze's italics). The implicit meanings become explicit by virtue of 'becoming conscious and by being perceived' (Jung in Pauli, 1994, p. 159).

It is the archetypal symbolism that presents us with those inner unconscious meanings that, while being outside of the conscious thought, are nonetheless 'located' within our embodied experiences, in which the archetypal patterns are embedded. Deleuze presents the paradoxical relationship between the inside and outside, inner and outer, in terms of the dynamical field of forces whose action (the action of the archetypes, in Jung's parlance) can lead to deterritorialization, that is, approaching and traversing the narrow boundaries of a personal Cogito. Such a limit-experience would be equivalent, for Deleuze, to *becoming-other* in the process of individuation. 'The other in me' (Deleuze, 1988a, p. 98) is ultimately implicated because of the twisted and folded relationship between a rational thought and a non-thought—or as yet 'unthought', unconscious and affective, dimension. This 'unthought' dimension belongs not to the conscious *Ego* expressing itself with an a priori given certainty in the form of a Cartesian 'I think', but to 'the fractured I of a dissolved Cogito' (Deleuze, 1994, p. 194). Jungian self-education then should be understood as constituting the developmental and learning—individuating—process when the fractured pieces of a dissolved Cogito will be put together in analysis or integrated into consciousness in the process of becoming-other and achieving, for Jung, a 'greater personality' (Jung CW 7. 136).

The traces of the collective unconscious are perceived indirectly, via their *effects* that, as we said earlier quoting Jung, do come into consciousness (Jung, 1954) and manifest themselves across cultures, times and places. Jung insisted that it is through the integration of the unconscious that we might have a reasonable chance to make experiences of an archetypal nature providing us with the feeling of continuity not only throughout our life-experiences but also in a spiritual sense before and after our existence. The better our understanding of the reality of the archetypes, the more we can participate in this reality progressively realizing the archetypes' eternity and timelessness. For Deleuze (and Guattari), it is the 'proper names of history' that are akin to the Jungian archetypes within the field of the collective unconscious—like Deleuze's infamous Body without Organs—and which are recognized as extending throughout a socio-cultural milieu and becoming demonstrable indirectly by virtue of their effects at the level of cultural, historical and collective, consciousness:

> It is a question of ... identifying races, cultures, and gods with fields of intensity on the body without organs, identifying personages with states that fill these fields, and with effects that fulgurate within and traverse these fields. Whence the role of names, with a magic all their own: there is no ego that identifies with races, peoples, and persons in a theatre of representation, but proper names that identify races, peoples, and persons with regions, thresholds, or effects in a production of intensive quantities. The theory of proper names should not be conceived in terms of representation; it refers instead to the class of 'effects': effects that are not a mere dependence upon causes, but the occupation of a domain, the operation of a system of signs. This can be clearly seen in physics, where proper names designate such effects within fields of potentials: the Joule effect, the Seebeck effect, the Devlin effect. History is like a physics: a Joan of

Arc effect, a heliogabulus effect—all the *names* of history, and not the name of the father. (Deleuze & Guattari, 1983, p. 86)

How We Learn

What the archetypal patterns seem to register is what Deleuze dubbed a 'profound complicity between nature and mind' (Deleuze, 1994, p. 165) at the level of our experience. As he argues in *Difference and Repetition* (1994), experiential learning is not a matter of carrying into action some a priori representation (say, by passing to the act of swimming from forming a representation of a teacher's movements). Rather, learning is, on Deleuze's account, a matter of indexing all possible conjunctions, i.e. a body in conjunction with a wave: a body *and* wave. Deleuze (1995) refers to new sports, like surfing, windsurfing and hang-gliding that require one to enter into an existing wave as if establishing a shared bond or indeed 'complicity' founded on the conjunction 'and' as the outline of 'creative line of flight' (Deleuze, 1987, p. 10) that traverses a particular experience. For Deleuze,

> When a body combines some of its own distinctive points with those of a wave, it espouses the principle of a repetition which is no longer that of the Same but involves the Other—involves difference, from one wave and one gesture to another, and carries that difference through the repetitive space thereby constituted. To learn is indeed to constitute this space of an encounter with signs, in which distinctive points renew themselves in each other, and repetition takes shape while disguising itself. (Deleuze, 1994, p. 23)

The very fact that we can learn at all, for Deleuze, points to this deep complicity between nature (body, the unconscious) and mind (consciousness). However, this complicity is not the Kantian one presented as a set of possibilities determined by the categories of our understanding and constitutive of phenomena. For Deleuze, it is not the possibilities of our conscious mind but the multiple and varying parameters of the unconscious body that continuously create novel relations in our real experience. They are the very problematic instances embedded in the archetypal patterns of our unconscious actions. Such problems appear at first only as subliminal or subconscious (as yet imperceptible or micro-perceptible) elements. Learning happens when a body actualizes its virtual potencies thus creating new assemblages. It is only in the real-life experiential singularity within an encounter with actual waves where the virtual 'essence' or 'idea' of swimming subsists thereby potentially allowing us to comprehend its meaning. Experience is thus paramount for learning, for creating novel meanings embedded in what Deleuze called the pedagogy of the concept. Experiential education will have paid attention to places and spaces, to retrospective as well as untimely memories, and to those dynamic forces that are capable of *affecting* and *effecting* changes thus contesting the very identity of subjects participating in this dynamical process. For Deleuze, philosophy is a practice of concept-creation, and the pedagogy of the concept 'would have to analyze the conditions of creation as factors of always singular moments' (Deleuze & Guattari, 1994, p. 12; cf. Peters, 2004). The relevance to education is tantamount: as Deleuze and Guattari (1994) assert, 'If the three ages of the concept are the encyclopedia, pedagogy, and commercial professional training, only the second can safeguard us from falling from the heights of the first into the disaster of the third' (Deleuze & Guattari, 1994, p. 12). It is the pedagogy of the concept that must educate us in becoming able to feel, to know, and to learn, that is, being able to *create concepts* as the meanings for experiences.

For Deleuze there is no 'representable concept' of swimming (at least not one from which anything new could be learned). There is only a dynamic *event* in which the distinctive points of a body combine with those of a wave. Swimming is thus not a static notion transmitted by a generic instructor to a generic student, but a dynamic form of *becoming* modulated across the body of the teacher *through* the body of the student. The essence of swimming is never a stable, representable 'solution' to the problem of what to do in water. Rather, swimming poses a problem or introduces a 'problematic field' in which we can learn: where can I swim? When can I swim? How long and how fast can I swim? Will I swim or sink? These are the questions that determine the essence of swimming. Learning centers on problems, not on solutions:

> To learn to swim is to conjugate the distinctive points of our bodies with the singular points of the objective Idea in order to form a problematic field. This conjugation determines for us a threshold of consciousness at which our real acts are adjusted to our perceptions of the real relations, thereby providing a solution to the problem. Moreover, problematic Ideas are precisely the ultimate elements of nature and the subliminal objects of little perceptions. As a result, 'learning' always takes place in and through the unconscious, thereby establishing the bond of a profound complicity between nature and mind. (Deleuze, 1994, p. 165)

Jung's archetypal patterns that make us act unconsciously nevertheless lead us to learning because their '[p]roblematic structure is part of objects themselves, allowing them to be grasped as signs, just as the questioning or problematizing instance is a part of knowledge allowing its objectivity and its specificity to be grasped in the act of *learning*' (Deleuze, 1994, p. 64). Therefore our unconscious is a necessary precursor (and quite often dark, as Deleuze would say) that indeed forces us to learn, to individuate, to become other. According to Deleuze, 'the intentionality of being is surpassed by the fold of Being, Being as fold' (Deleuze, 1988a, p. 110). In this respect, the unconscious perceptions are implicated (*le pli* in French means the fold) as little, or micro-, perceptions; as such they form a constitutive part of Deleuze-Guattarian schizoanalysis of establishing 'an unconscious psychic mechanism that engenders the perceived in consciousness' (Deleuze, 1993, p. 95) partaking as such on Jungian psychology.

Becoming-other

Deleuze's pragmatic (Semetsky, 2006) and future-oriented epistemology is oriented towards the creation of concepts 'for unknown lands' (Deleuze, 1995, p. 103), as well as meanings and values 'that are yet to come' (Deleuze & Guattari, 1987, p. 5). Similarly, Jung's synthetic method implies the emergence of new meanings as carrying the utmost significance in analysis thereby reflecting the future-oriented path to knowledge. According to Jung, archetypes hold some sort of foreknowledge: he emphasized the prospective function of the unconscious or what Deleuze, following Bergson, called the memory of the future. The synthetic, and not solely analytic, approach amplifies traditional psychoanalysis, which was considered reductive by Jung and Deleuze alike because of its sole orientation to the past marked by Oedipal conflict. Deleuze's philosophical method of transcendental empiricism functions on the basis of so-called transversal communication—akin to Jung's transcendent function—as a connection between nature and mind, between the unconscious and consciousness. The prefix 'trans' is significant: the unconscious dimension is transcended by means of an indirect, transversal, link of a symbolic mediation via the archetypal images. The transversal, as if intuitive, access to the unconscious makes Deleuze's method 'patterned after Bergson's intuition' (Boundas, 1996, p. 87). Intuition enables the reading of signs and symbols that might appear, for example in the process of Jungian active imagination or dream interpretation in analysis. As 'the presentation of the unconscious, [and] not the representation of consciousness' (Deleuze, 1994, p. 192), intuition leads to laying out what Deleuze called the plane of immanence aiming 'to bring into being that which does not yet exist' (Deleuze, 1994, p. 147), that is, novel concepts and new awareness due to which we acquire capacity to grow and develop. When Jung writes of Philemon—a persistent figure in his own dreams—he argues that 'there are things in the psyche which I do not produce, but which produce themselves and have their own life ... there is something in me that can say things that I do not know and do not intend, things which may even be directed against me' (1963, p. 183), that is, which act at the unconscious level beyond Jung's conscious will and voluntary control.

Human development engenders itself through both 'the psychic and the social' (Bosteels, 1998, p. 150), thus above and beyond verbal expressions of the conscious mind: 'it is not the personal human being who is making the statement, but the archetype speaking through him' (Jung, 1963, p. 352). In the 'Four Archetypes' Jung says:

> You need not be insane to hear his voice. On the contrary, it is a simplest and most natural thing imaginable ... You can describe it as mere 'associating' ... or as a 'meditation' [and] a real colloquy becomes possible when the ego acknowledges the existence of a partner to the discussion. (Jung CW 9. 236–237)

It is through a developing symbolic dialogue with such a 'partner' implicit in the archetypal dynamics—when it appears that 'something [is] passing through' (Deleuze, 1995, p. 141) and we can perceive its so far imperceptible 'voice'—that we can achieve a certain level of self-knowledge crucial for self-education and for ultimately becoming-other, that is, becoming our authentic Selves above and over our narrow Cartesian *res cogitans*. Becoming-other is established via 'diversity, multiplicity [and] the destruction of identity' (Deleuze, 1995, p. 44). Individuation presupposes transforming our old, unconscious, habits of thinking and acting alike: archetypes as symbols of transformation and 'system[s] of readiness for action' (Jung CW 9.199) are postulated by Jung to serve as a deep ground for our habits. Deleuze (1987) describes a conversation between Jung and Freud where Jung points out to Freud the importance of multiple elements constituting a particular context as they appear in the unconscious. Individuation, as always already becoming-other, is bound to collective assemblages: people do not become 'without a fascination for the pack, for multiplicity' (Deleuze & Guattari, 1987, p. 240), for the entangled lines of flight that bring to awareness meanings that were as yet unperceived. The unpredictable lines of transversal connections presuppose not the transmission of the same but the creation of the different: the process that has important implications for education understood as holistic, that is, as a generative practice of/for creation of new concepts, new meanings and values for experience which thus contributes to self-education and human development towards becoming a whole person.

Deleuze and Guattari (1987) emphasize *metamorphosis* with regard to Jung's theory of the transformation of the libido, which is defined as spiritual energy irreducible, we repeat, to Freud's limited definition of the libido as a sex drive. A play of unconscious affects may reach 'a point of excess and unloosening' (Deleuze & Guattari, 1987, p. 134). At this crucial turning point there are two options: a subject must 'either annihilate itself in a black hole or change planes. Destratify, open up to a new function, a diagrammatic function' (Deleuze & Guattari, 1987, p. 134), such a diagram functioning symbolically as a transversal link. The critical philosophical framework is too narrow: Deleuze posits philosophy as an enterprise both critical and clinical (Deleuze 1997) indeed tending towards the level of analysis as deep as analytical psychology. Jung's depth psychology merges with Deleuze and Guattari's schizoanalytic, or rhizomatic, method of tracing (symbolically or diagrammatically) the multiple lines forming a rhizomatic network of connections. Rhizome as a model of thinking includes a somewhat 'underground', unconscious, dimension. Indeed, Jung used the same biological metaphor of a rhizome as Deleuze:

> The life of a man is a dubious experiment ... . Individually, it is so fleet-ing ... Life has always seemed to me like a plant that lives on its rhizome. Its true life is invisible, hidden in the rhizome. The part that appears above ground lasts only a single summer. Then it withers away—an ephemeral apparition ... . Yet I have never lost a sense of something that lives and endures underneath the eternal flux. What we see is the blossom, which passes. The rhizome remains. (Jung, 1963, p. 4)

Jungian process of individuation proceeds in accord with Deleuze's positing transfor-mation, or change in nature, to be a precondition for subject-formation. We learn from the signs implicit in problematic events that make our very experience of such an event *problematic* and, by becoming able to read and interpret them—to become conscious of them—we can transform the problem, to make sense out of it so that its disjointed fragments ultimately form a unified whole. Deleuze admired Jung for describing the unconscious in terms of problems rather than in terms of solutions to the problems. Freud had insisted, against Jung, that psychic life can be reduced to sexual desire, and to the oppositional conflicts that both inspire and thwart such desire. For Freud, psychic life is fundamentally structured by being allowed or not allowed wish-fulfillment: being prohibited or being indulged, being restricted or being liberated, all in the end having to do with a desire satisfied or unfulfilled, the record of which lies in personal unconscious fixations. For Jung, the psyche *questions* as well as desires (Deleuze, 1994, p. 316). So the multiplicity of answered and unanswered questions has the correlates in the unconscious just as much as do the conflicts of desire. Deleuze noted that there is a perspective from which the argument between Jung and Freud can be superseded; a transcendental perspective from which that which is fundamental to psychic life is a series of *problems*, indeed. For Deleuze, the unconscious is essentially the site of an indefinite series of problems, and psychic life is organized around questions.

There is something like an Augustinian paradox here: a paradox for desire that reiterates the paradox of new knowledge (also called the learning paradox; cf. Semetsky, 2009) in Plato's famous *Meno* dialogue leading to his theory of recollection: how can I desire what I do not know (Augustine, 1991)? For Freud, one does not realize that one desires until one is prohibited in satisfying this wish. And 'I' will only emerge into an awareness of 'who I am' insofar as I will have realized that my desire is thwarted. For Jung, on the other hand, individuation is the confrontation with, and the integration of, the archetypal forces. Sexuality is only one among the powers in which the psyche participates, and libido as psychic or spiritual energy is an investment motivated by a desire for knowledge-in-depth, for inner Gnosis, ultimately modeled on initiation rites and the alchemical quest for a symbolic transformation of baser into nobler elements. For Jung, the psyche fully individuates only when it has embraced the totality of the elements to which it belongs. The archetypes represent various aspects of the personality, both natural and cultural, mental and material, sexual and spiritual; ultimately embracing alchemical Sophia as mediatrix in the form of Spirit permeating both nature and culture and confirming Jung's insight that 'psyche and matter are two different aspects of one and the same thing' (Jung CW 8. 418). They are united in analysis thus defying the ghost of the dualistic split haunting us since the days of Descartes both in theory and, importantly, in practice.

New Ethics

The level of practice as encompassing human behaviour, decision making or choosing a particular course of action is of utmost significance. Reflecting on what psychologist Erich Neumann (1969) called, in the aftermath of WWII, 'a new ethic', Jung commented that the presupposed universal rules of human conduct are 'at most provisional solutions, but never lead to those critical decisions which are the turning points in a man's life. As the author [Erich Neumann] rightly says: "The diversity and complexity of the situation makes it impossible for us to lay down any theoretical rules for ethical behaviour" '(Jung in Neumann, 1969, p. 13). Analogously, for Deleuze, an ethical behaviour cannot be prescribed in advance as according to some pre-existing moral code or in terms of how well our values might fit some higher moral ideal. Instead values and meanings are created in experience in accord with Deleuze's pedagogy of concepts. For Deleuze, human experience is ultimately educative: it is a long experiential process requiring wisdom in a Spinozian sense, that is, wisdom as practical and ethical, and overcoming in this process the limitations of narrow subject-centred knowledge. Ethics is inherent in the production of subjectivity, and subjectivation is 'ethical and aesthetic, as opposed to morality' (Deleuze, 1995, p. 114). Because experience is not confined to the individual Cogito of a Cartesian subject but is socio-cultural and always involves the other, the integration of such a generic 'other' is paramount for understanding and re-valuation of such an expanded experience. That is what one author (Semetsky, in press) calls the ethics of integration in education. The ethics of integration purports to overcome the dualistic split inherent in simple 'moral algebra' with its traditional binary division into 'good' versus 'evil', or 'right' versus 'wrong', or 'I' versus 'other'. It enables us to move beyond good and evil so that ultimately bring 'nature and culture together in its net' (Deleuze & Guattari, 1987, p. 236) towards the integration of those habitual dualistic opposites that are still deeply ingrained in the individual and cultural consciousness.

Typos, as the composite of the 'archetype', means imprint, stamp or pattern. Archetypes as dynamic patterns acting in the collective unconscious 'exist', according to Jung, only *in potentia*; they are beckoned forth by our experiences and, despite their a priori status, they are, as part of experiential field, categories of potential functioning only. Wolfgang Pauli, a Nobel prize winning physicist, who collaborated with Jung on their work on synchronicity, posited the unconscious as tending to the notion of ' "field" in physics [in terms of] a more general form of "connections" in nature' (Pauli, 1994, p. 164) and addressed archetypes as potentially meaningful patterns generated in nature and culture alike along the multiple paths of human experiences. For Deleuze, the objects that take the form of *Ideas* may exist, or rather subsist, in the preconscious, out of awareness, state of virtual potentialities or tendencies. The realm of the virtual is reminiscent of, but not limited to, the Jungian archetype of the Shadow (or, at the level of language, as Deleuze would put it, the shadow around the words). But it can be actualized, or brought into consciousness that is, *reterritorialized* when *becoming-other* during the process of individuation. While not all virtualities may become actualized in the present, they are nevertheless real; as such they confirm Jung's pointing out the [psychic] reality of the archetypes and the objective character of the collective psyche. Those activated archetypal forces 'seized *in actu*, liberated from substances that function as their support and vehicle, do seem better candidates for a diagrammatic mapping out of becoming' (Boundas, 1994, p. 105).

There are indeed real social and political ramifications to the concept of the unconscious as collective and to the idea of individuation and education linked to a confrontation with and passage through the unconscious Shadow. Jung realized that his own peculiar obsession with the Faust myth was neither strictly personal, nor strictly familial, but in fact grounded in the cultural and world-historical archetypal dynamics. Jung experienced himself as torn between the Faustian capacity for abstract and rational analysis, with its hypocritically rigid code of abstract morality, and the Faust's Mephistophelian Shadow, the spirit of amoral hedonism and lust for total domination. Yet, the Shadow is not strictly the devil it seems to be. Mephistopheles-the-devil borders on a distorted image of the one 'who in spite of his negating disposition represents the true spirit of life as against the arid scholar who hovers on the brink of suicide' (Jung, 1963, p. 235). Jung's entire life was a quest to access that supreme archetype, the Self, that would constitute a philosopher's stone, the image of Holy Grail, or alchemical *lapis* whose power would both draw from and eventually transform the binary opposition between Faust and Mephistopheles thus achieving a mystical union, a conjunction of opposites. Far from being a solely personal problem or an isolated neurosis, Jung's struggle for integration both echoes the unresolved tensions and unanswered questions of previous generations and also attempts to ward off the kinds of historical disasters precipitated by the likes of the Faustian Kaiser Wilhelm, whose hubris, according to

Jung, 'alienated Europe and paved the way for the disaster of 1914' (Jung, 1963, p. 235) or, we may add today, for the disaster of 9/11 in America.

At the collective level, the symbolic Shadow often encompasses those outside the moral 'norm' of the established order and the prevailing social system. Yet, while the ego-consciousness focuses on indubitable and unequivocal moral principles, these very principles crumble under the '*compensatory significance of the shadow* in the light of ethical responsibility' (Jung in Neumann, 1969, p. 12). The neglect of this responsibility tends to precipitate multiple consequences that manifest in the form of designated 'criminals, psychotics, misfits, scapegoats' (Samuels, 1985, p. 66). It is not only that they appear to stand outside the culture, but importantly the dominant culture or nation itself fails to assimilate its own Shadow, thus succumbing to a moment of psychological denial and the implementation of scapegoat politics while in the meantime projecting onto some generic Other one's own inferior and shadowy qualities. The scapegoat psychology is associated with what Neumann called the *old* ethic as the adherence to illusionary perfection and the absolute Good that necessarily leads to the appearance of its exact opposite, the absolute Evil. The new ethic, however, demands the recognition of our own shadowy side. The old ethic is 'partial' (Neumann, 1969, p. 74) as belonging solely to the Ego; but a new ethic devoted to the integration of the Shadow is holistic and is ideally a mode of existence of the individuated Self in terms of actually *becoming-other* in a Deleuzian sense. Indeed, *becoming-other* is by all means a condition of possibility for human learning and development despite (or perhaps due to) the fact that it often represents 'the harshest exercise in depersonalization' (Deleuze, 1995, p. 6). Yet ultimate self-knowledge would be achieved, for Deleuze, only through our 'experimentation on ourselves [as] our only identity, our single chance for all the combinations which inhabit us' (Deleuze, 1987, p. 11) and which may be hiding in the unconscious in the form of Jungian archetypes, including the Shadow. Becoming aware of one's shadow is a step towards individuation.

A Concluding Remark

To make a concluding remark, let us return to the problematic of self-education addressed at the very start of this paper. Jung was adamant that 'the education of the educator ... will eventually rebound to the good of [the] pupils' (Jung, 1954, p. 47). A teacher's self-education, however, should not be defined in terms of currently popular professional development or life-long training, but 'should make him properly conscious of himself' (Jung, 1954, p. 46). But: did anything change in the education system since Jung articulated his concerns more than half a century ago?

> At present we educate people only up to the point where they can earn a living and marry: then education ceases altogether, as though a complete mental outfit has been acquired ... Innumerable ill-advised and unhappy marriages, innumerable professional disappointments, are due to this lack of adult education. (Jung, 1954, p. 47)

Yet, the adults *are* educable; however, such education should not proceed along the lines of compulsory 'schooling'. Jung considered the analysis of dreams whose constancy of meanings is indeed exhibited by archetypal images to be 'an eminently educational activity' (Jung, 1954, p. 94) and asserted that symbolism has today assumed the proportions of a science. For both Jung and Deleuze, it is becoming conscious of the archetypal field of dynamic forces that constitutes the method of *indirect* adult education as a 'process resulting from the independent activity of the unconscious' (Jung, 1954, p. 49). For Deleuze and Jung alike, such a dynamic inquiry originates in the middle of real-life, often conflicting and baffling, human experiences that can be traversed by the lines of flight 'articulating' the deep meanings embedded in these experiences. The language of the archetypal symbolism is 'always heterogeneous, in which style carves differences of potential between which ... a spark can flash and break out of language itself, to make us see and think what was lying in the shadow around the words, things we were hardly aware existed' (Deleuze, 1995, p. 141), but that were nonetheless enfolded in the assemblages of the unconscious.

References

Augustine (1991) *Confessions*, H. Chadwick, trans. (Oxford, Oxford University Press).

Bosteels, B. (1998) From Text to Territory, Felix Guattari's cartographies of the unconscious, in: E. Kaufman & K. J. Heller (eds), *Deleuze and Guattari: New mappings in politics, philosophy, and culture* (Minneapolis, MN, University of Minnesota Press), pp. 145–174.

Boundas, C. V. (1994) Deleuze: Serialization and subject-formation, in: C. V. Boundas & D. Olkowski (eds), *Gilles Deleuze and the Theater of Philosophy* (London, Routledge), pp. 99–116.

Boundas, C. V. (1996) Deleuze-Bergson: The ontology of the virtual, in: P. Patton (ed.), *Deleuze: A critical reader* (Cambridge, MA, Blackwell), pp. 81–106.

Jung, C. G. (1953–1979) *Collected Works of C. G. Jung*, Vols. I-XX, R. F. C. Hull, trans., H. Read, M. Fordham & G. Adler (eds), W. McGuire, exec. ed., Bollingen Series XX (Princeton, NJ, Princeton University Press) [cited as CW throughout].

Jung, C. G. (1954) *Psychology and Education*. Vol. 17 (Princeton, NJ, Princeton University Press).

Jung, C. G. (1959) *The Archetypes of the Collective Unconscious* (London, Routledge).

Jung, C. G. (1963) *Memories, Dreams, Reflections*. R. & C. Winston, trans., A. Jaffe (ed.). (New York, Pantheon Books).

Deleuze, G. (1987) *Dialogues* (with C. Parnet), H. Tomlinson & B. Habberjam, trans. (Minneapolis, MN, Minnesota University Press).

Deleuze, G. (1988a) *Foucault*, S. Hand, trans. (Minneapolis, MN, University of Minneapolis Press).

Deleuze, G. (1988b) *Spinoza: Practical philosophy*, R. Hurl, trans. (San Francisco, CA, City Lights Books).

Deleuze, G. (1993) *The Fold*, T. Conley, trans. (Minneapolis, MN, University of Minnesota Press).

Deleuze, G. (1994) *Difference and Repetition*, P. Patton, trans. (New York, Columbia University Press).

Deleuze, G. (1995) *Negotiations 1972–1990*, M. Joughin, trans. (New York, Columbia University Press).

Deleuze, G. (1997) *Essays Critical and Clinical*, D. W. Smith & M. Greco, trans. (Minneapolis, MN, University of Minnesota Press).

Deleuze, G. & Guattari, F. (1983) *Anti-Oedipus: Capitalism and schizophrenia*, R. Hurley, M. Seem, & H. R. Lane, trans. (Minneapolis, MN, University of Minnesota Press).

Deleuze, G. & Guattari, F. (1987) *A Thousand Plateaus: Capitalism and schizophrenia*, B. Massumi, trans. (Minneapolis, MN, University of Minnesota Press).

Deleuze, G. & Guattari, F. (1994) *What is Philosophy?*, H. Tomlinson & G. Burchell, trans. (New York, Columbia University Press).

Kerslake, C. (2007) *Deleuze and the Unconscious* (London and New York, Continuum).

May, T. & Semetsky, I. (2008) Deleuze, Ethical Education and the Unconscious, in: I. Semetsky (ed.), *Nomadic Education: Variations on a theme by Deleuze and Guattari.* (Rotterdam, Sense Publishers), pp. 143–158.

Neumann, E. (1969) *Depth Psychology and a New Ethic* (London, Hodder and Stoughton).

Pauli, W. (1994) *Writings on Physics and Philosophy.* C. P. Enz & K. von Meyenn (eds), R. Schlapp, trans. (Berlin, Springer-Verlag).

Peters, M. (2004) Editorial: Geophilosophy, education and the pedagogy of the concept, in: I. Semetsky (ed.), Deleuze and Education, *Educational Philosophy and Theory*, 36, pp. 217–226.

Samuels. A. (1985) *Jung and the Post-Jungians* (London and New York, Routledge).

Semetsky, I. (2006) *Deleuze, Education and Becoming* (Rotterdam, Sense Publishers).

Semetsky, I. (ed.) (2008) *Nomadic Education: Variations on a theme by Deleuze and Guattari* (Rotterdam, Sense Publishers).

Semetsky, I. (2009) Deleuze as a Philosopher of Education: Affective knowledge/Effective learning, *The European Legacy: Toward New Paradigms*, 14:4, pp. 443–456.

Semetsky, I. (2010) Towards an Ethics of Integration in Education, in: T. Lovat, R. Toomey & N. Clement (eds), *International Research Handbook on Values Education and Student Wellbeing* (Dordrecht, Springer), pp. 319–336.

7

'The Other Half' of Education: Unconscious education of children

SHIHO MAIN

Introduction

Ideas about child education are inevitably underpinned by particular assumptions about children, including their nature and development, and are closely linked with certain expectations about the role of adults as well as of children, and the relationship between children and adults. This paper will discuss C. G. Jung's account of child education in relation to his psychological theory on children. Jung argues that the formal curriculum provides only half of education. The other half, which cannot be taught directly, is effected through the personality of the teacher and means 'guiding the child into the larger world and widening the scope of parental training' (Jung, 1928a, para. 107a). The other half of education helps children to develop their own sense of judgement and frees a child 'from his unconscious attachment to the influences of his early environment (Jung, 1910, para. 1013). Through the personal relationship with the teacher, unconscious education also provides continuity both with the home (see Jung, 1928a, para. 107a; 1943, para. 249) at an ontogenetic level and with the history of the human psyche (see Jung, 1943, para. 250) at a phylogenetic level.

Jung holds that in the relationship between two people, there are conscious as well as unconscious interactions going on in both directions (Figure 1). He borrows this idea from an alchemical text where the relationship is between the psyche of the alchemist and the matter being transformed (the stone) (Jung, 1946). He applies the idea to clinical contexts where the relationship is between a doctor and a patient, or an analyst and an analysand (1946, paras. 410–449).

Likewise, Jung believes that parents and teachers unconsciously influence children by what they are rather than what they say and do. In particular, Jung argues that the unconscious problems of adults are transmitted to the child's psyche and may have 'a poisonous effect' (Jung, 1926/46, para. 216). Jung also holds that in a relationship between two people, e.g. doctor and patient or a married couple, the psychologically more mature person can help the other, and this also applies to a teacher-student relationship (Jung, 1925, paras. 331c–334; 1943, para. 240). Nevertheless, this may not necessarily apply to every adult-child relationship, as Jung criticises the immaturity of many adults (Jung, 1934, para. 284), including those who are in authority and power, like teachers (Jung, 1926/46, para. 211).

Therefore, Jung recommends continuous education for adults through their becoming aware of their unconscious problems: 'Anyone who wants to educate must himself be

Jung and Educational Theory, First Edition. Edited by Inna Semetsky.
Chapters © 2013 The Authors. Book compilation © 2013 Philosophy of Education Society of Australasia.
Published 2013 by Blackwell Publishing Ltd.

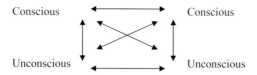

Conscious   Conscious

Unconscious   Unconscious

Figure 1: The conscious and the unconscious interactions between two psyches[1]

educated' (Jung, 1934, para. 284). Concerning the role played by the teacher in this unconscious education, Jung writes that 'It is not true that the educator is always the one who educates, and the child always the one to be educated' (Jung, 1926/46, para. 211). In Jung's account, as adults influence children by what they are, they need to become aware of their own shortcomings so that the adults' unconscious problems are not transmitted to the children. The aim of 'the other half' of education, as an unconscious process, could be contrasted with conscious, formal education. In order to discuss the nature and the extent of children's involvement in the other half of education, I will examine Jung's view on children, in particular, children's psyche and their psychological development. Consideration of Jung's view on the psychology of children will help to clarify why he thinks self-education is only suitable for adults and not for children, and consideration of Jung's view on children's psychological development will help in exploring the possible effects of adults' self-education upon children.

Children's Psyche

When Jung's view on the psyche of children is discussed, what is often emphasised is the immaturity of the children's psyche and its dependence upon the parents' psyche. This could be seen as the reason why self-education is not recommended for children.

The difference between the psyche of children and that of adults could be explained by what Jung calls *participation mystique* (also primitive identity or unconscious identity with parents) together with his view of the gradual development of ego-consciousness in early years.

Jung's use of *participation mystique* derives from Lévy-Bruhl's use of the same expression, which originally referred to the unconscious identity of primitive humans with the universe, without differentiation between subject and object (see Segal, 2007). Jung argues that until the child develops consciousness of its ego 'In his early years the child lives in a state of *participation mystique* with his parents' (Jung, 1928a, para. 107) and that 'The *participation mystique*, or primitive identity, causes the child to feel the [unconscious] conflicts of the parents and to suffer from them as if they were its own' (Jung, 1926/46, para. 216).[2] For this reason, when childhood neuroses are suspected, Jung recommends first analysing the parents (ibid., paras. 133; 179), pointing out that 'The infectious nature of the parents' complexes can be seen from the effect the mannerisms have on their children' (1928a, para. 107). In Jung's view, the process by which the individual consciousness frees itself from primitive identity occurs only gradually (ibid., para. 107a).[3]

These characteristics of the child's psyche build up a picture of the child as dependent, immature, and vulnerable, being originally fused with the parents. The unsuitability of self-education for children could be due to these structural differences of the child's psyche from the adult's psyche.

However, although Jung states that during the first years of the child's psychological life its individual psychology is 'only potentially present' (ibid., 1928a, para. 106) due to the child's fusion with the parents' psyches, he does acknowledge the existence of an individual psyche from the moment ego-consciousness arises, which is marked by the child referring to itself as 'I' (ibid., 1928a, para. 107). For Jung, the beginning of children's independence, or the end of their total dependence, can be identified with the age at which consciousness of the ego emerges, which Jung considers to be between the third and fifth year or earlier (ibid.). However, the end of children's dependence, or the beginning of their total independence, does not seem to be as clearly indicated in Jung as the emergence of ego-consciousness. Jung writes that 'the greatest and most extensive development takes place during the period between birth and the end of psychic puberty' (ibid., para. 103) but 'from puberty onwards it becomes slower, and fewer and fewer fragments of the unconscious are added to consciousness' (ibid.). Nevertheless, he argues that the process continues throughout life (ibid.) even though it is at a much slower pace. This implies that there is a long period in life when dependence and independence cohabit in the psyche.

When it comes to children's individuality, Jung implies that this is inborn: 'a child is not a mere appendage, but a new and individual creature, often furnished with a character which is not in the least like that of the parents and sometimes seems to be quite frighteningly alien' (Jung, 1926/46, para. 222). He explains how children's individuality could be disturbed by disharmony in the family relationship: 'The disharmony between the parents on the one hand and between the parents and the child on the other seemed especially liable to produce psychic currents in the child which were incompatible with this individual way of life' (1913, para. 307). As well as children as distinctive individuals, Jung also presents children as competent and knowing when he writes: 'children have an almost uncanny instinct for the teacher's personal shortcomings' (Jung, 1926/46, para. 211).

These images of children, competent and knowing, and being individuals from early on, are contrary to the images of children based on their weak ego-consciousness and fusion with the parental psyche. While the latter represent an undeveloped child dependent upon its parents, the former represent a developing, autonomous child. Contrary to the general belief about Jung's view on children, for Jung, children are not totally dependent on the parental psyche but are in one way potentially independent from them early on.

Therefore, even though it is the dependency of the child's psyche upon the parents' psyche that is often accepted as Jung's view on the child's psyche, this should not be mistaken as the sole image of the child that Jung holds. There seem to be contradictory concepts of the child's psyche co-existing in Jung's view on children. Accordingly, these contradictory images of children could create expectations about different roles of adults depending on the particular image of the child employed. For dependent children, what adults need to do might be to protect them, whereas for autonomous children adults might need to help them to participate in their world. It is not usually the case that contradictory concepts of the child support the same idea of education. I shall come back to this point later.

Children's Psychological Development

When Jung argues that the effects of adults' self-education are made indirectly upon children, his view of recapitulation needs to be understood. In relation to psychological development, Jung supports the idea that ontogeny (the course of individual development) recapitulates phylogeny (human evolution).[4] He explains children's psychological development in terms of 'the first half of life' for an individual person on the one hand and in terms of the early/ier phase of the history of the human psyche on the other hand.

Like the global parallelism prevalent in the late 19th century between the thought process of the child and what is thought to be 'savage' (Morss, 1990, pp. 23–4), Jung uses a parallelism between children and the unconscious, dreams, insanity, animals, prehistoric humans, and what are sometimes called 'primitive' tribes[5] (1911–12/52, 1913, 1926/46, 1927/31, 1930/50, 1943—see Miyagi, 2000, pp. 12–15; Main, 2008a, pp. 65–68). However, it is often misunderstood that Jung considers children's psyche, along with the other terms in the parallelism, to be inferior.

Jung's view on psychological development is different from other psychologists in his time because his understanding of recapitulation is different from others. Jung's models of development and recapitulation are both non-progressive and non-linear due to the continuous and cyclical relationship with the collective unconscious of every individual and of human beings as a whole (Miyagi, 2000; Main, 2008a, pp. 61–80). In this model of development, children's psyche is characterised as, rather than something inferior, the earlier and deeper layer of the psyche, which in fact goes beyond children's psyche or the psyche of prehistoric human beings.[6]

At this point Jung's key concepts in relation to his theory of psychological development need to be explained. Each concept is controversial, but the working model we employ here is as follows. In Jung's view, the psyche consists of consciousness and the unconscious, the latter of which is further divided into two layers: the collective unconscious and the personal unconscious. The collective unconscious is considered inherently common to all human beings regardless of time, place, and culture (1926/46),[7] whereas the personal unconscious 'contains everything forgotten or repressed or otherwise subliminal that has been acquired by the individual consciously or unconsciously' (1926/46, para. 207) and therefore 'has an unmistakably personal stamp' (ibid.).

The psyche of children starts with total identification with the unconscious, then goes through separation of consciousness of the ego from the unconscious, and finally arrives at full consciousness of ego. Nevertheless, this does not mean that the unconscious disappears in the place of the ego-consciousness. This earlier and deeper layer of the psyche, the collective unconscious (see, e.g., Jung, 1936), contains the archetypes,[8] the universal human behavioural patterns or the bases of myths and mythological images,[9] which Jung considers as objective facts,[10] and it remains in one's psyche throughout life.

The personal unconscious, in contrast, largely consists of complexes that are related closely to the inferior functions of one's personality and relationships with others in everyday life. In this model children could be thought not to have the personal unconscious or complexes at the beginning but to acquire and accumulate them through their experiences. Some contents of the personal unconscious are transmitted from parents to children in the state of unconscious identity and consist of complexes that have been passed on unresolved from generation to generation. The importance of the continuous relationship, even if only recognised later, between the earlier and deeper layer of the psyche and consciousness is apparent when viewing development as one cycle in both ontogeny and phylogeny. Jung calls the whole cycle of self-realisation the individuation process (1928b, paras. 266–268).

When Jung describes children's psychological development as 'the first half of life', what are expected in the first half of life are, at an ontogenetic level, according to Jung:

a) the emergence of ego-consciousness and separation from the unconscious (1928a: para. 103,[11] 107);
b) accumulation of complexes in the personal unconscious (1907, para. 90; cf. 1921, para. 201);
c) a shift from archaic thinking to directed thinking[12] and adaptation to the external world (1926/46, para. 211); and
d) an enlarging of the personality (1940/50, para. 215).[13]

Similarly, when Jung explains the development of the human psyche in parallel with development of the child's mind, what he observes has occurred at a phylogenetic level are:

a) differentiation of individual consciousness from the collective unconscious (1926/46, para. 207);[14]
b) a transfer of complexes from generation to generation (1926/46, para. 154);[15]
c) a shift from archaic thinking to directed thinking (1911–12/52, para. 17)[16] and hence also towards technical development and civilisation (1928a, para. 105).

The child's psyche is considered to go through the earlier phase of this human development. However, Jung also suggests as the goal in this process (at a phylogenetic level):

d) culture, namely, spiritual development, integration of the unconscious by using the ego-consciousness acquired in one's life and in human history (1926/1931, para. 160; 1947/1954, para. 375).

This cultural aspect of psychological development could be further explained in terms of ontogeny. While the changes in the first half of life are considered to be the tasks of nature, Jung considers the tasks set in the second half of life as 'culture'.[17] Nature and culture are, for Jung, biological and spiritual aspects of the human being. They do not equate with the biological and socio-cultural aspects which are often associated with the nature/nurture debate. (see Main, 2008a.) The tasks of the second half of life at an ontogenetic level are,

a) to integrate the unconscious with consciousness (1911–12/52, para. 459);
b) to face to, work on, and resolve the complexes in the unconscious by making them conscious (see 1930–31, para. 771);

c) to integrate (ever-lasting, continuous) archaic thinking by using directed thinking (which has been acquired) (1911–12/52, paras. 37–39) in order to adapt to the inner world (1917/26/43, para. 114; 1930–31, para. 785); and

d) to work on realising the whole personality for the sake of cultural development (1928c, para. 113; 1934, paras. 284–323).

These tasks could all be seen as paths to gaining an *objective* view of oneself. Jung holds that whereas the first half of life is an unconscious, natural process, the second half of life should be a process in which one has to make a conscious effort.[18] Although the second half of life is usually emphasised as crucial for the individuation process, psychological development is, in Jung's view, a process throughout life. The first half is indispensable for the second, for personality to be complete. Therefore, the first and the second half need to be viewed as a cycle of nature and culture together, in which each is indispensable for the completion of the other.

How well the tasks in the second half of life are achieved by individual adults becomes important in phylogeny as a high level of achievement could raise the cultural goal of psychological development at a collective as well as individual level. Jung writes: 'the child, in his psychic development, passes through the ancestral stages and is only educated up to the modern level of culture and consciousness. The adult, however, stands firmly on this level and feels himself to be the upholder of contemporary culture' (1928a, para. 109). Therefore, psychological development of the child cannot be considered without that of adults both in terms of ontogeny and phylogeny.

These relationships between the child and adult in one's lifetime and the child and adult in human history suggest two cycles which are actually connected. The first is a compensatory relationship within one person, and the second is an educational relationship between two people: the first can be attended by self-education in the second half of life, and the second by 'the other half of education'. Jung also talks about cultural education distinguished from education for the sake of progress.[19] In Jung's view, a purely technical and practical education alone is insufficient and education should not take less account of culture which is based on the continuity of the history of the human psyche (see Jung, 1943, para. 250). The formal curriculum and 'the other half' of education might correspond with progressive education and cultural education respectively, both of which are equally significant in Jung's view.

The unsuitability of self-education for children, which we considered earlier as possibly due to the dependence of the child's psyche, may also be due to the tasks set in the first half of life. Inner adaptation through self-education may hinder the fulfilment of the tasks of outer adaptation in the first half of life. In Jung's view: 'For a young person it is almost a sin, or at least a danger, to be too preoccupied with himself; but for the ageing person it is a duty and a necessity to devote serious attention to himself' (1930–31, para. 785). The teacher's self-education could have an effect on children via the collective unconscious through the indirect route of recapitulation. In unconscious education, the teacher alone will not make education possible; only the teacher and student together (student-teacher as nature and culture) can make education possible. A student and a teacher could be seen as a pair, one unit, working in partnership: both, in their being, fulfil an indispensable role in the completion of one task.

The effect of the teacher's self-education upon children—albeit unconscious and indirect—has a double meaning: it resolves the complex for the teacher's inner life on the one hand and it works on the personal unconscious that is passed on from generation to generation on the other. The teacher's self-education influences the students unconsciously in the here and now relationship and at the same time sets a higher goal for the students' future development of personality.

The Nature and Extent of Children's Involvement in 'the Other Half' of Education

Children's involvement in unconscious education could be seen as mainly passive, according to Jung's view that the child's psyche is largely unconscious and dependent upon their parents' unconscious psyche. However, children cannot be considered passive to the extent that the goal of unconscious education, i.e., the development of personality, is achieved by teachers or parents for the children. Jung's alternative view of a child's psyche—as autonomous and individual—suggests that children play an active role in their development of personality. These contradictory images of children are normally in conflict. They suggest different roles of adults and therefore do not support the same idea of education.

For instance, in the common debates about the tension between children's protection and participation rights, where these two contradictory images of children are discussed, opposite kinds of interventions are suggested by the different views about children: either to protect vulnerable and innocent children from harm or to advocate that autonomous and competent children should participate in their world (e.g. Burr and Montgomery 2003: 144–51; Cunningham, 1995; Fottrell, 1999; Freeman, 1992, pp. 34–5; King, 1985; Veerman, 1992, pp. 51, 396; see further Main, 2008a, pp. 118–146; Main, 2008b). However, unlike the conflicting images of children underpinning children's rights issues, Jung's contradictory views of the child can co-exist without conflict, and both the image of children as dependent and the image of children as autonomous could be sustained. For protecting dependent children from adults' repression of their individuality and supporting autonomous children's participation in their partly dependent psychological world are, in Jung's view, serving the same purpose of fulfilling nature, clearing away the obstructions to children's natural development and enabling an enlarging of the personality through outer adaptation. More specifically, in this view the teacher's role of providing children with continuity of the affectionate state of the home environment secures the child from suffering its parents' unrealised psychological problems through enabling the child to project and process its parental imagos. At the same time, the teacher's freeing the child from the home environment creates a space in the child's psyche which is independent from the parents' psyche and where his or her individuality can grow.

Similarly, the extent of children's involvement in unconscious education might seem limited when we consider that children remain unconscious in this process. Children scarcely seem in charge in a situation where adults are required to be more responsible by being consciously involved in self-education. Jung recommends only the teacher to become aware of his or her unconscious teaching and put it in practice by examples. The teacher's engagement with self-education is partly for the teacher's own development of personality (direct effect) and partly for the student's (indirect effect). However, children's involvement is not so limited that the adults' conscious effort and providing of examples have exactly the same effect upon every child. If unconscious education is viewed as collaboration between students and the teacher, working together as one unit, the state of being of children will be crucial. Again, it is not adults that make children into personalities.

Ultimately, in Jung's view, it is the nature of children themselves that enables their development of personality and not that adults develop the children's personality for them. Jung does not value personality which is artificially shaped by external means. Rather, as he writes: 'those who have a higher conception of education will prize most the method of cultivating a tree so that it fulfils to perfection its own natural conditions of growth' (1913, para. 442). If the development of personality is viewed as ultimately up to the child itself, or up to the nature of childhood, then the child's involvement in unconscious education will be significant, and the effect of unconscious education upon children will not be permanently fixed but could be changeable depending on the child itself.[20]

The view of the relationship between teacher and student as forming a unity is vital for 'the other half' of education, and the role that the child plays is essential in the partnership between teacher and student. In this relationship, the teacher and the student each hold their own psychological balance between the unconscious and consciousness, though each could also be unconsciously influenced by the other—by what is to come for the child and by what once was for the adult. Thus the aim of unconscious education seems specific to each person and can only be realised by the child himself or herself—even if only much later in life. As each individual's personality is different, the aim of unconscious education cannot be known at the outset more specifically than as the general aim of development of personality.

Some Problems with Jung's Account of 'the Other Half' of Education

There are some remaining questions about the applicability of Jung's notion of 'the other half' of education to conscious education. For instance, what can adults do for children and what can children do for themselves in preparation for unconscious education? In the current climate, emphasis is often placed on improving the quality and outcome of education, which includes promoting teachers' professional development as well as listening to children's voices.[21] However, unconscious education is unlikely to operate in the same framework as the formal curriculum, and these questions might be a wrong kind of questions to ask in relation to the unconscious. Unconscious education therefore may not be of any use for improving or changing conscious education.

In order to improve the quality of unconscious education, recognising the importance of 'the other half' of education and trying to support the teacher's self-education could seem important. But such external support is extremely difficult in practice due to the unobservable, non-assessable, and unmanageable nature of the teacher's role in this unconscious process. Trying to provide external support also risks defeating the point of self-education, which is to be internally motivated and self-reliant whatever the circumstances. However, not being able to regulate unconscious education also means that the teacher's autonomy and freedom are not interfered with. In unconscious education the teacher's personality and what is taught through the teacher's personality cannot be controlled or regulated by any institution or government, or even by the teacher himself or herself. Standardisation and regulation risk making teachers instruments of method and restricting their autonomy, but in unconscious education teachers remain free from such external pressure.

Inclusion of children at the conscious level, which would mean to inform them of the process of unconscious education and to consult them, would not work either, in Jung's view, as this is precisely the kind of thing that he discourages as an inappropriate projection of adults' responsibility. Jung offers no concrete advice to children about what they should or can do, nor does he make any particular statement directed to children themselves. However, from his account of 'the other half' of education and his views of children, we can speculate that, respecting their autonomy, he might have advised children to trust their own nature and seek out answers to their questions in the outer world. They need not be troubled yet with their inner problems which are not even their own but originate from their parents or even further back. Jung may seem irresponsible to suggest that a child is not accountable for its unconscious problems, as it may sound as though children have no responsibility for their behaviour and actions.[22] But in Jung's view, the innocent child (innocent, that is, of the problems which have been passed on from generation to generation) co-exists with the child who has 'every opportunity for individual responsibility', unless such opportunity is taken away by excessively strong attachment to the parents (Jung, 1928a, para. 107a). In this picture responsibility for their own development of individuality seems to emerge when children are left with autonomy.

Jung's account of unconscious education seems of no practical use for improving current educational systems. But there might be some usefulness in his psychological theory of education. For instance, Jung's account of 'the other half' of education as 'the real psychological education' could be recognized universally whatever the formal curricula, part of the world, particular educational needs or groups of children, or particular construction of childhood. As an unconscious process between a student and a teacher, unconscious education does not specify any particular conditions and therefore is inclusive of often marginalized groups. This universality has to be distinguished from the kind of naïve universalism which neglects diversity (cf. Main 2008a; 2008b). Jung does not seem to believe in the definition of universality as something absolute, clear-cut, and definite, which would be polarised with diversity. Instead, for Jung, universality, as represented in his multifaceted archetypal theory, is always there in the collective unconscious, paradoxically independent of and yet embracing social or cultural factors.

In Jung's view, diversity is the expression of universality. Therefore, in his view, universality and diversity are connected and are both multifaceted. Jung's model of the psyche and such concepts as the collective unconscious and the archetypes might not be easily accepted outside Jungian circles. But his account of unconscious education, because it is purely psychological, is inseparable from his psychological theory. If Jung's psychological theory is accepted, the goal of unconscious education, i.e. the development of personality, could be seen as a universal phenomenon (as emerging out of the core of all human psyches) while its particular meaning will differ for each individual (as it manifests in various forms in individual psyches, albeit sustaining a continuous relationship with the collective unconscious in each case).

It might be possible to see a complementary relationship between socio-culturally diverse systems of formal education and the unconscious, true human relationship between the teacher and the student found across cultures. This possible complementary relationship could add another dimension to evaluating both educational settings and children's experience of education, which is very different from the ways in which formal curricula are assessed. Such a perspective could also take account of the long-term effect of education. For while it may not be possible for a child (or anyone else) to understand the process of 'the other half' of education while in it, what is taught may become clearer to the child in his or her later life. In such ways, Jung's account of 'the other half' of education could provide fresh insights about the meaning and quality of education. Unconscious education might be difficult to relate to conscious education in one way, but it could be seen as complementary in another way.

Conclusion

As the debate about Jung's account of education has hitherto largely focused on adults and not children, this paper has explored the nature and extent of children's involvement in what Jung calls 'the other half' of education. It has explained 'the other half of education', that is, unconscious education, which works through the teacher's personality and *indirectly* affects the student's development of personality. It has been demonstrated that Jung holds a view of children as autonomous individuals, which differs from his more widely known view of children as dependent on their parent's psyche, and that accepting both views has implications for his account of education. Children are in an important sense *in charge* of the goal of unconscious education, i.e., the development of personality. The paper has demonstrated that the relationship between a student and a teacher could be seen in a different light when considering Jung's views of psychological development at both individual and collective levels (ontogeny and phylogeny). Adults and children are seen in one way as separate parties, having different psychologies and roles in unconscious education, and yet they are seen as forming one *cycle* (of the first and the second halves of life), a *union* (of opposites), and a *totality* (of nature and culture) to work towards the unconscious educational goal, i.e., the development of personality.[23] It is the view of this complementary and collaborative relationship in which both the student and the teacher retain autonomy that enables children's being to be seen as an active and provocative agency and the part children play in unconscious education to be taken as significant.

Although it may not be useful in a practical way and might even be counterproductive if one attempted to incorporate it in current educational systems, Jung's perspective could provide valuable insights for the teacher, contributing to the real human relationship between the students and the teacher. Jung's account of unconscious education is applicable to any educational contexts and is, in particular, inclusive of often marginalised groups regardless of culture, socio-economic background, special needs, and so forth. Jung's model of the psyche with such concepts as the collective unconscious and the archetypes may be challenging to non-Jungians. But his idea of 'the other half' of education cannot be separated from his psychological theory—in particular his placing of the collective unconscious as the core of all human psyches beyond cultural variations and social constructions. If utilised for understanding children's wellbeing in educational contexts, Jung's perspective might widen the way in which the meaning and quality of various kinds and forms of education are understood and valued.

Notes

1. This is based on the diagram which illustrates the marriage of the King and Queen in an alchemical text (Jung, 1946, para. 422).
2. Jung argues that the plasticity of the child's mind 'lies at the base of all education' which he explains is 'commonly compared with soft wax, taking up and preserving all impressions' (Jung, 1913, para. 310). Yet the child's mind is not a blank slate: 'He [the/a child] is not born as a tabula rasa, he is merely born unconscious' (1909/49, para. 728).
3. Jung's idea of the development of consciousness is elaborated in Erich Neumann (1954).
4. For discussion of Jung's understanding of recapitulation theory, see Miyagi, 2000; Main, 2008a.
5. Jung's use of these parallels persists through his work: children (infantile thinking), dreams (dream-thinking), and primitives (earlier evolutionary stage) in terms of mythological thinking (1911–12/52); children, dreams, and dementia praecox in terms of mythological references (1913); childhood and prehistory of the race and of mankind in terms of possession of animal instincts (1927/31); children in parallel with primitives and animals (1913, para. 470); childish fear (fairy tales) and primitive psychology ('night religion' of 'primitives') in terms of myth (1927/31); dreams, primitive levels of development, mental disturbances, the unconscious in terms of earlier stages of evolution (1930/50); and childhood and a state of the past in terms of the pre-rational, pre-scientific world, i.e. the 'world of the men before us' (1943).
6. Jung writes: 'The personal layer ends at the earliest memories of infancy, but the collective layer comprises the pre-infantile period, that is, the residues of ancestral life. [... .] When ... psychic energy regresses, going beyond even the period of early infancy, and breaks into the legacy of ancestral life, the mythological images are awakened: these are the archetypes' (Jung, 1917/26/43, para. 117).
7. Jung also calls the collective unconscious the impersonal layer of the psyche (Jung, 1926/46, para. 207). 'There is a layer of the unconscious which functions in exactly the same way as the archaic psyche that produced the myths' (ibid., para. 209).
8. Jung explains archetypes: 'in accordance with phylogenetic law, we still recapitulate in childhood reminiscences of the prehistory of the race and of mankind in general. Phylogenetically as well as ontogenetically we have grown up out of the dark confines of the earth; hence the factors that affected us most closely became archetypes, and it is these primordial images which influence us most directly, and therefore seem to be the most powerful' (Jung, 1927/31, para. 55).
9. For the differences between the archetypes and the archetypal images, see Jung, 1938/54, para. 155.
10. Jung argues: 'we are concerned with primitive or archaic thought-forms, based on instinct, which naturally emerge more clearly in childhood than they do later ... . The instinctive, archaic basis of the mind is a matter of plain objective fact' (1911–12/52, para. 38). Jung describes these as 'a highly important psychological fact: that the power which shapes the life of the psyche has the character of an autonomous personality' (1909/49, para. 727).
11. Jung writes: 'We reinforce this process in children by education and culture. School is in fact a means of strengthening in a purposeful way the integration of consciousness' (1928a, para. 103).

12. Jung writes: 'We were speaking of the ontogenetic recapitulation of phylogenetic psychology in children, and we saw that archaic thinking is a peculiarity of children and primitives. We now know that this same thinking also occupies a large place in modern man and appears as soon as directed thinking ceases. Any lessening of interest, or the slightest fatigue, is enough to put an end to the delicate psychological adaptation to reality which is expressed through directed thinking, and to replace it by fantasies' (1911–12/52, para. 32).

13. Jung argues: 'The personality is seldom, in the beginning, what it will be later on. For this reason the possibility of enlarging it exists, at least during the first half of life' (1940/50, para. 215). He continues that 'a considerable increase of personality may be experienced' by assimilation of new vital contents found outside (ibid.).

14. Jung proposes: 'The unconscious is the ever-creative mother of consciousness. Consciousness grows out of the unconscious in childhood, just as it did in primeval times when man became man' (1926/46, para. 207).

15. Jung talks about the phylogenetic effect of unconscious problems from generation to generation (1926/46, para. 154).

16. In Jung's words, 'Directed thinking or, as we might also call it, thinking in words, is manifestly an instrument of culture, and we shall not be wrong in saying the tremendous work of education which past centuries have devoted to directed thinking, thereby forcing it to develop from the subjective, individual sphere to the objective, social sphere, has produced a readjustment of the human mind to which we owe our modern empiricism and techniques' (1911–12/52, para. 17).

17. Jung proposes: 'Could by any chance culture be the meaning and purpose of the second half of life?' (1930–31, para. 787) He claims that the transition leading from the first half of life to the second is 'a transformation of nature into culture, of instinct into spirit' (1925, para. 335).

18. Jung writes: 'Man has two aims: the first is the natural aim ... . When this aim has been reached a new phase begins: the cultural aim. For the attainment of the former we have the help of nature and, on top of that, education; for the attainment of the latter, little or nothing helps ... . What youth found and must find outside, the man of life's afternoon must find within himself ...' (1911–12/52, para. 114).

19. Jung cites a Swiss educationist, Johann Pestalozzi (1927) regarding the distinction in value between culture and civilisation: 'Culture has the power to unite men as individuals, in independence and freedom, through law and art. But a cultureless civilization unites them as masses, without regard to independence, freedom, law or art, through the power of coercion' (Jung, 1945, n. 10). For Pestalozzi human culture would not be advanced by any form of education established for the masses; our race develops only by means of humane education for the individual, not for the masses or for civilisation (ibid., n. 8). Jung seems to view the process of civilisation in terms of changes to the primitive psyche and the process of culture in terms of changes to the modern psyche. In agreement with Pestalozzi, Jung considers that culture requires greater conscious effort than civilisation, which is merely a one-sided enhancement of consciousness. In Jung's view, swinging from one extreme to the other, e.g. from archaic to directed thinking, is not an achievement.

20. Jung writes: 'We know that the first impressions of childhood accompany us inalienably throughout life, and that, just as indestructibly, certain educational influences can keep people all their lives within those limits. In these circumstances it is not surprising that conflicts break out between the personality moulded by education and other influences of the infantile milieu and one's own individual style of life.' (1913, para. 310) But he also continues: 'It is a conflict which all those must face who are called upon to live a life that is independent and creative' (ibid.).

21. All countries in the world that have ratified the 1989 United Nations Convention on the Rights of the Child (which is every country except the United States and Somalia) have responsibility to ensure children's participatory rights, which includes informing and consulting with children about matters that affect them (see Fottrell, 1999; UNICEF, 2009).

22. The United Nations Convention on the Rights of the Child (CRC) suffers from the same criticism, not pointing out children's responsibility by focusing solely on their rights (Burr and Montgomery, 2003, pp. 157–164).

23. Jung also writes about 'the child in the adult' (1934, para. 286), i.e. the archetype of the child (e.g. 1940), which he considers as a 'symbol of the self' (1946, par. 378). This could be further discussed in relation to both adults' self-education and the relationship between 'the child in the adult' and actual children. But to do so is beyond the scope of the present article.

References

Burr, R. & Montgomery, H. (2003) 'Children and Rights', in: M. Woodhead and H. Montgomery (eds), *Understanding Childhood: an interdisciplinary approach* (Milton Keynes, Open University; Chichester, John Wiley).

Cunningham, H. (1995) *Children and Childhood in Western Society since 1500* (London and New York, Longman).

Fottrell, D. (1999) Children's Rights, in: A. Hegarty & S. Leonard (eds), *Human Rights: An agenda for the 21st century* (London, Cavendish).

Freeman, M. (1992) The Limits of Children's Rights, in: M. Freeman & P. Veerman (eds), *The Ideologies of Children's Rights*, International Studies in Human Rights, vol. 23 (Dordrecht, Martinus Nijhoff Publishers).

Jung, C. G. (1907) The Psychology of Dementia Praecox, in *The Collected Works of C. G. Jung*, 20 vols. H. Read, M. Fordham, and G. Adler (eds); W. McGuire, executive ed.; R. F. C. Hull, trans. (London, Routledge and Kegan Pau) 20 vols, (1953–1979) [hereafter *CW*], vol. 3.

Jung, C. G. (1909/49) 'The Significance of the Father in the Destiny of the Individual', in *CW4*.

Jung, C. G. (1910) 'The Family Constellation', in *CW2*.

Jung, C. G. (1911–12/52) *Symbols of Transformation*, *CW5*.

Jung, C. G. (1913) 'The Theory of Psychoanalysis', in *CW4*.

Jung, C. G. (1917/26/43) 'On the Psychology of the Unconscious', in *CW7*.

Jung, C. G. (1921) *Psychological Types*, *CW6*.

Jung, C. G. (1925) 'Marriage As a Psychological Relationship', in *CW17*.

Jung, C. G. (1926/46) 'Analytical Psychology and Education: Three lectures', in *CW17*.

Jung, C. G. (1927/1931), 'Mind and Earth', in *CW10*.

Jung, C. G. (1928a) 'Child Development and Education', in *CW17*.

Jung, C. G. (1928b) 'The Relations Between the Ego and the Unconscious', in *CW7*.

Jung, C. G. (1928c) 'On Psychic Energy', in *CW8*.

Jung, C. G. (1930–31) 'The Stages of Life', in *CW8*.

Jung, C. G. (1930/50) 'Psychology and Literature', in *CW15*.

Jung, C. G. (1934) 'The Development of Personality', in *CW17*.

Jung, C. G. (1936) 'The Concept of the Collective Unconscious', in *CW9 (i)*.

Jung, C. G. (1938/54) 'Psychological Aspects of the Mother Archetype', in *CW9 (i)*.

Jung, C. G. (1940) 'The Psychology of the Child Archetype', in *CW9 (i)*.

Jung, C. G. (1940/50) 'Concerning Rebirth', in *CW9 (i)*.

Jung, C. G. (1943) 'The Gifted Child' in *CW17*.

Jung, C. G. (1945) 'Psychotherapy Today', in *CW16*.

Jung, C. G. (1946) 'The Psychology of the Transference', in *CW16*.

King, M. (1985) Are Rights Relevant?, *Educational and Child Psychology*, 2:2, pp. 49–57.

Main, S. (2008a) *Childhood Re-imagined: Images and narratives of development in analytical psychology* (London, Routledge).

Main, S. (2008b) Re-imagining the Child: Challenging social constructionist views of childhood, in: L. Huskinson (ed.), *Dreaming the Myth Onwards: Revisioning Jungian theory and thought* (London, Routledge).

Miyagi [m. Main], S. (2000) 'Recapitulation' and 'Development' in Analytical Psychology, *Harvest: Journal for Jungian Studies*, 46:2, pp. 7–32 (London, Karnac).

Morss, J. R. (1990) *The Biologising of Childhood: Developmental psychology and the Darwinian myth* (Hove, Lawrence Erlbaum Associates).

Neumann, E. (1954) *The Origins and History of Consciousness* (2nd printing with corrections and amended bibliography, 1964), Bollingen Series, vol. 42 (New York, Pantheon Books).

Pestalozzi, J. H. (1927) *Ideen* [*Pestalozzi's Werk*, M. Hürlimann, ed.] (Zurich, Insel).

Segal, R. A. (2007) Jung and Lévy-Bruhl, *Journal of Analytical Psychology*, 52:5, pp. 635–658.

Veerman, P. E. (1992) *The Rights of Children and Changing Images of Childhood*, International Studies in Human Rights, vol. 18 (Dordrecht, Martinus Nijhoff Publishers).

UNICEF (2009) Convention on the Rights of the Child, http://www.unicef.org/crc/, accessed 29 May 2009.

8

Complex Education: Depth psychology as a mode of ethical pedagogy

Robert Romanyshyn

The First Experiment

In 1991 I published an article entitled 'Complex Knowing: Towards a psychological hermeneutics'. The article was based on a graduate level class I was teaching that was focused on reading some of Freud's case histories. The question that I wanted to explore was how one reads these texts that contain so much potentially psychoactive material. In the background of this question was my curiosity about those moments in reading any kind of text where in one way or another the reading was slowed down, where it was perhaps interrupted by some intellectual puzzlement or some felt bodily reaction to the text. Specifically, I was curious about those moments when a person would underline a passage, or write marginal notes, or discover that they had just misread a passage, or realize that for the last ten minutes or so they had fallen into a state of reverie. These pauses, it seemed to me, were pregnant with possibilities and I wondered about 'who' was present in those moments.

To phrase my curiosity in terms of this question 'Who' might seem a bit odd, but my point is that reading a text is a complex affair. In my own graduate education in clinical psychology I had studied phenomenology and hermeneutics and I understood how the work of making sense of a text involved the circular dynamic between text and reader. The ideas of Paul Ricœur (1970) and Hans-Georg Gadamer (1975) were particularly important for me, but, educated as well in the traditions of Freudian and Jungian psychology, I also felt that when faced with the 'other-as-text' in the therapy room, the circular dynamic seemed more complex. In the therapy room the field between 'reader' and 'text' was a transference field whose dynamics were more than a matter of one's presuppositions and prejudices, whose dynamics were rooted also in the unconscious. Between the site of the classroom and the site of the therapy room, the hermeneutic circle would twist into a hermeneutic spiral. Did philosophical hermeneutics make a place for the unconscious in the 'Hermes' process, and if so how? These questions arose in this first experiment, but were not adequately addressed by me until the second experiment and the publication of *The Wounded Researcher* (2007), which I will take up in the next section.

This 'who' question is a psychological move. It is a move into the depths that personifies one's behavior and experience. It complicates things and it differs quite radically from the question of 'why'. The latter asks for reasons, for a reasoned and

Jung and Educational Theory, First Edition. Edited by Inna Semetsky.
Chapters © 2013 The Authors. Book compilation © 2013 Philosophy of Education Society of Australasia.
Published 2013 by Blackwell Publishing Ltd.

reasonable explanation. It tends to look for answers outside oneself. The former situates such explanations in a field *between* 'you' and 'other' that opens the possibility for a dialogue. This psychological move informs the title of my essay, specifically the two terms 'complex' and 'ethical'. It says in effect that reading a text is as much a complex affair as is falling in love, or writing an article, and that, if our pedagogical practices are to be ethical, educators have to take this psychological complexity into account.

The question of 'who' acknowledges the complex character(s) of one's identity at levels that are often quite unconscious. It is a challenging question, because it acts like a solvent that dissolves our Cartesian dream of the person whose sense of self is guaranteed by a 'cogito' that is singular, isolated and a spectator of an inanimate world-as- spectacle mapped in terms of univocal and determinable meanings (Romanyshyn, 1989/2000).[1] As educator David Jardine, however, persuasively argues, this challenge is hardly ever acknowledged. He writes, 'We are silently living out Descartes's dream-turned-nightmare' (1998, p. 9).

In this dream-turned-nightmare so much of our educational practice forgets or ignores that the student who comes *to* the classroom is and is not the character(s) who come *for* an education. 'Who' is present is a complex question. The same complexity, of course, applies to the teacher. Here too one has to avoid confusing the person who comes to teach with the character(s) who are teaching. In my own life the teachers who deeply educated me were characters who also had character, my first philosophy professor, for example, who on hot summer days with the sleeves of his starched white shirt rolled up kept young men of 19 and 20 enthralled with the arcane mysteries of Thomas Aquinas' *Summa*. Through him Aquinas and the world he inhabited entered the classroom, and because of that it did not seem so arcane to me that Aquinas would ask how many angels could fit on the head of a pin?

When I teach my introductory psychotherapy class to clinical students I begin with this challenge to the assumption of univocal identity. So, I say upfront that the first thing one must do is to avoid confusing the person who comes *to* therapy with the characters who come *for* therapy, with those characters whose abode are the symptoms. And, I emphasize that the same caution applies to the therapist. Jung's diagram of the transference aptly describes the complexity of this field (*CW* 16, para. 422). Analyst and patient interact not only at the level of their conscious egos, but each is also engaged with their own unconscious complexes. In addition, the ego of the patient is dynamically in touch with the unconscious of the analyst and vice versa. Finally, the unconscious of the patient interacts with the unconscious of the analyst and vice versa. Six variations of who is present inform this complex transference field. Six characters set the stage, as it were, for this dramatic encounter.

Starting here the education of a therapist who makes a place for the unconscious begins with learning how to read the signs not only of the other 'who' is present, but also of the 'others' who implicitly inform of his or her presence. The biggest obstacle in this work is the literal frame of mind that is corollary to the assumption of identity as univocal in the manner of Cartesian *Cogito*. And what works best here in the education of a therapist is the move to a metaphoric sensibility. I will say more about this later but for the moment I can easily illustrate what I mean with this simple example. Learning to read the differences between the person and the character(s) is no different from what happens when one goes to the theater. In that place one does not confuse the person of the actor with the character(s) portrayed, unless the actor is very bad. When Dustin Hoffman, for example, shuffles on stage as Willy Loman,[2] a tired, broken and beaten man, it is Willy who is present and who evokes from the person in the audience some character(s) whose emotional responses to Willy's tragedy companion that person when he or she leaves the theater. Within the context of this 'who' question the therapy room becomes a theater, a place for the characters to tell their tales.

The same, I would argue, is true of the classroom if we begin with this question of 'who'. The classroom is also a theater whose landscapes transform the neutral, architectural space of the room into a place where the characters meet. In both sites the work of imagination is taking place, and education becomes to a great extent a matter of leading and being led into other worlds of possibility. Even subjects like science or mathematics, which in devotion to facts and rules would seem to be well beyond the ken of imagination, can become in the hands of a teacher-as-character an awakening of the heart.[3]

For example, many years ago when my oldest son was in the first grade his teacher, who was in her first assignment, was introducing the students to the science of the solar system. She was enthusiastic but quite bound to the facts. So, when my son came home one afternoon and simply threw his paper on the table as he dashed outdoors to play, I saw that she had given him a zero for his remarks about the earth's relation to the sun. In response to the question—'Does the earth move?'—he had checked 'yes' and 'no'. Inviting him on a walk I asked him to tell me about his answer. He said with all the innocent confidence of one who was 6 years old, that when he and I were walking the earth did not move. He went on to explain to me that it moved only if we took a rocket ship into space.

Of course, he was correct, but his answer flew in the face of the facts of science as his teacher was presenting them. I knew that what he was speaking about was science as a perspective, as a way of knowing the world and being in it, but from the point of view of science what is real and true is that the earth is a planet in motion. My son did not, of course, use this language of perspective. He was simply staying faithful to the fact that living as an astronaut on a planet in space is not the same as living on the ground of earth as an embodied being. He was being 'who' he was, two different 'characters' in two different worlds. He had not yet been led out of himself into that place of mind that leaves the body behind (Romanyshyn, 1989/2000).

Children are wonderful educators and I realized that here was a challenge that I had to take. I had become deeply interested in the theme of science as a perspective and in the issue of how it was being taught in primary schools. Thus I offered to come to his class and his teacher happily accepted.

On the appointed day I came with a microscope and several prepared slides. My intent was not to challenge the validity of the facts of science. Rather, I wanted to demonstrate a difficult philosophical point: that science was a perspective that required a specific attitude toward the world and the body. But how should I do that? And for whom? 'Who' were six-year-olds? What was it like to be six and sitting at a desk listening to someone who, like their parents, was an adult? 'Who' should come into the classroom? That day 'I', father to my son, became a magician. Saying this I need to add that this character was as much created by the circumstances, as it was a conscious, deliberate choice. I lived in the space of the classroom as a magician. It was not a technique.

As I showed each slide I made a drama about the attitude necessary to see the world with a microscopic eye. Before I would bend down to look through the microscope I would wave and say 'goodbye'. Then I would pop up quickly and say, 'Oops! I forgot to close one eye' and then I would wave again and repeat my goodbye. The final moment was a loud, amazed 'Wow' as I looked at the slides I had prepared.

Every child in that room wanted to see what was under the microscope, and as each in turn took their place at the microscope they repeated the entire performance, culminating in their amazed 'wows'. In addition many of them made up stories about what they saw, the grain of pepper, for example, became a rock that they put on their hamburgers.

Something magical had happened, that kind of magic that happens at the theater, that kind of magic that releases us from the tyranny of the 'real', that kind of magic that is the work of imagination. In addition, in their enthusiasm the students had learned that microscopic vision was a special way of being embodied in the world. They had learned this attitude by enacting it; they had built what they had learned into their bodies through the gestures of taking leave of their surroundings, repeating what Isaac Newton had done in 1666, when to study light he went into a dark room, cut a small hole in his window shade and placed between that portal and his singular, fixed eye a small prism through which, to the dismay of the poet John Keats, he unwove the rainbow and rewove it as a spectrum (Romanyshyn, 1980).

To be sure, another poet, Alexander Pope, praised Newton for this singular vision, when he said, 'Nature and Nature's laws lay hid in night,/God said, "Let Newton be!" And all was light' (Nicolson, 1960, p. 154). Both poets, of course, were right. In that moment when the rainbow became a spectrum something was *lost and gained*. Too often, however, we forget the cost and education becomes indoctrination. When no child is to be left behind, still—tested, measured, mapped and regulated—what is left behind is the imagination. In this context history is no longer a living reality and figures like Newton, Keats and Pope are no longer characters who live on in the imagination.

On this day, however, they were there, invisible companions bending over the microscope with those children, haunting that *third* world between the world of sense and the world of intellect that the philosopher Henri Corbin termed the *imaginal*, and which for Jung is the landscape of the psyche, a world that is neither a matter of fact nor an idea of mind, but which is as real as these other two. Hillman (1975, 1981), drawing on Corbin, has explored this autonomous reality whose organ of perception is the heart and which opens to the creative imagination. Others like Watkins (1986/2000), Goodchild (2001, 2006) and Raff (2000) have deepened our understanding of this domain of reality and it is at the heart of the imaginal approach to research in *The Wounded Researcher*. It is also at the heart of an approach to education that makes a place for the many levels of the unconscious and all those characters 'who' dwell there.

Of course, the children of this day did not know any of this in any conscious or self-conscious way and the lesson of science as a perspective still needed to be taught. The magician had to give way to someone else, but 'who?'

Here I need to anticipate a point about the imaginal approach to education, which I will explore again later: the place in education for what Jung calls the feeling function. In the enthusiasm of what had happened something was lost and a sense of sadness informed my final question to them. But how to bring this *feeling-toned* question into the room without spoiling the enthusiasm?

I had also come with a pair of scissors and a fresh slide, and when all the prepared ones were finished I asked for a volunteer who would allow me to snip a strand of hair. A girl with a flaming red mane of hair quickly raised her hand. Carefully, like Newton had cut that small hole in his shade to admit only a ray of light, I cut one piece of that red hair and placed it on the slide. I repeated the earlier performance, but this time in place of the amazed 'wow' I ended with a puzzled look on my face. The absence of 'wow' caught their attention, and a few actually spoke it for me. But I glanced back and forth a few times between the single strand of hair under the microscope and the wavy fullness of the girl's red hair. The difference that I knew to be the case had to be felt in the moment lest it be only a technique. It had to be embodied by the one who was living the difference as if experienced for the first time. I waited, lingering in my puzzlement. Then I asked my final question.

Is there anyone, I asked, who could think of something that could not be put and seen under a microscope. The question was not greeted with silence. On the contrary, there was almost unanimous agreement that anything could be cut up and placed under the microscope. One boy even said he could do that to his brother, a rather clear and disturbing indication of the complexity of education. But I waited and repeated my question, wanting to illustrate now how science as a perspective had to look at things separated from their living context. And then from the back of the room a hand was raised. A blond haired girl with a soft lisp said that she knew something that could not be seen under a microscope. She paused—embarrassed?—and said, 'a smile'.

I grant that six-year-olds can be an embarrassment to philosophers and psychologists with our grand theories of education. I also grant that the classroom landscape of six-year-olds and that of sophisticated graduate students are not quite the same thing, and yet I would argue that a place for embodied education and the feeling function to open the imagination applies in both situations. Indeed, if we enter any classroom unknowingly ensconced within the Cartesian dream, not only does imagination wither, it also stays outside the door where the body is left behind. Education then becomes a matter of imparting information by a teacher-as-cogito, disembodied and disconnected from a feeling and passionate connection to his/her words. Teaching as a *vocation* becomes reduced to a narrow *profession* designed to educate its members into a set of skills that can be observed, quantified, measured and organized within a set of goals that lay out the territory even before one has entered into it.

It is not surprising, therefore, that within the space of this dream-turned-nightmare David Jardine tells the tale of another smile, of a student teacher whose students seemed to be disinterested. Commenting on his observations that during the class she seemed herself to be elsewhere, he reports that her response to this observation was to ask him if she should smile more. Here is technique with a vengeance and it illustrates that when we lose touch with the embodied characters of 'who' is teaching, with the *complexity of this vocation*, we also lose touch with those who seek to learn. Within this dream-turned-nightmare and with skills in hand we remain disconnected from the others 'without', from those who are our contemporary existential companions. And disconnected from them we also remain disconnected from the others 'within'. We lose touch with our complex psychological companions who haunt our presence and inform our ways of being with our existential companions, who are themselves also complex ways of being *with us*.

In the Cartesian dream-turned-nightmare, education becomes a matter of method and technique designed to ward off the messy ambiguity of complexity. As I showed in *The Wounded Researcher* this warding off is the psychological function of method when method is made primary. It is, moreover, the point that the ethno-psychoanalyst George Devereux (1967) made more than forty years ago in his sadly neglected book, *From Anxiety to Method in the Behavioral Sciences*. His title says it all.

But no precision of method can dispel the anxiety that comes from giving a place to the embodied complexities of encounter. Gaston Bachelard alludes to this point when he writes, 'I am not the same man when I am reading a book of ideas ... as when I am reading a poet's book ...' (1969, p. 65). *Bachelard's 'I' is anything but singular or isolated.* Indeed, it is informed by—formed in relation to—a field, and the two different texts correspond to two different others who read these texts. The Bachelardian 'I' is a paradox of identity within difference: the man who reads a book of ideas or a book of poems *is and is not* the person of Gaston Bachelard. We have, I would assert, an ethical obligation to take into account this complexity in our educational praxes. We have an ethical obligation to make a place for the educator 'who-is-a-character'.

Attending to this issue of the characters that we are is an initial step toward becoming aware of the connection between being a character and having character. This step is an encounter with the unconscious, with those characters who dwell in the margins of a text and draw us into reveries. In this regard, an ethical pedagogy based in Jung's work would seem to converge with that specific subfield in educational philosophy called moral or character education.

After a certain point in life a person, according to Albert Camus, is responsible for their face. Those lines and marks are traces of the characters that are etched in the flesh. True objectivity is not gained by ignoring these characters who borrow our eyes. True objectivity comes from engaging them. *True objectivity comes through deep subjectivity.*

It is not my intention here to discuss the results of this first experiment except to say that after I finished the article I took up its themes in my teaching and writing at Pacifica Graduate Institute. Hired in 1992 to lay a foundation for an approach to research that would fit within the institute's Jungian orientation, I published in 2007 *The Wounded Researcher*, the culmination of a fifteen-year effort to make a place for the complex unconscious and its correlates in the classroom. But as I realized along the way, this work was at its core a book about ethics, specifically about *an ethics rooted in the unconscious*. In this context, the issue of research has been and is the means by which this work becomes a reflection on education and the task of making the bodies of knowledge we create and teach into *ethical epistemologies*.

Today, this obligation to build ethical ways of knowing the world and being in it is, perhaps, the primary issue, because as I have tried to show in some reflections on technology (Romanyshyn, 1989/2000, 1993, 1994) the absence of such ethical episte-mologies leads to epistemological violence. Education cannot continue in that context. Education has to be subversive of the conventional order, and one of the ways to achieve that is to attend to the place of unconscious dynamics in the classroom, and to the ways that in its being ignored perpetuate violence. Jung makes this point when he writes:

> The teacher must not be a merely passive upholder of culture; he must actively promote that culture through his own self-education. His culture must never remain at a standstill, otherwise he will start correcting in the children those faults which he has neglected in himself. This is manifestly the antithesis of education. (*CW* 17, para. 110)

Jung's deepening of the unconscious is particularly important in this process of *self-education* because in his formulation of the *psychoid* archetype the unconscious links not only all humanity at a collective level, but also all of us to nature. And so, for example, we have to make a place in our teaching for the melting polar ice caps (Romanyshyn, 2008), because education as a matter of mind divorced from body is also education divorced from nature. Such education, which leaves things as they are, not only fails to be responsive to these complex webs, it is also irresponsible.

Between 1991 and 2007 the task of complex knowing became personified as the wounded researcher. Along the way one issue that has remained pivotal is the necessity to avoid identifying education with therapy or worse reducing education to therapy. If both are sites of theater, they are different theaters: *the classroom is not the therapy room.*

Jung is quite clear about this point. Speaking of the practical application of the methods used in analytical psychology, he says, 'The practical application of these would be out of the question for the ordinary teacher, and an amateurish or half-serious use of them is to be severely discouraged, although some knowledge of them on the part of the teacher is certainly desirable' (*CW* 17, para. 108).

The point then is not the direct application of the principles of analytic therapy by the teacher to the classroom. The point is that *the educator has to be educated* in such a way that he or she does not perpetuate in the classroom the complex dynamics of an unconscious life. *The question of teacher preparation is central.* Just as we expect a surgeon's hand to be free of germs, we should expect the educator's psyche to be as free as possible of complex contaminants of an unconscious life. Addressing some of the fundamental questions of psychotherapy, Jung notes with respect to the therapist, 'for only what he can put right in himself can he hope to put right in the patient' (*CW* 16, para. 239). *Educating the other has to begin with and continue to be educating oneself.* So, if we do not ignore—cannot afford to ignore!—the unconscious complexities of education, then how do we make a place for the unconscious in the classroom without turning the classroom into the therapy room? How do we make a place for the *wounded educator? The Wounded Researcher* is and has been the second experiment with this issue.

The Second Experiment

> No investigator, however unprejudiced and objective he is, can afford to disregard his own complexes, for they enjoy the same autonomy as those of other people. As a matter of fact, he cannot disregard them because they do not disregard him. Complexes are very much a part of the psychic constitu-

tion, which is the most absolutely prejudiced thing in every individual. His constitution will therefore inexorably decide what psychological view a given observer will have. Herein lies the unavoidable limitation of psychological observation: its validity is contingent upon the personal equation of the observer. (Jung, *CW* 8, para. 213)

With one small change of terms from investigator/observer to educator, Jung's words apply to education as a complex affair. His diagram of the complex transference field in psychotherapy also depicts the transference field of the classroom. When one crosses the threshold of the classroom, one's complex constitution does not magically fade away; it is not deposited on the other side of that threshold.

Moreover, while Jung's statement clearly shows that his psychology belongs to the tradition of hermeneutics, and, while it also indicates a radical break with that tradition because it gives a place to the complex constitution of 'who' does the work of interpretation, it also betrays Jung's own complex constitution. The use of the masculine personal pronoun throughout the quote shows the cultural-historical complex of patriarchy in his work. No one is exempt from this complex 'personal equation' and a sense of self as *a-priori* identity.

The Wounded Researcher makes a place for a *complex hermeneutics*. Modeling itself on the procedures in depth psychology that make a place for the unconscious in psychotherapy, it makes a place for the unconscious in the research process. However, since the educator is also a complex psychological being, *a place must also be made for the unconscious in the processes of education*. Indeed, as I mentioned earlier, *making such a place is an ethical obligation*, a point to which I will return in the final section of this essay. Jung establishes the ground for this obligation:

> The present day shows with appalling clarity how little able people are to let the other man's argument count, although this capacity is a fundamental and indispensable condition for any human community. Everyone who proposes to come to terms with himself must reckon with this basic problem for, to the degree that he does not admit the validity of the other person, he denies the 'other' within himself the right to exist—and vice versa. The capacity for inner dialogue is a touchstone for outer objectivity. (*CW* 8, para. 187)

Jung wrote those words in 1916 and so the present day that he refers to was nearly one hundred years ago. It is very doubtful if in that span of time things have gotten any better. Indeed, given the pace of technology over this period of time, especially with respect to its capacity to increase our powers of destruction, things have gotten worse. *The Wounded Researcher* makes a place for the unconscious in multiple ways. In this part of my essay I want to summarize some of these contributions, which I have employed with students and which are equally applicable to *the education of the educator*.

Cultivating a Metaphoric Sensibility

Earlier I mentioned that in the education of a psychotherapist who would make a space for the unconscious in the therapy room, the cultivation of a metaphoric sensibility is an essential first step. It is so because, in undoing one's unexamined assumptions about the univocal identity of 'who' a patient is, it opens up an image of 'who' that patient might be like, an image of the patient-as-a-character with a story. The cultivation of a metaphoric sensibility is also the first step if one is to make a place for the unconscious in the classroom. Such a sensibility leads one out of an addiction to fixed, linear and literal ways of thinking. It fosters a disposition that is hospitable to paradox and ambiguity. It develops that attitude of negative capability that John Keats described as the ability 'of being in uncertainties, Mysteries, doubts, without any irritable reaching after fact and reason' (Barnard, 1973, p. 539).

The image quality of a metaphor taxes the irritable mind. It situates that mind in the space where meaning is unhinged from its usual moorings to either things or thoughts, where meaning is neither a matter of fact about things, events or persons in the world nor an idea of mind. It places one in that *imaginal* domain, which, as I indicated earlier was explored by Henri Corbin, and which was described by him as '... the intermediate world ... between the intellectual and the sensible, in which the Active Imagination as *imaginatio vera* is an organ of understanding mediating between intellect and sense ...' (Bloom, 1958/1969, p. xvi).

In this intermediate domain the logic of either/or gives way to another logic, to a neither/nor way of knowing the world and being in it. This shift is essential to changing the culture and climate of the classroom. It begins the work of transforming education from being a matter of transmitting information and/or imposing values to education as an awakening of the curious and creative imagination. The neither/nor logic of a metaphoric sensibility is a provisional way of knowing and as such it offers an epistemological foundation for Jung's psychology of the unconscious.

In one of his most seminal essays, 'On the Nature of the Psyche', Jung affirms the radical implications of the unconscious. Its discovery, he says, 'is of absolutely revolutionary significance in that it could radically alter our view of the world'. It would do so, he adds, because any serious consideration of it would force us to acknowledge that, 'our view of the world can be but a provisional one' (*CW* 8, para. 369–370). Susan Rowland amplifies this point when, commenting on Jung as a writer, she writes, 'Anything derived merely from rationality risks being profoundly inauthentic unless it also bears witness to the destabilizing presence of the unconscious'. Attending to this destabilizing influence, she says, Jung's psychology was 'an attempt to evoke in writing what cannot be entirely grasped: the fleeting momentary presence of something that forever mutates and reaches beyond the ego's inadequate understanding' (2005, p. 3).

Jung's psychology does move through several iterations, and one can find in his work traces of a Cartesian metaphysics, a Kantian influence and Platonic overtones. And yet there is a *telos* in his work grounded in the reality of the image and perhaps best realized in his works on alchemy. The metaphor of alchemy is a bridge between his earlier Gnostic interests and his later explorations into the relations between his psychology of the unconscious and quantum physics. For our purposes I want only to underscore that this metaphor of alchemy places *the image* at the center of Jung's vision of psychological life. Any education, then, which would take into account the psychological depths of mind has to attend to the realty of the image.

What does so is a metaphoric sensibility. It emphasizes how the alchemy of metaphor releases the image in the experience. Via the image, this alchemy of metaphoric language works between the construction of meaning and its de-construction. Every metaphor is, as it were, like the 'vas' of alchemy where the material being worked on was transformed, where the lead was turned into gold. According to Jungian analyst Edward Edinger (1984) of all the processes at work in this work of transformation two were essential: *coagulatio* and *solutio*. The therapist—or the educator—who would be master of metaphor, who would make use of metaphor with awareness, is an alchemist, who on one hand coagulates or fixes a meaning and on the other hand dissolves it *into a possibility of creating ever-new meanings*.

In educating my students into this domain of the image, I often use the simple example offered by the literary critic Howard Nemerov. 'What is a purple finch?' I ask, and for anyone who is not a bird enthusiast the question is a puzzle. Following Nemerov I read them the factual description found in Peterson's field guide, but note that Nemerov himself is not convinced by these matters of fact that the bird that he sees in his garden while thinking about the mystery of metaphor is a purple finch. Then I read the last statement in the field guide: a purple finch is a sparrow dipped in raspberry juice! Nemerov then says that through this image he is certain that the bird he sees in his garden is a purple finch. And he says that this recognition is not quite canny.

Of course! The claim is uncanny. It is an irritating claim but that is the point. It destabilizes the comfortable ways in which we have settled into thinking in terms of either things out there or thoughts in here, of either a world of facts or a mind full of ideas. It challenges us to think about how we think about the world. On one hand, the metaphor of a sparrow dipped in raspberry juice is not a fact that one can validate with empirical tests. No photo would show any traces of a bird soaked with juice, and even if in a fit of empirical frenzy one managed to rush into the garden and take hold of the bird, one's hands would not drip with juice.

On the other hand, the metaphor is not simply an idea in Nemerov's mind. The metaphor turns Nemerov toward the world—the purple finch is there in his garden! The metaphor escorts him, as it were, into the world. It is the *subtle bridge between perception and thought*, the bridge that connects matter and mind. The image quality of the metaphor opens a vision. It is the lens of the eye of imagination that sees through the density of the world, an eye so different from Newton's prismatic eye that took him into his darkened room away from the world. It is an eye that led the visionary poet William Blake to pray, 'May God us keep/From Single Vision and Newton's Sleep' (Erdman, 1981, p. 693), an eye that sees into the invisible depths of the world, that invisible of the visible that is at the heart of Merleau-Ponty's phenomenology of embodied perception (1964/1968).

In addition to Nemerov's metaphor I often also use the example of Magritte's painting entitled '*Ceci n'est pas une pipe*'. It is a wonderful visual metaphor that shows a pipe but whose title undoes what one is seeing. In the very act of perception what is shown to be a pipe is not a pipe. Here the painting itself is that alchemical 'vas' where the categories of reality and representation are open to question. One looks at the painting and these fixed categories are dissolved. One is forced to wonder again. The alchemy of metaphor resides in the tension between the 'is' and 'is not' of metaphor. On the side of the metaphoric 'is' a metaphor seems to adhere to the logic of A=A, the logic of identity. A thing is what it is. A person is who he is and about this 'what' or 'who' there hovers no ambiguity. The identity pole of a metaphor affirms that things and people have self-identity. On the other side of this tension, however, the metaphoric 'is not' undoes these adhesions. It erases the = sign; it dissolves the self-identity of the thing and the person.

The 'is not' pole of metaphor makes a big difference. Hidden, as it were, in the shadow of the 'is' of metaphor, the 'is not' of metaphor does its work of opening the imagination. It works its alchemy in the darkness of the light that shines forth from the 'is' pole of a metaphor. It works its alchemy one might say in twilight or in dark light. In this dark light the 'is not' pole trails a question that annoyingly lingers and asks if A is not A, then what is it? What is A (like) if it is not itself? This 'is not' pole takes one into thinking about paradoxes and correspondences, about similarities and differences, about relationships and resemblances. In this respect David Jardine makes an excellent point when he cites the work of Wittgenstein on the nature of analogical language. He says that Wittgenstein's work portrays the 'deeply *dialogical* and *analogical* character of lived-experience, the deeply conversational nature of life as it is actually lived, with its irresolvable and potent "family resemblances" and kinships' (1998, p. 26, his italics). A metaphoric sensibility seems to be not only an epistemological foundation for Jung's psychology, but also the foundation for a psychology that stays rooted in embodied life.

In the climate of education today where emphasis is placed on the establishment of clear goals and objectives and the measurement of competencies, the cultivation of a metaphoric sensibility in service to the imagination with its delight in paradox and ambiguity seems foolish. Indeed, its cultivation seems as foolish as alchemy and as useless as a poem. Elsewhere (Romanyshyn, 2002) I have written in defense of being a fool and in defense of being useless, but the best defense comes in the very enactment of these qualities in the classroom. One has to risk being a fool if education is to have the depth of the psyche, if it is to have the courage to dissolve fixed and unexamined knowledge—unconscious metaphors that function as projections—if it is to begin with how we are addressed by what is unknown. And so, I often use a poem as a third way of cultivating a metaphoric sensibility.

The poem is 'Thirteen Ways of Looking at a Blackbird' by Wallace Stevens. My intention is to show how the blackbird as an object of perception in this poem is a matter of perspective, and then by analogy to suggest that one is always in some perspective, myth, dream, fantasy or complex even though one does not know what that is. To give weight to the point I set the stage with a fable, suggesting that each of the thirteen stanzas are spoken by experts in ornithology who have come together at a conference to present their definitive findings on the nature of the blackbird. Inviting each of thirteen students to speak one of the thirteen stanzas, I let the process unfold and then ask, 'Which expert is correct?' 'Which of the thirteen views is the truth?'.

More often than not the students have a living, felt sense of the hermeneutic circle in the work of understanding, and they come to appreciate the necessity of dialogue with the other's point of view. In *The Wounded Researcher* this fable appears in the final chapter of the book devoted to the issue of what constitutes an ethical epistemology. My argument there is that the capacity to hear the other is inseparable from the capacity to regard one's position as a point of view and vice versa, the point that Jung makes and which I quoted earlier in this paper. But as I also said and as Jung also makes quite clear this capacity to allow the other person's argument to count is difficult and rare. It requires that one is able to make a place for the reality of his/her complexes. In the context of education it requires the capacity, courage and commitment to make a place for the unconscious.

A metaphor is a perspective. It is a way of 'seeing' that betrays 'who' one is who lives within that metaphor. Moreover, we dwell within metaphors whose roots reach deeply into personal, familial, and cultural-historical depths. A good example here would be the Western cultural-historical metaphor of technology, which in being lived out unconsciously has functioned as a symptom and collective dream (Romanyshyn, 1989/2000, 2008). The cultivation of a metaphoric sensibility is this first step toward making a place for the unconscious. Insofar as that first step requires the capacity to hear the other, making a place for the unconscious also involves an education in learning how to listen.

Education as Awakening Vocation

For Jung the symbol is a bridge between the unconscious and consciousness. It is a manifestation of the transcendent function, the language of the dream, the means by which 'the unknowable substance ... of the unconscious always represents itself to consciousness ...' (*CW* 11, para. 810) The symbol also serves the same function in Freud's work, connecting and translating the unconscious into consciousness, a work of translation that in turn requires translation, situating the encounter with psyche within the tradition of hermeneutics and, as I argued above, necessitating the cultivation of metaphoric sensibility as the epistemological counterpart of the ontological reality of the psyche as a matter of symbols and their images.

Any education, therefore, that would address the whole person—the embodied mind in its psychological depths—would have to make a place for *symbolic ways of knowing alongside empirical and rational ways of knowing*. In this respect, I would claim that the therapy room that appears at the end of the 19th century marks a new threshold between the academic classroom with its education of mind and the medical clinic with its treatment of the body. In this gap between mind and body the first neurotics address us from the abyss of Descartes' nightmare, blindly stumble across the threshold into Freud's consulting rooms, and, with their abysmal hysterical symptoms that now re-fuse and con-fuse the material body and the unconscious mind, offer a new form of education. Paul Ricœur in his now classic work on Freud alludes to this point when he says:

> After the silence and forgetfulness made widespread by the manipulation
> of empty signs and the construction of formalized languages, the modern
> concern for symbols expresses a new desire to be addressed. (1970, p. 31)

To be addressed is to be summoned by something or someone other than oneself. *Education that begins with this summons is an education that awakens a vocation. Jung's psychology of individuation is this kind of education.*

In his essay, 'The Development of Personality', Jung situates his call for a pedagogy that would serve the whole person within a trenchant critique of the educational practices of his day, which continue into our own time to the degree that such practices leave out of the picture the unconscious depths of mind. He says of those who employ such practices that they 'are half-baked educators who are not human beings at all, but walking personifications of method', not unlike the example of the student teacher cited above by David Jardine who asked if she should smile more. Continuing, he says, 'Anyone who wants to educate must himself be educated', which means coming to know one's own complex presence in the classroom. Indeed, Jung argues that to the degree that we shirk this responsibility we foster an image of the educated adult as one who has 'a solid conviction of his own competence', which would remove 'Any doubt or feeling of uncertainty ... undermining the necessary faith in his own authority'. But the end result of this program he says is that, 'The professional man is irretrievably condemned to be merely competent' (*CW* 17, para. 284).

While the education of psychotherapists is woefully guilty on this score—competence in technique dominates over the shaping of character—I suspect that a similar condition exists in the field of pedagogy. But, Jung says, 'Children are not half as stupid as we imagine' (*CW* 17, para. 286). They are imagined as such only because we regard them in the shadow of the image of the one condemned to be merely competent, a regard that Jung suspects harbors the unconscious complexes of adult life that are projected onto the child. Cultivating the imagination then becomes a casualty of a system of education that unconsciously imposes upon the child this task of becoming merely competent.

But, and this is Jung's point, education cannot and should not ask of the 'other' what one has not done oneself. Education cannot and should not perpetually pass on to the next generation the task of making a place for the unconscious. In his essay he equates becoming aware of one's unconscious dynamics with the development of the individuated personality, about which he says the following:

> The achievement of personality means nothing less than the optimum development of the whole individual human being. It is impossible to foresee the endless variety of conditions that have to be fulfilled. A whole lifetime is needed. Personality is the supreme realization of the innate idiosyncrasy of a living being. It is an act of high courage flung in the face of life, the absolute affirmation of all that constitutes the individual, the most successful adaptation of the universal conditions of existence coupled with the greatest possible freedom for self-determination. To educate a man to *this* seems to me no light matter. (*CW* 17, para. 289, his italics)

Education that does take up this task as no light matter aims toward the development of the individuated human being, who in the context of the above quote, is one who can take up the universal conditions of human existence in a manner that is transformative not only of himself or herself but also of those same conditions. Such an individual is not the monstrosity of the one who is a law unto himself or herself, which is only the superficial and narcissistic form of the individuated personality. This is education in bad taste. On the contrary, he or she is the one who is faithful, as Jung puts it, 'to the law of one's own being' (*CW* 17, para. 295), and this fidelity, he says, is more than a matter of courage and necessity. In the final analysis, what induces a person 'to rise out of unconscious identity with the mass as out of a swathing mist', is 'what is commonly called vocation: an irrational factor that destines a man to emancipate himself from the herd and from its well worn path' (*CW* 17, paras. 299–300).

Education that too tightly scripts the program, that too early and too rigidly maps the path leaves no room for such irrational factors, for those moments that would allow one to be addressed by the law of one's own being, to that vocation fidelity to which not only affirms one's destiny but also puts one in service to something other and larger than oneself. The mythic figure of Orpheus is an archetypal background for this form of education. As the only poet who was allowed back into the city by Plato, Orpheus personifies that shaman-poet-lover whose words simultaneously awaken the slumbering soul from its forgetfulness and align it with its destiny. In this respect, he is the poet of anamnesis, which is a term that connotes a movement upward into memory, a movement of return from a state of being without memory, a movement upward and back from forgetting.

Orpheus is a poet whose education is against forgetting, a poet whom Plato contrasts with the mimetic poets like Homer and Hesiod whose words induce in their listeners a life of imitative identification with traditional values. Welcoming Orpheus into the polis, Plato is creating a new form of education in Greek life. In an essay on the Orphic roots of Jung's psychology, I argued that Plato's reform of education reappears in Jung's approach to psychotherapy. 'The creation of the therapy room at the end of the nineteenth century' I said, 'was a creation of a new form of the Polis where the symbolic speech of dreams was spoken in a voice that is closer to the poet than it is to anything else' (2004, p. 57). I also showed how in that place the symptomatic expression of the suffering soul, its psychopathology, was and is the reappearance of the mimetic and the Orphic poets, and how Freud's and Jung's psychologies are related but different forms of education.

Freudian psychotherapy is a form of education that attends to the symptom as a matter of enslavement to repetitive patterns, which chains a person to a life of unconscious mimetic identification. There is a stoic aspect to this form of education. One learns here to suffer one's fate with tragic resolve.

Jung's psychotherapy, on the other hand, attends to the symptom as vocation and as such it is a form of education that awakens soul to its Orphic voice and leads it into the law of its own being, thus placing it in service to something other and larger than itself. One's life becomes part of a story that has archetypal resonances and one discovers how the many forms of 'who' one is in life are like those archetypal characters who become our companions along the way. This is the *creative* aspect of the symptom, the way in which a wound in life can become a work, the way in which education might even come to be a matter of homecoming.

Regardless of whatever preference one might have for one or the other of these forms of education, my point in that article was that the therapy room has given us an opportunity for a new form of education, one, as I said earlier, that spans the abyss between a mind cut off from its own psychological depths, the reasonable mind cut off from its own shadows, the enlightened mind oblivious of its darkness, and a body severed from that mind. It is a form of education, which in attending to the mimetic and Orphic voices of 'who' dwells in the symptom, is a *poiesis*, a term that emphasizes education as a creative act with all the attendant consequences of risk, of being the fool who, to borrow the apt title of an essay by David Miller, has 'Nothing to Teach! No Way to Teach It! Together with the Obligation to Teach', is useless. Miller's essay 'is a critique of the imposition of the language of assessment and accountability onto those realms of human experience that cannot be counted but which nevertheless do count' (Miller, 2006, p. 217). As such it is a form of education that is counter not only to education as indoctrination, but also to any forms that place their emphasis only on either dispensing information or training in techniques.

The opportunity has been squandered. The therapy room has remained cut off from the classroom, the suffering soul as a form of education not only imprisoned there but also indoctrinated with the very same cultural-historical dreams that made its presence inevitable. Speaking in this way I am not, as I said before, advocating that the classroom become a therapy room. That would not only be dangerous, it would also be unethical. The differences between these two sites of education have to be honored. And yet, any form of education that would ignore the reality of the unconscious in its shadow and creative aspects is also dangerous and unethical. Jung clearly spoke to this dilemma and the cautions that must be exercised in his essay 'The Significance of the Unconscious in Individual Education' (*CW* 17); in *The Wounded Researcher* I acknowledged these same issues.

If we are to recover what has been squandered, then ways have to be found that do make a place for how we are addressed by the unconscious in its many manifestations. *The Wounded Researcher* has been and is an attempt in that direction. It is a beginning. The alchemical hermeneutic method, for example, makes a place for dreams, symptoms and other expressions of the unconscious in the educational process, including the functions of feeling and intuition as Jung describes them. It also makes a place for the body in the process. But to present all that material would double the size of this essay, and there is a final and crucial point to be made about education as a matter of vocation. Therefore, I can say only that the book offers numerous examples from my students whose work illustrates these and the other points raised in this essay.

Vocation and Response-ability

To be addressed, to be summoned into thinking requires that one have the capacity to listen if one is to be able-to-respond to what one has heard. As able to respond one becomes responsive; one becomes responsible. But listening in a responsible way is a complex affair. How often does one hear a question that arouses an emotional reaction against the question and the one who raised it? 'Who' is hearing the question here? And, from the other side, 'Who' is asking it? The dynamics here are as complex as they are in the case of two lovers. Being psychologically deaf is not so uncommon. Complex unconscious residues build up in the ear like wax does. Mary Shelley's *Frankenstein* is, as the subtitle to the tale suggests, a modern myth for our time. Victor Frankenstein who personifies the spirit of enlightened reason is a 'deaf' man. He hears but fails to listen to the entreaties of his creation and as consequence brings ruin upon those whom he loves and himself.

If education awakens us to how we are addressed by the 'other' both within and without, then procedures need to be in place that will help us to remove the complex obstacles impeding our ability to listen. *The Wounded Researcher* developed some of these procedures within the context of an approach to research that makes a place for the unconscious and which, in doing so, differentiates the researcher's conscious intentions for the work from what is unfinished in the work. This process of differentiation takes place within a transference field between a researcher and his or her work.

Perhaps even more than the value of dreams, the notion of a transference field between an analyst and the patient was and is the most significant insight of a depth orientation to psychotherapy. Its acknowledgement undercuts Descartes' nightmare of an interior Cogito, of a dis-embodied self that is separated from the other. This field is a field of contagion where we infect, as it were, each other with our unexamined desires, fantasies, complexes, and other unconscious dynamics, and it functions as much in the relation between teacher and student as it does between analyst and patient.

In the beginning, Freud understood this complex arena as a matter of the patient's projection onto the analyst, but in time he admitted the reciprocal character of this dynamic and spoke of the analyst's projections onto the patient as counter-transference. Through his studies of alchemy and his deepening of the unconscious beyond the personally repressed to the collective unconscious, Jung, in his essay 'The Psychology of the Transference' (*CW* 16, 1946/1954), extended this field beyond projections to include archetypal dynamics, which, like the invisible lines of force that arrange a magnetic or gravitational field, structure the field between the participants. In addition, he further deepened our understanding of the unconscious and its impact on the transference when, in his essay 'On the Nature of the Psyche' (*CW* 8, 1946/1960), he developed in his dialogues with quantum physics the idea of the deepest, psychoidal, level of the unconscious.

Jung's essay, which is discussed in detail in chapter one of *The Wounded Researcher*, is very difficult. But it is also extremely important because in it he offers from many sources evidence that what depth psychology originally named the unconscious is more than a psychological reality. At the psychoid level the unconscious is the consciousness of nature. It is what used to be known as the *lumen naturae* or the *anima mundi* long before we took leave of our senses and, parting company with the natural world, declared it inanimate (cf. Romanyshyn, 1989/2000). To take leave of our senses is to break the natal bond between what Merleau-Ponty called the flesh of the body and the flesh of the world (1964/1968), an aesthetic bond of reciprocal desire, which is the starting point of his phenomenology. I refer to Merleau-Ponty because phenomenology, as a necessary companion to depth psychology, also contributes to our understanding of the transference field in two ways. First, through its recovery of the lived body as opposed to the body as object, it re-imagines the transference field as a gestural field (Romanyshyn, in press). Second, in the works of J. H. van den Berg (1961, 1970, 1971) phenomenology moves beyond its essentialist biases and addresses itself to cultural and historical differences.

The transference field as it arose in the therapy room is composed of multiple levels from the repressed complexes through the collective-archetypal and cultural-historical to the psychoid levels. This deepest and most archaic level where psyche and nature are *one* indicates that the natural world has its dynamic presence in the transference field. Since at all levels this complex field functions, by definition, outside conscious awareness, the presence of the natural world in this field is a *symptomatic* one. Today one cannot, and ethically should not, deal with our suffering apart from its connection with the suffering of nature. Our depressions, for example, are inseparable from what is happening to the environment in the same way that our cancers are. The same point applies to our systems of education. Our pedagogies impose upon us the ethical demand to be responsive to voices other than our own and it is in response to this ethical obligation that I have attempted to translate this notion of the transference field from the therapy room to the classroom.

The Wounded Researcher offers a detailed description of transference dialogues, which are the procedures employed at the four levels of the transference field. Designed to make a place not only for the voices of cultural diversity, but also for all the complex voices of psychological life, these dialogues are modeled on Jung's process of active imagination. In addition, I draw upon the work of Jungian analyst August Cwik who showed the connection between active imagination and D. W. Winnicott's description of play as a transitional space that mediates between psyche and world. This last point is important because it shifts somewhat the negative emphasis that is usually associated with the unconscious and affirms, as Jung does, its creative potential. Of course, the former cannot be ignored and I acknowledge the safeguards that are necessary in this work.

At each of four levels the intention of the dialogues is to open a space where one can be addressed by the 'other'. It is a way of systematically challenging one's fixed and unexamined assumptions about one's perspective, a way of showing that one is always 'located' in some perspective even if one does not consciously know what that is. These dialogues, therefore, are a process that helps toward the development of a metaphoric sensibility, which, as I showed above, opens one to the necessity for dialogue that situates 'who' one is within a field of listening. In these dialogues one is asked to be responsible by being responsive to the other. This process, which consists of two phases the second of which has five steps, is detailed in *The Wounded Researcher* and many examples of the process are cited. A preliminary version was also published in *Harvest: International Journal of Jungian Studies* (2006). Here I will give a basic description of how the process starts at each level in order to illustrate its contributions toward a mode of pedagogy as fundamentally ethical.

At the *personal* level of the unconscious one invites 'others' from their family constellation, familial history and personal biography to bring their perspective to the work. The encounter can be recorded as a script, or drawn, painted or even enacted in a bodily fashion. This level of engagement with the 'other' is often the easiest one to do, and generally the cast of characters who are part of this field are fantasies that personify an individual's complex projections. At the *cultural-historical* level, however, one invites 'others' of a different gender, race, economic class, culture or period in history to bring their perspective to the work. Already, the process has further de-centered the position of the ego as the singular voice of the work, and on occasion literary figures become part of the encounter.

These figures can also be complex projections embedded in the cultural unconscious of the individual, but they might also be imaginal figures as discussed earlier in this essay. As such these characters are autonomous; they are not projections of the individual's complex unconscious. It is not always possible to say with certainty whether these figures who enter the transference field are complex or imaginal characters. But in the end this judgment does not matter, since the intention here is to make the unconscious as conscious as possible in service to the ethical obligation to be as responsive to the 'other' as one is able to be.

This de-centering of the ego continues as one next invites 'others' from the *archetypal-collective* level of the unconscious to take their place. Here the encounter is with the imaginal 'other'. This field might include mythological, literary or historical characters whose presence feels as real as one's contemporaries but who belong neither to the material nor mental domains. Jung's encounter with Philemon, which he describes in his autobiography, offers a good example of this type of field (1965). This level of encounter, along with the next one, is most difficult to engage, because it so deeply challenges the ego's positions of control and authority. It invites one to enter a space where one's sense of identity as univocal, centered and fixed is put into question. For the ego this level is in effect the nightmare side of Descartes' dream of reason, which, as we have seen, has itself become a nightmare. At the *psychoidal* level of the unconscious one invites any of the 'others' with whom one shares creation to bring in their perspective. It is not uncommon here to encounter the wise animal (as a kind of spirit guide) found in fairytales and who shows a path into the work.

This process of transference dialogues is an on-going experiment in service to making a place for the unconscious in education. While it is still a work in progress with numerous questions to be considered, it does show that 'who' one is as author is companioned by 'who' one is in many ways as an agent in service to some larger issues beyond the self and its conscious intentions. In this respect, education might more directly serve the purpose of making one responsive to the unfinished issues of the day. Ellen MacFarland's book (2008) is an excellent example of this point. A psychotherapist, who specialized in the treatment of early childhood abuse and whose own complex vocation to her work was rooted in the abuse she suffered, she made use of the transference dialogues in her dissertation work with me at Pacifica Graduate Institute. In the context of these dialogues she became responsive to the deep connections between childhood abuse and our abuse of nature and has become now an avowed spokesperson for the natural world.

Toward an Ethical Pedagogy

Considering the implications of Gilles Deleuze's philosophy for ethical education, May and Semetsky note, 'it is what we do *not* know, rather than what we do, that is of educational significance' (2008, p. 143; italics in original). This lacuna in our knowledge is not just an absence of information that can be remedied by more education. Rather this not-knowing is, as they assert, attributable to the fact that 'much of our world, as well as our learning, are unconscious rather than conscious' (2008, p. 143). My intention in this essay has been to show how making a place for the complex unconscious dynamics in the educational process lays a foundation for an ethical pedagogy. Along these lines I have applied a Jungian approach to this task, which I have been developing the past fifteen years. There is, as I said earlier, an urgency to this task for we cannot solve the political, economic, environmental, and other problems we face today at the same level at which they were created: a way of knowing and being that leaves out of the picture the radical insights about the unconscious first articulated in the therapy room more than a hundred years ago, that place that was and remains a new form of education.

In *Depth Psychology and a New Ethic*, Erich Neumann makes this point:

> The old ethic is a partial ethic ... it fails to take into consideration or to evaluate the tendencies and effects of the unconscious ... Within the life of the community, this takes the shape of the psychology of the scapegoat; in international relations it appears in the form of those epidemic outbreaks of atavistic mass reactions known as war. (1973, p. 74)

In 1946 Jung wrote that the hypothesis of the unconscious 'is of absolutely revolutionary significance in that it could radically alter our view of the world' (*CW* 8, para. 369). That revolution has not happened in education or anywhere else. And now the need seems even greater. Some twenty years later in one of his last works, his autobiography, Jung emphasized that the images of the unconscious place a great responsibility upon a man and that developing insight into them 'must be converted into [our] ethical obligation' (1965, p. 193). Our pedagogical practices bear this responsibility today as their greatest challenge. How can we expect to be responsive to the other if we who educate are still irresponsible? The transference dialogues could be a start toward the self-education of the educator.

Notes

1. Editor's note: in educational philosophy, John Dewey criticized a spectator theory of knowledge firmly grounded in Cartesian dualism.
2. Editor's note: Dustin Hoffman played Willy Loman on the Broadway stage and in the 1985 TV movie 'Death of a Salesman'.
3. Editor's note: Nel Noddings, in her many works, has advocated enriching mathematics and science curriculum with the elements of the ethics of care.

References

Bachelard, G. (1969) *The Poetics of Reverie* (Boston, MA, Beacon Press).

Barnard, J. (1973) *John Keats, The Complete Poems* (New York, Penguin).

Bloom, H. (1958/1969) Preface, in *Alone with the Alone: Creative imagination in the Sufism of Ibn'Arabi* (Princeton, NJ, Princeton University Press).

Devereux, G. (1967) *From Anxiety to Method in the Behavioral Sciences* (The Hague, Mouton and Co.).

Edinger, E. (1984) *Anatomy of the Psyche: Alchemical symbolism in psychotherapy* (La Salle, IL, Open Court).

Erdman, D. V. (1981) *The Poetry and Prose of William Blake* (Berkeley, CA, University of California Press).

Gadamer, H-G. (1975) *Truth and Method* (New York, The Seabury Press).

Goodchild, V. (2001) *Eros and Chaos* (York Beach, ME, Nicolas-Hays).

Goodchild, V. (2006) Psychoid, Psychophysical, P-subtle! Alchemy and a new world view, *Spring 74: Alchemy*.

Hillman, J. (1975) *Re-Visioning Psychology* (New York, Harper and Row).

Hillman, J. (1981) *The Thought of the Heart* (Dallas, TX, Spring Publications).

Jardine, D. (1998) *To Dwell with a Boundless Heart: Studies in the postmodern theory of education* (Berlin, Peter Lang).

Jung, C. G. (1916) The Transcendent Function, in *The Structure and Dynamics of the Psyche, The Collected Works of C.G. Jung*, vol. 8 (Princeton, NJ, Princeton University Press, 1960).

Jung, C. G. (1923) Child Development and Education, in *The Development of Personality, The Collected Works of C.G. Jung*, vol. 17 (Princeton, NJ, Princeton University Press, 1954).

Jung, C. G. (1928) The Significance of the Unconscious in Individual Education, in *The Development of Personality, The Collected Works of C.G. Jung*, vol. 17 (Princeton, NJ, Princeton University Press, 1954).

Jung, C. G. (1932) The Development of Personality, in *The Development of Personality, The Collected Works of C.G. Jung*, vol. 17 (Princeton, NJ, Princeton University Press, 1954).

Jung, C. G. (1934) A Review of the Complex Theory, in *The Structure and Dynamics of the Psyche, The Collected Works of C.G. Jung*, vol. 8 (Princeton, NJ, Princeton University Press, 1960).

Jung, C. G. (1939) On 'The Tibetan book of the Great Liberation', in *Psychology and Religion: East and West, The Collected Works of C.G. Jung*, vol. 11 (Princeton, NJ, Princeton University Press, 1958).

Jung, C. G. (1946/1954) The Psychology of the Transference, in *The Practice of Psychotherapy, The Collected Works of C.G. Jung*, vol. 16 (Princeton, NJ, Princeton University Press, 1954).

Jung, C. G. (1946/1960) On the Nature of the Psyche, in *The Structure and Dynamics of the Psyche, The Collected Works of C.G. Jung*, vol. 8 (Princeton, NJ, Princeton University Press, 1960).

Jung, C. G. (1951) Fundamental Questions of Psychotherapy, in *The Practice of Psychotherapy, The Collected Works of C.G. Jung*, vol. 16 (Princeton, NJ, Princeton University Press, 1954).

Jung, C. G. (1965) *Memories, Dreams, Reflections* (New York, Vintage Books).

MacFarland, E. (2008) *The Sacred Path Beyond Trauma: Reaching the divine through nature's healing symbols* (Berkeley, CA, North Atlantic Books).

May, T. & Semetsky, I. (2008) Deleuze, Ethical Education and the Unconscious, in: I. Semetsky (ed.), *Nomadic Education: Variations on a theme by Deleuze and Guattari* (Rotterdam, Sense Publishers), pp. 143–158.

Merleau-Ponty. M. (1964/1968) *The Visible and The Invisible* (Evanston, IL, Northwestern University Press)

Miller, D. (2006) Nothing to Teach! No Way to Teach It! Together with the Obligation to Teach!, quoted in R. Romanyshyn, 'Yes, But Who is Going to Convince the Chicken?': Meditations on the *Inside* and the *Outside*, in: C. Downing (ed.), *Disturbances in the Field: Essays in Honor of David L. Miller* (New Orleans, LA, Spring Journal Books).

Neumann, E. (1973) *Depth Psychology and a New Ethic* (New York, Harper and Row).

Nicolson, M. H. (1960) *The Breaking of the Circle: Studies in the effect of the 'new science' in seventeenth-century poetry* (New York, Columbia University Press).

Raff, J. (2000) *Jung and The Alchemical Imagination* (York Beach, ME, Nicolas-Hays).

Ricœur, P. (1970) *Freud and Philosophy: An essay on interpretation* (New Haven, CT, Yale University Press).

Romanyshyn, R. (1980) Looking at the Light: Reflections on the mutable body, *Dragonflies: Studies in Imaginal Psychology*, 2:1.

Romanyshyn, R. (1989/2000) *Technology as Symptom and Dream* (London, New York, Routledge).

Romanyshyn, R. (1991) Complex Knowing: Toward a Psychological Hermeneutics, *The Humanistic Psychologist*, 19:1, pp. 10–29.

Romanyshyn, R. (1993) The Despotic Eye and Its Shadow: Media image in the age of literacy, in: D. Levin (ed.), *Modernity and the Hegemony of Vision* (Berkeley, CA, University of California Press).

Romanyshyn, R. (1994) The Dream Body in Cyberspace, *Psychological Perspectives*, 29:1, pp. 90–103.

Romanyshyn, R. (2002) *Ways of the Heart: Essays toward an imaginal psychology* (Pittsburgh, PA, Trivium Publications).

Romanyshyn, R. (2004) Anyway Why Did it Have to Be the Death of the Poet?' The orphic roots of Jung's psychology, *Spring 71: Orpheus*.

Romanyshyn, R. (2006) The Wounded Researcher: Levels of transference in the research process, *Harvest: International Journal of Jungian Studies*.

Romanyshyn, R. (2007) *The Wounded Researcher* (New Orleans, LA, Spring Journal Books).

Romanyshyn, R. (2008) The Melting Polar Ice: Revisiting technology as symptom and dream, *Spring 80: Technology, Cyberspace, and Psyche*.

Romanyshyn, R. (in press) The Body in Psychotherapy: Contributions of Merleau-Ponty, in: R. Jones (ed.), *Body, Mind and Healing After Jung* (London, Routledge).

Rowland, S. (2005) *Jung as a Writer* (New York, Routledge).

Van den Berg, J. H. (1961) *The Changing Nature of Man* (New York, Dell).

Van den Berg, J. H. (1970) *Things: Four Metabletic Reflections* (Pittsburgh, PA, Duquesne University Press).

Van den Berg, J. H. (1971) Phenomenology and Metabletics, *Humanitas*, 7:3, pp. 279–290.

Watkins, M. (1986/2000) *Invisible Guests* (Woodstock, CT, Spring Publications).

9

Jung and Tarot: A theory-practice nexus in education and counselling

INNA SEMETSKY

Since Aristotle, the relationship between theory and practice has been controversial. Theory is derived from *theoria*—defined as a philosophical contemplation of higher truths and as such disengaged from practical, political contexts and social life; that is from *praxis*, which is defined as the process of putting theoretical knowledge into practice and is embedded in actions, relationships and experiences that by definition have an ethical or moral dimension. The research presented here represents a theory-practice nexus. It originated long ago as the action-project representing a type of research analogous to what Jungian scholar Robert Romanyshyn will have called years later *research with soul in mind* (Romanyshyn, 2007). Referring to the *Imaginal*, Romanyshyn emphasised the role of this third dimension between the senses and the intellect as enabling an embodied way of being in the world within the context of complex mind reaching into the whole of nature. It was philosopher Henry Corbin who coined the *Imaginal world—Mundus Imaginalis* or *mundus archetypus*, the archetypal world—as a distinct order of reality corresponding to a *distinct mode of perception* in contrast to purely *imaginary* as the unreal or simply utopian. The archetypal world comprises what Carl Jung posited as the collective unconscious or *objective* psyche that manifests itself through symbols and images and is shared at a deeper, *psychoid*, level by all members of humankind (Jung, 1959) thereby transcending cultural, temporal or language barriers.

The symbolic meanings of human experiences are 'always grounded in the unconscious archetype, but their manifest forms are moulded by the ideas acquired by the conscious mind. The archetypes [as] structural elements of the psyche ... possess a certain autonomy and specific energy which enables them to attract, out of the conscious mind, those contents which are better suited to themselves' (Jung CW 5. 232) thus helping in achieving much wider scope of awareness than rational thinking, in terms of solely cognitive reasoning—deprived of what Jung called feeling-tone—is capable of providing. The integration of the unconscious into consciousness contributes to the practical manifestation of the ultimate Jungian archetype of wholeness called the Self. For Jung, the profound relationship between the soul of the world, *Anima Mundi*, and an individual human consciousness remained a great mystery. He did not distinguish between the *psyche* and the material world: they represent two different aspects of the *Unus Mundus*, or one world. Archetype is seen by Jung as a skeletal pattern, filled in with imagery and motifs that are 'mediated to us by the unconscious' (CW 8. 417), the

Jung and Educational Theory, First Edition. Edited by Inna Semetsky.
Chapters © 2013 The Authors. Book compilation © 2013 Philosophy of Education Society of Australasia.
Published 2013 by Blackwell Publishing Ltd.

variable contents of which form different archetypal *images*. The archetypal images are the vehicles for/of information embedded in the collective unconscious, and the unconscious is capable of spontaneously producing images 'irrespective of wishes and fears of the conscious mind' (Jung CW 11. 745). The archetypal images are 'endowed with a generative power; [the image] is psychically compelling' (Samuels *et al.*, 1986, p. 73). Contemporary post-Jungians consider the archetypes to be both the structuring patterns of the psyche and the dynamical units of information implicit in the contents of the collective unconscious. Archetypal psychologist James Hillman called for the rescue of images which are capable of 'releasing startling new insights' (Hillman, 1989, 25), and Jung pointed out that a 'symbolic process is an experience *in images and of images*' (Jung CW 9i, 82; italics in original).

A specific subject matter of my research is the set of images comprising a Tarot deck (e.g. Semetsky, 2006a, 2009, 2011) and representing in the symbolic form the very archetypes 'inhabiting' the Imaginal world. It is our cognitive function enriched with creative imagination that provides access to the Imaginal world with a rigor of knowledge specified since antiquity as knowing by analogy. The method of analogy defies the privileged role allotted to the self-conscious subject that observes the surrounding world of objects—from which the epistemic subject is forever detached—with the cool 'scientific' gaze of an independent spectator so as to obtain a certain and indubitable knowledge, or *episteme*. Rather, the method of analogy presupposes *participation*—contrary to observation—in the process of subjects and objects together forming a relational network as an interdependent holistic fabric with the world, thus overcoming the dualistic split that has been haunting us since the time of Descartes and is still confining us to what Corbin used to call the banal dualism of matter versus spirit. This relational approach agrees with Nel Noddings' ethics of care as a feminine alternative to the traditional model of character education (Noddings, 1984). Noddings points to such common global human experiences as birth, marriage, motherhood, death or separation, even while denying moral universals as predestined rules for our actions. These experiential events are fundamental; thus, they can be considered to have universal meanings for humankind, even when they are happening in different places across the globe, geographically, or in different periods in history. These common human experiences are symbolically represented by the images in Tarot pictures.

A typical Tarot layout comprises a particular pattern with each position having some specific connotations that become clear when an experienced reader creates an imaginative narrative out of the pictorial story. Non-incidentally, *imaginative narrative* is one of the methodologies employed by the innovative interdisciplinary field called *Futures Studies*, which also uses utopian thinking, forecasting and strategic planning. M. Peters and J. Freeman-Moir (2006) dedicate their recent volume, *Edutopias: New utopian thinking in education*, to future generations of educators capable of understanding that, with *imagination*, education can indeed transform individuals, raise collective consciousness and contribute to the development of global civic society. In this respect, Tarot represents an example of post-formal (Steinberg *et al.*, 1999) education grounded in an existing *cultural practice*—called, in popular parlance, Tarot readings—during which the pictorial 'language' of the unconscious is converted into verbal expressions, thereby facilitating the 'widening and deepening of conscious life [as] a more intense, disciplined, and expanding realisation of meanings ... And education is not a mere means to such a life. Education is such a life' (Dewey, 1916/1924, p. 417).

The word education derives from the Latin *educare*—to lead out as well as to bring out something that is within. The word therapy derives from the Greek *therapeia*, in terms of human service to those who need it. Education and counselling alike involve either implicit or explicit inquiry into the nature of the self and self-other relations. Carol Witherell notices that, ideally, each professional activity 'furthers another's capacity to find meaning and integrity' (1991, p. 84) in lived experience. Importantly both practices are 'designed to change or guide human lives' (Witherell, 1991, p. 84). This was the focus of my research: to investigate a potential of Tarot as a transformative, at once educational and counselling, tool informed by a Jungian conceptual framework. For Jung, archetype is a symbol of transformation, and symbols—like those represented by the Tarot imagery—function as transformers capable of raising the unconscious contents to the level of consciousness: the implicit meanings become explicit by virtue of 'becoming conscious and by being perceived' (Jung in Pauli, 1994, p. 159).

Jung's biographer Laurens van der Post, in his introduction to the book *Jung and Tarot: an Archetypal Journey* by Sallie Nichols' (herself Jung's student in Zurich), notices the contribution made by Nichols to the profound investigation of Tarot, and her 'illuminated exegesis of its pattern as an authentic attempt at enlargement of possibilities of human perceptions' (in Nichols, 1980, p. xv). Andrew Samuels mentions 'systems such as that of the *I Ching*, Tarot and astrology' (1985, p. 123) as possible, even if uncertain, resources in analytical psychology and quotes Jung writing: 'I found the *I Ching* very interesting. ... I have not used it for more than two years now, feeling that one must learn to walk in the dark, or try to discover (as when one is learning to swim) whether the water will carry one' (in Samuels, 1985, p. 123). Irene Gad (1994) has connected Tarot pictures with the process of human development—what Jung called individuation—and considered their archetypal images to be 'trigger symbols, appearing and disappearing throughout history in times of transition and need' (p. xxxiv).

Tarot pictures are called Arcana, and the meaning of the word Arcana derives from Latin *arca* as a chest; the verb *arcere* means to shut or to close; symbolically, Arcanum (singular) is a tightly shut treasure chest holding a secret, its deep meaning. Nearly every one of the 78 Arcana in a deck—22 Major and 56 Minor—has an image of a living being, a human figure situated in different contexts. This figure is not just a physical body but the mind, soul and spirit as well. And while a body goes through life and accomplishes different tasks, the psyche goes through transformations, as human experience itself calls for the constant renewal and enlargement of our consciousness. The journey through Tarot imagery is at once learning and therapeutic as each new life experience contributes to self-understanding and self-knowledge. Noddings (2006) emphasises the importance of self-knowledge as the very core of education: 'when we claim to *educate*, we must take Socrates seriously. Unexamined lives may well be valuable and worth living, but an education that does not invite such examination may not be worthy of the label *education*' (Noddings, 2006, p. 10, italics in original). When symbolically represented in Tarot images, human experiences become reflected upon; thus indeed *examined*. The archetypal realm is brought, so to speak, *down to earth* by virtue of its *embodiment* in physical reality, confirming Jung's insight that 'psyche and matter are two different aspects of one and the same thing' (Jung CW 8. 418). The apparent binary opposites are united in the process of reading and interpretation, thus defying Cartesian dualism both in theory and, significantly, in practice! The levels of *praxis* as encompassing human behaviour, decision-making or choosing a particular course of action is of utmost significance. Jung insightfully commented that the general rules of human conduct are

> at most provisional solutions, but never lead to those critical decisions which are the turning points in a man's life. As the author [Erich Neumann] rightly says: "The diversity and complexity of the situation makes it impossible for us to lay down any theoretical rules for ethical behaviour" ... The formulation of ethical rules is not only difficult but actually impossible because one can hardly think of a single rule that would not be reversed under certain conditions ... Through the new ethic, the ego-consciousness is ousted from its central position in a psyche organized on the lines of a monarchy or totalitarian state, its place being taken by *wholeness* or the *self*, which is now recognized as central" (Jung, 1949 in Neumann, 1969, p. 13; italics in original).

To achieve such wholeness, we have to evaluate real-life social situations as they arise in our very *practice* and learn the lessons embodied in the Tarot archetypal journey through what I call a symbolic school of life. Each and every Tarot reading as a mode of informal pedagogy becomes a step toward the conscious realisation of the deepest meaning (*corpus subtile*) of a particular situation; subsequently, an enlargement of consciousness itself becomes a step towards individuation. The true means of communication between the conscious mind and the unconscious is a language of symbols: 'symbols act as *transformers*, their function being to convert libido from a "lower" into a "higher" form' (Jung CW 5. 344). It is Tarot symbolism as a universal, even if 'silent' language (Semetsky, 2006b, 2010, forthcoming) that establishes such an unorthodox communicative link. The meanings of the symbols embedded in the pictures are not arbitrary but accord with a specific grammar of this universal language above and beyond verbal expressions of the conscious mind: 'it is not the personal human being who is making the statement, but the archetype speaking through him' (Jung, 1963, p. 352). In *Four Archetypes* Jung says: 'You need not be insane to hear his voice. On the contrary, it is the simplest and most natural thing imaginable ... [A] real colloquy becomes possible when the ego acknowledges the existence of a partner to the discussion' (CW 9. 236–237).

An expert reader transforms this implicit colloquy into an explicit dialogue when she functions as a 'bilingual' interpreter, converting the pictorial language of the unconscious into verbal expressions, thus facilitating the trans-formation of in-formation into consciousness. What takes place is an indirect, mediated, connection akin to the active principle of synchronicity posited by Jung in collaboration with the famous physicist and Nobel laureate Wolfgang Pauli. Synchronicity addresses the problematic of meaningful patterns generated both in nature and in human experience, linking the concept of the unconscious to the notion of '"field" in physics [and extending] the old narrow idea of "causality" ... to a more general form of "connections" in nature' (Pauli, 1994, p.164). Pauli envisaged the development of theories of the unconscious as overgrowing their solely therapeutic applications by being eventually assimilated into *natural* sciences 'as applied to vital phenomena' (1994, p. 164). In his 1952 letter to Jung, Pauli expressed his belief in the gradual discovery of a new, what he called *neutral*, language that functions symbolically to describe the psychic reality of the archetypes and would be capable of bridging the psycho-physical dualism. Jung described synchronicity not only in terms of a coincidence between mental content, or a dream, or a vision with the physical event, but also as a premonition about an event, '*a foreknowledge of some kind*' (Jung CW 8. 931; italics in original). The reality of this implicit 'self-subsistent "unconscious" knowledge' (Jung CW 8. 931) of what we are meant to be and where we stand within the individuation process demonstrates itself *empirically* in the archetypal constellations of Tarot images during readings.

Archetypes 'residing' in the dynamic field of the collective unconscious form an unorthodox *virtual* foundation for moral knowledge upon which many individual real-life experiences lay down their own structures. Multiple combinations of innumerable experiences—the constellations of the actualised archetypes—produce diverse archetypal images that manifest overtly through their effects at the level of the body in the form of particular unconscious patterns of feelings and actions that are symbolically represented in the Tarot imagery. Archetypes do have two complementary poles, one expressing a 'positive, favorable, bright side [and the other a] partly negative ... partly chthonic' (Jung CW 9i. 413). It is 'a natural process [as] a manifestation of [psychic] energy that springs from the tension of opposites' (Jung CW 7. 121) expressed in the dark and light archetypal aspects, both pertaining to Tarot imagery not unlike *yin* and *yang* as an interplay of opposites in the Chinese Book of Changes. The difference between the opposites gives rise to the Jungian transcendent, unifying, function. By bringing to our awareness many initially unperceived and latent meanings, the unconscious contents of the archetypal images become *amplified* via their representation in the material medium of the pictures. Because of the amplifying, synthesising, nature of symbols, the meanings expressed in the multitude of images hiding in the unconscious can be elucidated, interpreted, narrated and potentially integrated into consciousness. The amplifying and synthetic character of symbols reflects the dynamical and evolutionary approach to knowledge and, for Jung, a 'psychological fact ... as a living phenomenon ... is always indissolubly bound up with the continuity of the vital process, so that it is not only something evolved but also continually evolving and creative' (Jung CW 6. 717) as a function of our lifelong learning from experience in the process of 'Re-symbolization of the Self' (Semetsky, 2011).

Many typical life experiences are represented in the patterns that appear and can be discerned when the pictures are being spread in this or that layout, and a person can learn from their experience when it is being unfolded in front of their eyes in the array of images. Respectively, the latent meanings of experience become available to human consciousness, and a person can discover in practice a deeper, spiritual or *numinous*, as Jung would say, dimension of experience. Thus Tarot, in terms of its archetypal dynamics, and despite being traditionally considered irrational and illogical, helps us achieve an intense scope of awareness exceeding narrow instrumental rationality. It is what educational psychologist Jerome Bruner called an intuitive sense of rightness that allows a genuine reader to articulate the implicit meanings of Tarot images and symbols. For Bruner, intuition 'implies the act of grasping the meaning or significance or structure of a problem without explicit reliance on the analytic apparatus of one's craft' (Bruner,

1966, p. 61). A symbolic, intuitive, approach creates a dialectical relationship between consciousness and the unconscious. In this respect, Tarot images may be viewed as a bridge between the personal unconscious, via the archetypal field of the collective unconscious, to the conscious mind. Similar to the interpretations of dreams in Jungian analysis, Tarot hermeneutic (Semetsky, 2011) as reading and interpreting pictorial images becomes the core means of assisting people in the process of individuation. Etymologically, the Greek words *hermeneuein* and *hermeneia* for interpreting and interpretation are related to the mythic god Hermes, a messenger and mediator between gods and mortals, who crosses the thresholds and traverses the boundaries because he can 'speak' and understand both languages, the divine and the human, even if they appear utterly alien to each other.

Understanding the symbolic meanings embodied in the archetypal images of Tarot Arcana and bringing them to consciousness contributes to the re-symbolisation of the Self in the process of gradually removing the Ego from its privileged, egocentric position and enriching the human mind with other ways of knowing that complement its solely rational functions. The task of the reader is to make available the information concealed in the unconscious; thus to facilitate a process of individuation for the subject of the reading who is an equal participant in the emerging therapeutic and learning relation! For Jung, the *intuitive* function is non-rational (but not irrational), and the contents of intuition 'have the character of being given in contrast to the "derived" or "deduced" character' (Noddings & Shore, 1984, p. 25) in a logical manner pertaining to two other, strictly rational, Jungian functions. For Hillman (1997, p. 45), it is the human soul that 'selects the image I live', and each image is what Plato called a *paradeigma* or pattern. When we look upon the patterns created by the Tarot pictures, we enter what Noddings and Shore (1984) call *an intuitive mode* of perception. Etymologically, intuition is derived from the Latin verb *intueri*, which means *to look upon*. In the Middle Ages, the word *intuition* was used 'to describe an ineffable mystical experience of identification with God' (Noddings & Shore, 1984, p. 11). Tarot hermeneutic is a process of reading and interpreting these implicit patterns embodied in the images of the Arcana and as yet concealed by the unconscious; the readings that encompass an intuitive mode of perception reveal them, thereby making them explicit and integrated in consciousness. While the 'fostering of intuition as an aid to learning and knowing was not on [Jung's] agenda' (Noddings & Shore, 1984, p. 27) explicitly, it is the Tarot symbolism that triggers the stream of the unconscious and serves as a device to educate and strengthen the human intuitive function invaluable for meaning-making.

The split between theory and practice led, in modern times, to a spectator theory of knowledge and strict disciplinary boundaries between sciences and humanities. The detached gaze at the 'spectacle' of antiquity is, rather ironically, a precursor to modernity's scientific method. Scientific, intellectually certain, knowledge as cognitive *episteme* became distinguished from, and opposed to, the creative arts as *techne* or τέχνη. Tarot pictures are artistic productions—*techne*; the pictures mastered by human skill inspired, in turn, by the creative imagination of the particular artist who designed a given deck. *Techne* is often translated as craftsmanship, handicraft or skill; the products of techne are artefacts, such as Tarot pictures. In its dimension as a *techne*, Tarot becomes a powerful, albeit alternative, educational aid in the context of post-formal holistic education and mental health alike. However, Tarot as *praxis* is equally if not more important. In Greek mythology, *Praxis* is also another name for Aphrodite, the goddess of love who was a central character in the story of Eros and Psyche. The myth tells us that it is by virtue of active learning from novel life experiences imposed on her by Praxis (or Aphrodite), rather than by a theoretical contemplation of the objects of knowledge *already possessed* by the conscious mind, that Psyche, as a personification of *human* soul, was eventually able to reunite with Aphrodite's son, the *divine* Eros.

In Plato's *Symposium*, Diotima the Priestess teaches Socrates that Eros or Love is 'located' *in-between* lack and plenty; it is a spirit or daemon that, importantly, can hold two opposites together as a whole, therefore to eventually reconcile that which analytic thinking habitually perceives dualistically, that is, as binary *irreconcilable* opposites. Jung used the Latin term *coincidentia oppositorum* for the apparently mystical coincidence of opposites, such as psyche and matter, which takes place in synchronistic experiences. It was Hermes, the messenger of the gods, who finally summoned the human Psyche to Olympus where she reunited with her beloved, divine Eros, having been granted a godlike immortality in this loving union. It is through being driven by Eros/Love that Psyche was able to meet multiple challenges and overcome the obstacles created by Praxis. *And it is only through love and compassion for the often suffering human spirit that an expert Tarot reader can intuit, understand and narrate the subtle meanings encoded in the symbolism of the pictures, hence making each reading a precious learning experience.*

It is our learning from life experiences embodied in the symbolism of the pictures that not only leads to human development and eventual individuation but can also reconnect an individual *psyche* with its symbolic origin in *Anima Mundi*, the soul of the world, because our unconscious ideas are archetypal in nature and partake of the collective unconscious. Jung noticed that such conceptualisation

> is particularly true of religious ideas, but the central concepts of science, philosophy, and ethics are no exception to this rule. In their present form they are variants of archetypal ideas created by consciously applying and adapting these ideas to reality. For it is the function of consciousness not only to recognise and assimilate the external world through the gateway of the senses, but to translate into visible reality the world within us (Jung CW 8. 342).

This is a prerogative of Tarot as an educational and counselling tool: to *translate into visible reality the deep and invisible, internal world within us* and to enrich human experience with deep spiritual meaning. As complemented by imagination and intuition, the interpretation of images, according to Jung, 'reflects a higher level of intellect and, by not forcibly representing the unknowable as known, gives a more faithful picture of the real state of affairs' (Jung CW 11. 417). Tarot images and symbols, when interpreted, create 'something that is ... in the process of formation. If we reduce this by analysis to something that is generally known, we destroy the true value of the symbol; but to attribute hermeneutic significance to it is consistent with its value and meaning' (Jung CW 7. 492). Each meaningful reading represents what Jean Watson (1985) called, in the area of nurse education, the occasions of caring. Noddings explains that the occasions of caring constitute the moments when nurse and patient, or teacher and student, meet and must decide what to do with the moment, what to share, which needs to express or whether to remain silent. This encounter 'needs to be a guiding spirit of what we do in education' (Noddings, 1991, p. 168); such a guiding, relational and caring spirit is ontologically preeminent in Tarot hermeneutic. As recently noted by philosopher and abbot Mark Patrick Hederman (2003, p. 86) in his remarkable book *Tarot: Talisman or Taboo? Reading the World as Symbol*, Tarot provides us with the symbolic system to fill the gaps produced 'where education and trained sensibility are in short supply'. Hederman insists that 'each of us should be given at least the rudiments of one of the most elusive and important symbolic systems if we are even to begin to understand human relationships. This would require tapping into a wavelength and a communication system other than the cerebral [that] covers the three Rs of traditional education' (2003, p. 87). I wholeheartedly share this urgent and noble task.

References

Bruner, J. (1966) *Toward a Theory of Instruction* (Cambridge, MA, Harvard).

Dewey, J. (1916/1924) *Democracy and Education* (New York, Macmillan Company).

Gad, I. (1994) *Tarot and Individuation: Correspondences with Cabala and Alchemy* (York Beach, ME, Nicholas-Hays, Inc).

Hederman, M. P. (2003) *Tarot: Talisman or Taboo? Reading the World as Symbol* (Dublin, Currach Press).

Hillman, J. (1989) *A Blue Fire: Selected Writings by James Hillman*, T. Moore (ed.) (New York, Harper Collins).

Hillman, J. (1997) *The Soul's Code: In Search of Character and Calling* (New York, Warner Books Edition).

Jung, C. G. (1949) Foreword (R. F. C. Hull, Trans), in: E. Neumann (1969) (ed.), *Depth Psychology and a New Ethic* (E. Rolfe, Trans.) (New York, Harper & Row Publishers), pp. 11–18.

Jung, C. G. (1953–1979) *Collected Works* (Vols. 1–20), H. Read & R. Hull, (trans.), M. Fordham, G. Adler & W. M. McGuire (eds), Bollingen Series (Princeton, NJ, Princeton University Press). *Cited as CW*.

Jung, C. G. (1959) *The Archetypes of the Collective Unconscious* (London, Routledge).

Jung, C. G. (1963) *Memories, Dreams, Reflections*, R. Winston, C. Winston, trans., A. Jaffe (ed.) (New York, Pantheon Books).

Neumann, E. (1969) *Depth Psychology and a New Ethic*, E. Rolfe, trans. (New York, Harper & Row Publishers).

Nichols, S. (1980) *Jung and Tarot, an Archetypal Journey* (York Beach, ME, Samuel Weiser, Inc).

Noddings, N. (1984) *Caring: A Feminine Approach to Ethics and Moral Education* (Berkeley, CA, University of California Press).

Noddings, N. (1991) Stories in Dialogue: Caring and Interpersonal Reasoning, in: C. Witherell & N. Noddings (eds), *Stories Lives Tell: Narrative and Dialogue in Education* (New York, Teachers College Press), pp. 157–170.

Noddings, N. (2006) *Critical Lessons: What Our Schools Should Teach* (Cambridge, Cambridge University Press).

Noddings, N. & Shore, P. (1984) *Awakening the Inner Eye: Intuition in Education* (New York & London, Teachers College, Columbia University).

Pauli, W. (1994) *Writings on Physics and Philosophy*, C. P. Enz & K. von Meyenn (eds), R. Schlapp, trans. (Berlin, Springer Verlag).

Peters, M. & Freeman-Moir, J. (2006) *Edutopias: New Utopian Thinking in Education* (Rotterdam, Sense Publishers).

Romanyshyn, R. (2007) *The Wounded Researcher: Research with Soul in Mind* (New Orleans, Spring Journal Books).

Samuels, A. (1985) *Jung and the Post-Jungians* (London and Boston, Routledge & Kegan Paul).

Samuels, A., Shorter, B. & Plaut, F. (1986) *A Critical Dictionary of Jungian Analysis* (London, Routledge).

Semetsky, I. (2006a) Tarot, in: E. M. Dowling & W. G. Scarlett (eds), *Encyclopedia of Religious and Spiritual Development* (Thousand Oaks, Sage), pp. 443–444.

Semetsky, I. (2006b) The language of signs: Semiosis and the memories of the future, *SOPHIA: International Journal for Philosophy of Religion, Metaphysical Theology and Ethics*, 45:1, pp. 95–116.

Semetsky, I. (2009) Whence Wisdom? Human Development as a Mythic Search for Meanings, in: M. de Souza, L. J. Francis, J. O'Higgins-Norman & D. Scott (eds), *International Handbook of Education for Spirituality, Care and Wellbeing* (Dordrecht, Springer), pp. 631–651. Vol. 3 of International Handbooks of Religion and Education.

Semetsky, I. (2010) Silent Discourse: The language of signs and 'becoming-woman, *SubStance #121*, 39:1, pp. 87–102.

Semetsky, I. (2011) *Re-Symbolization of the Self: Human Development and Tarot Hermeneutic* (Rotterdam, Sense Publishers).

Semetsky, I. (forthcoming) *The Edusemiotics of Images: Essays on the Art~Science of Tarot* (Rotterdam, Sense Publishers).

Steinberg, S. R., Kincheloe, J. L. & Hinchey, P. H. (1999) *The Post-Formal Reader: Cognition and Education* (New York and London, Palmer Press).

Watson, J. (1985) *Nursing: The Philosophy and Science of Caring* (Boulder, CO, Associated University Press).

Witherell, C. (1991) The Self in Narrative: A Journey into Paradox, in: C. Witherell & N. Noddings (eds), *Stories Lives Tell: Narrative and Dialogue in Education* (New York, Teachers College Press), pp. 157–170.

Index

active imagination 13, 106
adult education 14, 15–16, 63
affect freedom 56–8
affect science 54
Agassiz, Louis 47
alchemy 3, 4–5, 6, 8, 38, 76, 98–9
anima/animus 8, 38, 40–41
Anima Mundi 111, 117
animism 5
Aphrodite 27–8, 117
Apollo 25–6, 27
archetypes x, xi, 3, 16, 21–3, 36, 41, 65, 66,
    68–9, 72, 86n, 111–12
    see also Greek pantheon; Tarot
Ares 28–9
Arian controversy 40
Artemis 26–7
artistic process 4, 6
arts education xi, 29, 36–7
Athene 24–5
Augustine 71
Austen, Jane: *Mansfield Park* x, 9–11

Bachelard, Gaston 36, 95
Barthes, Roland 18
beauty 27, 29
Beebe, John 57, 58
Berehynya 42
Bergson, Henri 69
Bernstein, Jerome x, 1, 4, 6–7
biological adaptation 47, 50–51
Blake, William 99
Book of Changes (I Ching) 113, 115
Boyd, R.D. 14, 16
Bruner, Jerome 115

Cambridge Primary Review 12
Camus, Albert 95
caring 117–18
Cartesian *Cogito* 66, 71, 91, 105
    see also dualism
chaos 23, 30
charisma 27, 31
child's psyche 77–82
    contradictory images of the child 82–3
chora 41
Christianity 40, 42
citizenship 52, 56, 58
Clinton, Hillary 58
Cogito 66, 71, 91, 105

cognitive theorists 54, 55
collective unconscious 3, 4, 65, 66, 79, 86n,
    111
Collingwood, R.G. 36
competition 28, 29
complexes 21–2, 96–7
complexity theory 6
conflict 28, 29
Conforti, Michael 21
containment 30
cooperative teaching 25
Corbin, Henri 93, 98, 111, 112
creativity 6, 8.12.23.28
    artistic 5
    cultural 7
cultural diversity 106
cultural leadership 56, 58
Cwik, August 106

de-centering of the ego 106, 107, 116
de Paula, Claudio Paixào Anastácio 7, 8
de Tocqueville, Alexis 53
decision-making 25
Deleuze, Gilles xi–xii, 63
    becoming-other 65, 66, 68–71
    ethics 71–3, 107
    experiential learning 67–8
    personal and collective unconscious 64,
        66
Demeter x, 24, 41, 42, 43
democratic culture 25, 55
depth psychology 63, 65, 70, 105
Descartes, René 57, 112
    Cogito 66, 71, 91, 105
    see also dualism
developmental psychology xii, 47–8, 50–51
    children's psyche 77–82
        contradictory images of the child 82–3
Devereux, George 95
Dewey, John ix, xi, 37, 44
    continuity between the biological and
        psychocultural 47, 50–51
    humane social institutions 51–2
    Liberalism and Social Action 52–3
    Quest for Certainty 48
    subject/object dichotomy 48–50
Dionysus 30–31
Diotima 39, 117
Dirkx, John 14, 15, 16, 17–18
diversity 84

Divine Feminine 38
    see also Greek pantheon; Sophia
Dobson, Darrell 7, 8–9
dreams 64, 65, 69, 73
dualism 5, 19, 71, 72, 112, 114

ecstasy 29, 30
Edinger, Edward 99
'educated soul' x, 4–7
educational policy x
    current crisis 35–6
    Futures Studies 112
    profit-making 1, 2, 32–3
    universities 1, 7–8
Egan, Kieran 35–6
ego-consciousness 78, 79, 80
    de-centering 106, 107, 116
ego-inflation x–xi
emotion
    affect freedom 56–8
    affect science 54–6
    deprecation 52, 53, 54
    feeling function 93, 94
empiricism 53, 57
English teaching ix–x, 8
    healing fiction x, 9–11
Enlightenment 52, 54
Erikson, Erik 48
Eros 5, 8, 28, 117
esoteric philosophy 37
    see also Gnosticism
ethical pedagogy xii, xiii, 95, 106, 107–8
ethics 71–3
Eve 40
evolutionary theories 6, 47, 79
experience
    biological/psychocultural 50, 55
    cultural 48, 49, 57
    definition 48
    embodied 66
    emotional 56
    integration 14, 40
    learning from xii, xiii, 37, 63, 64, 65, 67–8,
        71, 72
    lived 100
    meaning and 68, 70, 71, 74
    of soul 18
    religious 31
    subjective/objective 49, 50

fairytales 42
Faust 72
feeling function 93, 94
    see also emotion
feminine archetype 38
    see also Greek pantheon; Sophia
feminism 39
Fish, Stanley 1, 2

Fosha, Diana 57
Frankenstein 104
Freud, Sigmund 47, 54, 57, 64, 65, 69, 70, 71,
        101, 103, 105
fun 23, 27, 31
Futures Studies 112

Gad, Irene 113
Gadamer, Hans-Georg 90
Genesis 5, 6
Giosa, Elenice 7–8
Glasser, William 23, 27
global catastrophe 1, 5
Gnosticism xi, 37–9
    Sophia 39–41, 42, 44, 71
Goddess 38
    see also Greek pantheon; Sophia
Greek pantheon x–xi, 22–3, 33–4
    Aphrodite 27–8, 117
    Apollo 25–6, 27
    Ares 28–9
    Artemis 26–7
    Athene 24–5
    Demeter x, 24, 41, 42, 43
    Dionysus 30–31
    Eros 5, 8, 28, 117
    Hephaistos 29–30
    Hades 43
    Hecate/Hekate 33, 41, 43
    Hera 23–4
    Hermes x, 32–3, 116, 117
    Hestia 30
    Kore 41, 42, 43
    Persephone 33, 41, 42, 43
    Prometheus 31–2
    Zeus x, 23
Greene, Maxine 35, 36, 37
group work 25
Guattari, F. 64, 67–8, 70

Hades 43
healing fiction x, 9–11
Hecate/Hekate 33, 41, 43
Hederman, Mark Patrick 118
Helen of Troy 40
Hephaistos 29–30
Hera 23–4
Heraclitus 19
hermeneutics 90, 97, 100, 101, 116
Hermes x, 32–3, 116, 117
Hestia 30
higher education 1, 7–8
Hillman, James 14, 18, 21–2, 93,
        112
holism ix, 2, 6, 65
    Mythos versus Logos 18, 19
humane institutions 51–2
humanities ix, 1, 7, 116

I Ching (Book of Changes) 113, 115
images
  pictorial language 113
  power of 14–16
imaginal world xii, 93, 98, 111
imagination xi, 12, 35, 36, 37
  active imagination 13, 106
  power of images 14–16
imaginative narrative 112
indigenous culture 6
individualism 53
individuation ix, x, 2, 3, 4, 5, 13, 52, 63, 69,
    70, 71, 80
integration xii, 72
internalization 51
intimacy 28
intuitive function ix, 69, 115–16

James, William 18, 47, 54
Jardine, David 91, 94, 100, 102
Jungian psychology
  Aion 38
  anima/animus 8, 38, 40–41
  anti-Oedipal 64
  archetypes x, xi, 3, 16, 21–3, 36, 41, 65,
    68–9, 72, 86n, 111–12
    see also Greek pantheon; Tarot
  complexes 21–2, 96–7
  convergence with Dewey *see* Dewey, John
  differentiation from collective
    unconscious 47–8, 49–50, 57, 80
  dreams 64, 65, 69, 73
  educational value ix–x, 2–4, 76–7
    children's psyche 77–82
    contradictory images of the child 82–3
    self-education xii, 63–4, 73, 76–7, 81–2,
      83, 96, 102
    therapy versus education 13–14, 96,
      104
    transformative learning ix, x, 2, 8–9, 14,
      16
  emotion 54
    feeling function 93, 94
  first and second half of life 80–81
  Gnosticism xi, 37–9
    Sophia 39–41, 42, 44, 71
    individuation ix, x, 2, 3, 4, 5, 13, 52, 63, 69,
      70, 71, 80
    internalization 51
    intuitive function ix, 69, 115–16
    recapitulation theory 79, 86n, 87n
  Sermons 38, 45
  Shadow xii, 3, 12, 72–3
    Mythos versus Logos 18, 19
  symptoms as education 103
  synchronicity 3, 114, 115, 117
  transference xii, 91, 105
  unconscious ix, 2, 64, 98, 108

collective unconscious 3, 4, 65, 66, 79,
    86n
teacher-student dynamics xii, 76–7,
    82–5

Keats, John 93, 98
Kerslake, Christian 63
Klein, Melanie 54
Kore 41, 42
Kristeva, Julia 39, 41

leadership 56, 58
learning paradox 71
liberalism 51–2, 53
libido 64, 70, 71
literary theory x
  healing fiction 9–11
Locke, John 57
Logos 5, 8, 18, 19, 39, 40

MacFarland, Ellen 107
magic 93
Magritte, René 99
maiden goddess 41, 42
marketplace 32
Mary 40
mass mindedness 53–4
Mead, George Herbert 17
meaning 37
  co-creation 3, 10, 11 16, 67, 70, 71, 71
  unconscious 64, 65–6, 68, 74
mechanisation 2
meditation 30
Mephistopheles 72
Merleau-Ponty, M. 99, 105
metaphors xiii, 1, 97–101
Mill, John Stuart 53
Miller, David 104
modernity xi, 3
monotheism 5, 6
Mother Goddess 24, 40, 41
mystical marriage 38
Mythos 18, 19

National Curriculum 2
nature 1, 5, 6, 26, 27, 105–6
Navajo 6–7
Nazism 4
Nemerov, Howard 99
Neumann, Erich 71, 73, 108
Newton, Isaac 93, 99
Nichols, Sallie 113
Noddings, Nel 112, 113, 117

Obama, Barack 58
Oedipal complex 64
Omer, Aftab 57, 58
Orpheus 103

Paganism 42
Pandora 29
participation mystique 77
participative decision-making 25
Pauli, Wolfgang 114–15
Persephone 33, 41, 42, 43
Pestalozzi, Johann 87n
phenomenology 90, 105
Philemon 69, 107
Philo of Alexandria 39
phylogeny 79, 81
pictorial language 113
Plato 14–15, 39, 71, 103, 117
political liberalism 51, 53
political psychology 55, 56, 58–60
political therapy xi, 58
polytheism 34
    see also Greek pantheon
Pope, Alexander 93
positive psychology 19
positivist paradigm xi, 50, 52
power 23
praxis 111, 115
prejudices xii
primitive psychology 79, 86n, 87n
Prometheus 31–2
Psyche 117
psychoidal unconscious 105, 107, 111
psychological citizenship 56, 58
psychotherapy 57, 59
    de-centering of the ego 106, 107, 116
    symptoms as enslavement or education 103
    technique 102
    therapy versus education 13–14, 96, 104
    see also Freud, Sigmund; Jungian psychology
public-private divide 51, 52, 53
purposive behavior 51
Pythagoras 39

quality school 23

rationalism 53, 57, 98
recapitulation theory 79, 86n, 87n
Reddy, William 55, 57
religion 5–6, 39, 40, 42, 57
Ricoeur, Paul 90, 101
ritual 51
Robbins, Lee 7, 8
Romanyshyn, Robert x, 1, 4–6, 111
Rowland, Susan 98

Said, Edward 10, 11
Samuels, Andrew 57, 58, 113
scapegoats 73
science teaching 92–4
scientific method 16–17, 52, 116
seduction 27, 28
self-directed learning 15

self-education xii, 63–4, 73, 76–7, 81–2, 83, 96, 102
self-knowledge xiii, 16, 69, 113
self-reflection 13
sentiment 53
sexual seduction 27, 28
sexuality 38, 64, 70, 71
Shadow xii, 3, 12, 72–3
    Mythos versus Logos 18, 19
Shelley, Mary 104
skills 32
Slavic culture 40, 42–4
social institutions 51–2
social sciences xi, 17, 52, 54, 59
Socrates xiii, 14–15, 113, 117
Sophia 39–41, 42, 44, 71
soul psychology x, 17–18
spirit guides 107
standardisation 2, 84
Stevens, Anthony 21
Stevens, Wallace 100
subject-object dichotomy xi, 3, 48–50, 52, 54
symbols 38, 101, 114, 115
    see also archetypes
synchronicity 3, 114, 115, 117

Tarot xiii, 112–13
    Arcana 113
    archetypal journey 113–14
    complementary opposites 115, 117
    readings 114, 115, 117–18
    techne and *praxis* 116–17
teacher-student dynamics xii, 76–7, 82–5
techne 116
technology 32
teleology 50
Tillich, Paul 53
Tomkins, Sylvan 55, 57
transference xii, 91, 105
transference dialogues 106–7
transformative learning ix, x, 2, 8–9, 14, 16

Ukrainian culture 40, 42–4
unconscious ix, 2, 64, 98, 108
    collective unconscious 3, 4, 65, 66, 79, 86n, 111
    teacher-student dynamics xii, 76–7, 82–5
United Nations Convention on the Rights of the Child 87–8n
universality 84
university education 1, 7–8
utilitarianism ix, 1, 53
utopian thinking 112

van den Berg, J.H. 105
van der Post, Laurens 113
visionary art 4

visionary reading 9–11
vocation 103, 104

Watson, Jean 117
Winnicott, D.W. 106
Wisdom 39

Wittgenstein, Ludwig 100
wonder 35
wounded healer 9, 59
Wundt, Wilhelm 47

Zeus x, 23